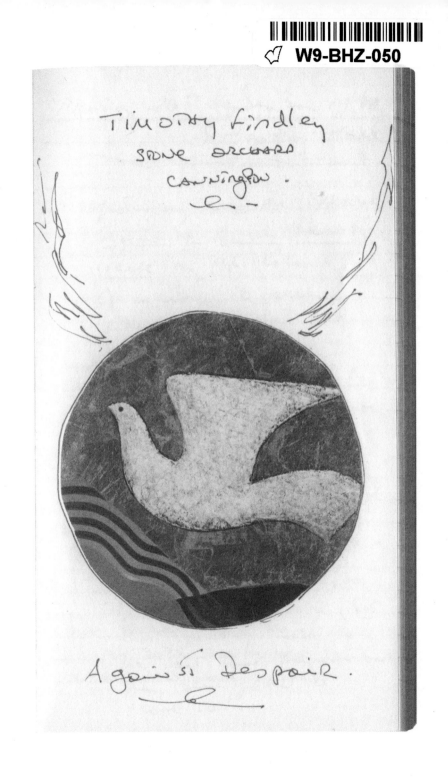

Timothy Findley
Stone Orchard
Cannington.

Against Despair.

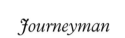

Journeyman

TIMOTHY FINDLEY

Journeyman

TRAVELS OF A WRITER

*Edited and Introduced
by William Whitehead*

Harper*Flamingo*Canada

Journeyman
© 2003 by Pebble Productions Inc. All rights reserved.

The publisher gratefully acknowledges the following sources: Thornton Wilder letter on page 293. This material is used by permission of Tappan Wilder and may not be reproduced without his prior written consent. Martha Henry letter on page 309. Reprinted by permission of the author.

First Edition

HarperCollins books may be purchased for educational, business, or sales promotional use through our Special Markets Department.

HarperCollins Publishers Ltd
2 Bloor Street East, 20th Floor
Toronto, Ontario, Canada
M4W 1A8

www.harpercanada.com

National Library of Canada Cataloguing in Publication

Findley, Timothy, 1930–2002
Journeyman: travels of a writer / Timothy Findley ; edited and introduced by William Whitehead. — 1st ed.

ISBN 0-00-200673-1

1. Findley, Timothy, 1930–2002 – Journeys.
2. Findley, Timothy, 1930–2002 – Diaries.
3. Authors, Canadian (English) – 20th century – Diaries.
I. Whitehead, William, 1931–
II. Title.

PS8511.I38Z53 2003   C818.'54
C2003-905560-4

HC 9 8 7 6 5 4 3 2 1

Printed and bound in the United States
Set in Monotype Plantin Light

Endpaper: This illustration by Timothy Findley appears on the opening page of his Sept.–Oct. 1988 journal. Several of his journals begin with this drawing and bear similar inscriptions. NATIONAL ARCHIVES OF CANADA, TIMOTHY FINDLEY/WILLIAM WHITEHEAD FONDS (MG31-D196, VOL. 124)

This book is dedicated to its readers,
to the memory of its writer
and to those who helped guide him
through his writing years:

Grace Bechtold at Bantam Books,
William Clarke of Clarke, Irwin,
Cynthia Good and her colleagues at Penguin Canada,
Iris Tupholme and her crew at HarperCollins Canada,
Larry Ashmead at HarperCollins, New York,
Mary Adachi, copy editor of all but two of his books
and Bruce Westwood and his agent cohorts
at Westwood Creative Artists
and W C A Film and Television.

Contents

PEN POWER

THEATRE TOURS
AND FINAL CURTAIN

Introduction

Timothy Irving Frederick Findley was known to his friends and family by his initials: TIFF. Since, more than forty years ago, he became my friend and, with recent changes in Canadian law, he also became part of my family, I shall call him Tiff.

You may find me referred to, in his writings, as Bill, WFW, Willy or Wolf.

We began our journey together in February 1962, when we were both working in the theatre, I as co-producer of a repertory season in Toronto, Tiff as an actor in our company. One day during rehearsal, he told me of having played the title role in a CBC television show based on Jules Pfeiffer's *Crawling Arnold*. The show was to be aired that evening, but Tiff had no television set. By any chance, could he . . . ? I quickly invited him to watch the piece at my place, but a few minutes later, began to regret it. The problem was, I had put most of my money into our repertory season, and so my pockets were in almost the same state as my completely empty refrigerator. Somehow, I had to have *something* to offer a guest. A quick check of resources showed I had just enough cash to buy some crackers and cheese or a six-pack of beer. The guest was Timothy Findley. No problem. The six-pack was duly purchased and installed in my fridge.

When Tiff arrived, I headed for the kitchen, confidently asking if he would like a beer. He stopped me cold. *Oh, I'm sorry, Bill. I started taking Antabuse this morning, and so I'd get very sick if I drank any alcohol. But I'm simply starving. Do you have anything to eat?*

The plain truth is that Tiff did not go home that night. In fact, he stayed for the rest of his life, which ended on the first day of summer 2002. In one sense, he never left. He can still be found in his books and in our hearts and memories.

Shortly after the 1990 publication of his memoirs, *Inside Memory: Pages from a Writer's Workbook*, we began to build up on the computer another collection of articles, speeches and journal entries—this time, on the subject of travel. Some of the writing was done at Stone Orchard, our farm near Cannington, Ontario. Later, Tiff worked in France at our writing retreat in the Provençal village of Cotignac, and at our new home in Stratford, Ontario. Fortunately, he even got to write a few pieces specifically for this book.

The careful reader may notice that four of the pieces bear the date 2003. These are "Four-Wheeled Companions," "A Moveable Feast," "Driven to Distraction" and "Translation Traps." These were written by me and consist of stories from our travels that I have heard Tiff tell privately and occasionally publicly. For that reason, I have written them in his voice, since the act of writing them was akin to taking dictation from memory.

Tiff was not a good traveller. He never wanted to leave home, wherever home was. He hated flying. He hated speed of any kind. His body reacted badly to any application of centrifugal force, which meant always slowing down on the curves. And yet he journeyed a good deal—by car, by train, by plane, occasionally by ship and often only in his mind. Many of these travels informed what he wrote—and how he wrote. Apprentice, journeyman or master, Tiff never stopped developing his craft—and these journeys were part of that process. We visited many countries, and some of these countries—along with some of the people we encountered along the way—were reinvented in Tiff's writings.

We decided on a four-part structure for this book. First, accounts of voyages made by land, water and in the air. Second, excursions into the past and the future, on the wings of memory, imagination or speculation. Third, journeys into the writing community—its people, their tools and craft—and their concerns, especially censorship and prejudice. Finally, a voyage into the world of theatre, with its plays, players and playwrights. In each of these four parts there will be hints of the other three, and in all of them, occasional observations about how these meanderings became the raw material of Tiff's fiction.

Within the first of the four sections, Going Places, the structure is mostly chronological, with the exception of the occasional journal entry placed according to its subject rather than its timing. In the rest of the book, subject determines structure, as outlined in the Table of Contents.

There are no words to express just what it has meant to journey through most of my life with Tiff—nor is it possible to articulate fully what it means that our travels together are over. I hope what follows will give some sense of both.

BILL WHITEHEAD
Stratford
Spring 2003

Prologue

The Countries of Invention

Stone Orchard
February 1984
Article

Most writers write from a private place: a nation or a country in the mind, whose landscape and whose climate are made up of what has been seized and hoarded from the real world—en passant.

No one is static. Not even dead, are we static. Stillness is something in the mind and nothing more, a part of forward movement. After death, decay and remembrance keep on moving us forward, who knows where, but certainly the living, by digging in the earth, can make a guess. And anyone who reads or listens or watches is perfectly aware of the dead who keep our company. This is because we have given them a place in the countries of our invention.

We are never still. If you live by the side of the road, as I do, you are very much awake to this fact (and, sometimes, awakened by it), since every time the shadows move it means that someone is passing. And my garden, my wall, my house and the cat asleep on the roof will all become images fixed in someone's mind—part of their private hoardings, their collection—because they have come this way seeking passage.

I, too, pass. It is only natural: making my own collection, lifting my images from here and there—vistas, faces, gestures, accidents—

carrying them forward with me, letting them rattle round my brain, my innards, until they have settled themselves, either as landmarks or as residents. I am a travelling country of invention. A roadshow. *Pay attention.*

Thornton Wilder used to say that, *pay attention,* if he caught you looking at the pavement, trying to avoid the cracks. *There's nothing down there but your feet, Findley. Look around you; it's much more interesting.*

Yes, and he was right. Thornton Wilder lived in fear of missing something, not in the gossipy sense (gossip is all too common knowledge) but in the sense of missing something no one else had noticed. That bridge that fell into the chasm at San Luis Rey . . . No one else had seen it falling. But he did. Paying attention to the landscape around him, it is more than likely Thornton Wilder, being a world traveller, saw the bridge falling (a ghost bridge only) into an Austrian valley. Or, perhaps it fell into the gorge at Crawford Notch. Where it was first "seen" falling doesn't matter. All that matters is that, paying attention en passant, he caught a glimpse of it superimposed on a foreign landscape; foreign, at any rate, to the landscape where it ultimately fell. The fact is, it fell in Peru. But Thornton Wilder had never been anywhere near Peru; never—until he went there in his mind, equipped with the image of a bridge that had fallen through his imagination somewhere in Europe or New Hampshire. It may be the image was prompted by the space between two peaks; the awesome depth of a gorge or the width of a valley and Wilder had thought (because he was paying attention): *what a dreadful distance to fall that would be. What a fearful height that is and, if one had to walk there over a bridge . . . And if the bridge fell, who would fall with it? Who would be fated to fall: or chosen . . . ? And why?* In an instant, glimpsing his imaginary bridge as it spanned the real space between two heights, the basis for a classic novel was laid in place—and cemented.

Thornton Wilder's work comes very close to providing the perfect example of the countries of invention: Caesarean Rome in

The Ides of March; 18th-century Peru in *The Bridge of San Luis Rey*; post-Platonic Greece in *The Woman of Andros*; the Ice Age and Noah's Flood in *The Skin of Our Teeth*; beyond the grave in *Our Town*. Wilder was no historian, in the academic sense; neither was he a time-traveller—yet, each of these places resonates with the sound of real voices and each of them is, at times alarmingly, alive with the textures of a life so vividly imagined that it becomes life. The countries of invention can be more real than any place we see and hear in our everyday lives: the ones we live outside of books and daydreams.

Everyone has memories: private memories and shared memories. One of the most poignant of human activities is the game that begins: *do you remember . . . ?* And there is also the sharing of private memories, the game that begins: *I remember . . .* Both of these games are vital to the theatre, and playwrights have employed them since Euripides first prompted Hecuba to recall the wonder of happiness as she surveys the ruin of Troy. And there is no more magical moment in the theatre than Justice Shallow's *Jesu! The days we have seen . . .* The conjuring of memory, as pure device—its theatrical impact aside—is equal to the closing of the circle, whether the circle be of fate or clarity around the shape of a character.

The whole of Chekhov's impetus as a playwright seems to have sprung from a desire to set people loose in a minefield of memory and to see which one of them, if any, might survive. His plays show us one unbroken line of men and women caught in this minefield—some of them stumbling and certain to perish; some of them gracefully waving aside the danger and stepping forth boldly into the past while others are transfixed, unable to move with any kind of joy into the past and, thus, unable to conjure any sense of the future at all. Chekhov sees, perhaps most clearly of all the great playwrights, the importance that memory plays in our ability to survive. He knew that much of what anyone remembers is not "real": that memory itself is a country of invention. But he also knew it was a source of solace and the basis of all reconciliation.

Memory provides a ground—however mined it might be—on which we can face reality, accommodate reality and possibly even survive it. If only we could believe the best of what we recall about ourselves and others, there might then be some chance to make something real in the here and now that is an echo of that better person. But the countries of invention can be treacherous, and most of Chekhov's people are beguiled by memory and they go to live there forever. This was not pessimism on Chekhov's part. The fact is, he saw it all for precisely what it is: a great ironic comedy at the end of which we all, as does the old retainer Firs at the close to *The Cherry Orchard*, lie down in memory, to pass away—forgotten—forever.

Forgotten forever. This, of course, is everyone's fear: not to be one of those people chosen, en passant, to be hoarded in someone's memory: not to be a resident in someone else's country of invention. Marie-Claire Blais has said that every writer is *un temoin*: a witness. One of the things they witness and record is the cryptic passage of people and events that, otherwise, would gain no place in memory. This is not only because, by paying attention, they see what others fail to see but, also, because they record what others resist remembering. We resist remembering what we cannot understand—what we cannot cope with—what is ugly—what is dangerous to our self-esteem and our way of life. What we fail to see can range from falling bridges to the peach we dare not eat. Our survival may not depend on falling bridges and uneaten peaches, but it may very well depend on our being reminded of their existence: J. ALFRED PRUFROCK THWARTS DESTINY BY PAUSING TO EXAMINE PEACH BEFORE SETTING FOOT ON THE BRIDGE AT SAN LUIS REY!

Paying attention pays off.

I was recently given the opportunity to reach back into the past in order to explore my beginnings as a writer. My publisher thought it was time to make a collection of my short fiction and this meant re-establishing contact with three decades of stories. The thing that struck me first was how consistent the images were. They had been gathered by a pack rat whose tastes and interests could be established just by running the eye over sentences written as far apart as 1956 and 1983. The country in my mind has a lot of distance in it, but the distance can be covered by the sound of a banging screen door or the barking of a dog or the voice of someone calling: *you'll be late if you don't hurry up!* Many of the people, the children and the men especially, turn up over and over again in white; the women wear colour—blue, orange, red and the darker shades of grey. Many of the people have the habit of shading their eyes—which implies a plethora of light. Certainly, there is endless heat; summer is the dominant season. All the roads are dusty and the rooms are filled with brass and copper lamps. I don't know why. Storms are important (the weather in my country is appalling) and they blow up from nowhere. People are terse with one another—mostly, that is, till one of them decides to talk for ten pages. Why? I don't know; I really don't know and I'm not going to ask. I only point it out because it tells something. It shows something. It shows what one writer's eyes have been scanning for thirty and more years and it shows that he has been looking for something, whether he knew it or not (he didn't), and it shows that, en passant, he has made a collection of remarkable cohesion. It also shows what the writer's ears have been listening for—a particular tone of voice, perhaps a way of speaking, always for the sound of someone trying to say something. It has not just been the inability to communicate that caught his attention—but the inability to communicate through speech. And the noises! All those screen doors—plus a lot of falling chairs and the sound of voices rising in argument in a distant room. These people, places, noises—all these voices belong in one country; even though the territory spans from Ontario to Austria and from Montreal to the Bahamas, New York to Hollywood. The maps of the countries of invention might be collected one day as an exercise in the destruction of reason. How can so much sameness be so disparate? There is nothing out of place in the countries of invention. This is their hallmark. The accidents, the mutilations, the deaths belong there alongside the people sitting behind the screens on their porches and the children playing in the tall grass and the rabbits giving birth on the lawn. There are no surprises in the countries of invention, but there is amazement and there is bewilderment at the behaviour of the inhabitants and the treachery of the climate. The real world is not like that. In the real world our lives are plagued by surprise and yet we are never amazed and, certainly, no one's behaviour bewilders us. We expect and even anticipate jeopardy in all its various shapes and perfidy in all its forms. In real life we are always saying: *there, you see? I told you so.* In the real world we are jaded—a nice old-fashioned word for a nice old-fashioned condition. But go and pick up someone else's world of invention and the odds are, the jade will fall away.

It is only in fiction, only in memory that our eagerness to be trusting is justified. This is one of fiction's—one of memory's and one of imagination's—bravest functions. It is by these media we are urged towards hope and sanity; maybe even compassion.

Is memory a medium?

Yes. In every sense. By promising continuity, it gives the present certainty and it gives the future an odds-on chance of making an appearance in our lives. It also broadcasts and publishes its daily reminder of better times and lost causes. Memory is not only in itself a country of invention; it is also that country's *Time* and *Maclean's* and its six o'clock news.

We cannot live in the countries of invention. We can only go there and come back. For those who choose to go and live there forever, who choose it as a way of life, there is always the grave danger of becoming merely reactionary. This is a dead end. The truth about the countries of invention is that everyone you put there is put there because they are posing questions. For the reactionary, the

questions take on the heat of answers. For the visitor who writes—
who goes there to write—the questions are all that matter. There are
no answers: none. If there were, there would be no reality.

This brings us back to Thornton Wilder's bridge, its imminent
collapse and the deaths of those who walk upon it. And the question.

And the question.

Why?

The answer is not in Thornton Wilder's country of invention.
The answer is in everyone who picks up *The Bridge of San Luis
Rey* and who reads it through to the end.

Going Places

Lake Henshaw, Ontario
May 1962
Journal

Our first journey together was taken at the end of May 1962—just over three months after Tiff came to watch televsion and never went home. We badly needed a holiday, having worked hard all winter and spring, including a season of repertory at the Central Library Theatre in Toronto. I had been invited by its producers, Jean Roberts and Marigold Charlesworth, to join them as co-producer, while Tiff played demanding roles in the three plays we offered: Sheridan's *The Rivals*, N.F. Simpson's *One Way Pendulum*, and Jean Genet's *The Balcony*. As soon as the season closed, we borrowed a car, drove up into the Muskoka region north of Toronto and rented a tiny cabin on the shores of Lake Henshaw. Although I have no memory of sketching a nude Timothy Findley basking on a rock, as I write this I am looking at my colour portrait of a Lake Henshaw Jumping Spider, which became one of Tiff's favourite possessions, and his ink drawing of the lake—which is still one of my most treasured mementoes. WFW.

Sitting at Lakeside. 7:10 p.m.
    Far end of Lake Henshaw—in bay. Very shallow. Bill and I have sketched all afternoon from the boat—then landed here and have explored the shoreline.

Saw a giant turtle (snapper) under a submerged log in the shallows. Enormous head about six or seven inches long, with very large body of shell. Probably quite old.

The wind is from the west—coming right towards us, but very light, and the sunshine is still strong, as the sun will not go down until after nine.

We have not seen a soul all day—it has been exquisitely quiet and peaceful. Both very very grateful for this and for being alone.

We brought sandwiches, milk, Coke and tonic water with us.

The air is indescribably clear and bright—everything is crystal clear even in the distance.

I have done some sketching in ink which is very pleasing and Bill has done some in pastel and Conté crayon—presently he is working on one of me sitting here on this rock quite naked with my book and feeling very much the bunches of stomach I'm afraid he'll draw. How weak we both are after the long winter!!

Here is what I can hear:

dragonfly buzz
song sparrow (near)
song sparrow (distant)
blackbird
water laps
bullfrog
dog in distance
a silvery-noted bird
wind in the trees behind me
Bill lighting a cigarette

Richmond Hill, Ontario
December 30, 1963
Journal

WE OWN A CAR!

A 1962 sage-green (beautiful) Valiant—with radio—snow tires—
excellent heater. Automatic—rides like a dream and WFW has a
gorgeous time driving it. I watched him go away this a.m. and it is a
very special prize for us, indeed. We've waited so long, but now we
have the perfect car at last. We are like two idiot children—always
looking out the windows at it in the driveway—and when we ride in
it all we do is laugh and play the radio very loud. It is wonderful!

Lake Superior, Ontario
July 7, 1965
Journal

We named the Valiant Gulliver and, after moving 120 kilometres
northeast of Toronto to a farm we called Stone Orchard, we
embarked on the first of Gulliver's Travels. It was a multi-purpose
trip to the west. First, we would deliver our Richmond Hill housekeeper, Mrs Agnes Mortson, to a village in southeastern
Saskatchewan—Wawota, near where Mrs Mortson and her parents
had homesteaded when she was a girl and the area was still known as
the Northwest Territories. Then, we would pay our first visit
together to my parents in Regina, after which we would make a cir-
cular camping trip through various parks in Alberta, Montana,
Wyoming and South Dakota before heading home. Tiff was
awestruck by his first panoramic views of the west. I had to keep
stopping so he could gaze out over the sweep of the prairies and the
magnificence of the mountains. Unfortunately, he was frequently
moved in a different way—saddened and angered all too often by
what we could see by simply looking down as we drove. WFW.

The dead by the road, or on it, testify to the presence of man. Their little gestures of pain—paws, wings and tails—are the saddest, the loneliest, most forlorn postures of the dead I can imagine. When we have stopped killing animals as though they were so much refuse, we will stop killing one another. But the highways show our indifference to death, so long as it is someone else's. It is an attitude of the human mind I do not grasp. I have no point of connection with it. People drive in such a way that you think they do not believe in death. Their own lives are their business, but my life is not their business. I cannot refrain from terrific anger when I am threatened so casually by strangers on a public road. I don't *want* to die yet—and I don't want Bill to, either.

Stone Orchard
April 17, 1977
Journal

"You've no need to be afraid," she said. "You're making a mountain out of a molehill."
   And I said: "no. You're wrong. I'm telling you—it's molehills I'm afraid of."

Glacier National Park
July 16, 1965
Journal

Last night we stayed at a camping site by Cameron Lake in Waterton National Park, Canada, and slept among the trees . . .
   In the middle of the night—very dark, but not pitch dark—I awoke and heard *noises*. I could hear clawing at tables and door handles and gentle but man-heavy footsteps. I was certain something "grizzly" was going to happen, if you know what I mean. I

turned over like a leaf—and, terrified, saw that it was only Bill. "Only Bill" is the understatement of the last year. I looked at him and, needless to say, my following words are now the watchword of our trip. They were spoken wide awake—like a statement at a cocktail party. "Oh. I thought you were a bear."

Black Hills, South Dakota
July 21, 1965
Journal

The Custer Battlefield has retained a great sense of period. They have kept it virtually intact without dotting the landscape with buildings and signs. At the top of the hill is a mass grave with one tombstone monument bearing all the names. Around the fields you see the little slab markers, upright in the grass, which show where each man fell and was found. The sun was hot—very bright—and a wind moved the grass. The view of hills and distance moved me. It was absolutely possible to relive the experience of the men who fell—and battled. Later, at night, farther away on their route march, it was again possible to sense their thoughts . . . so far from home and wondering.

As dark came we decided to spend the night in a state park which was marked on the map. So we drove there. (Understatement of the trip.) It turned out to be on an old road so ill-kept that it was worse than a flood road. As we progressed, we became more and more alarmed. It seemed impossible that we were really headed for a state park . . . this was virtually like one of my war nightmares. The rutted road—trees on either side—not a sign of habitation for miles—and when we did come upon a sign it would be some form of dilapidation—a broken-down truck or car—an abandoned, looming, broken, black-windowed house . . . We went through a set of gates—over cow-gates and down a hill. It began to seem like a madman's ambush or a robber's trap. The

signs were misspelled or broken and old and looked like the work
(in our, by now, reeling imaginations) of someone bent on a
trick—either serious or demented. We came to a bridge—and
hardly dared go over. We both felt that it would collapse—and
then, ditched, we would fall prey to a group of marauders . . . As
we progressed (we *did* cross the bridge and it rattled and shook
enough to double our expectations of danger) . . . we drove on
and came to the so-called "park." Deserted—there wasn't a soul.
We travelled a down-graded road and came to a sign saying
"WATER." At the foot of the road we reached a sluiceway. We got
out and I went to fill the Thermos. A sign read: "DANGER. TUR-
BULENT UNDERTOW. SURVIVAL IMPOSSIBLE." I ran back to
the car and got in. We then approached another sign, riding
now—not daring to walk—and the sign read: "WARNING." We
went closer. Surely it was a warning to watch for snakes—or
bears—or spiders. "WARNING." Closer. The car lights shone on
the words and we strained forward to read. "WARNING. This is
the property of the United States Government. Do not deface or
damage."

But there was nothing there *to* deface—nothing, but a bit of
stone and weed to damage. It was positively weird.

"I wonder . . ." I said, "where everyone *is*."

"I dunno," said Bill. "For a state park, this takes the cake. No
cars. No campfires. No trailers. No people . . ."

"Maybe it's condemned."

"Maybe."

"Isn't there supposed to be a dam here—a dam in the park?"

"Keyhole Dam."

"Get the map."

The map was consulted.

"Sure—here it is. Right here. Keyhole Dam."

"Well, you'd think everyone would come to see the dam."

The last dam we had seen (Hungry Horse) had been a great
attraction.

"Well. It beats me," Bill said—looking out through the front windshield. "It just doesn't . . . My God!!!"

"What? What? What? What? What?"

"The dam."

"Dam? Dam? What dam?"

"Keyhole Dam. We're right underneath it."

Indeed—we were. It loomed up over us—tall and impressive and thoroughly frightening. We had the answer to our earlier question. Who would bring their hordes of trailers, dogs, children and campfires to roost at the foot of a dam . . . ? An earth dam, at that.

We fled.

Stratford

2003

Four-Wheeled Companions

I have always been struck by the fact that a car can have a personality. Each car that Bill and I have enjoyed over the years is garaged in memory with a distinctive sense of identity. Something that involves make, model, year and colour—but even more, a sense of where we went together and how we were living at the time.

The first one was a '62 Valiant. I cannot say why we always considered our automobiles to be masculine, but we did. We ultimately called him Gulliver. This was meant to honour one of our favourite cats—a wanderer who was killed by another car on the street in front of our house. By then, we had had the car for over a year, and had begun our own version of Gulliver's Travels.

We all got together in 1963—over a year after Bill and I had left the world of actors and were trying to make a go of it in the world of writers. We were living in Richmond Hill, in a house we rented, at a pittance, from my parents. They had bought it as a retirement haven, but my father's health dictated that they remain in Toronto—for the time being, anyway. And so there we were: two aspiring writers and eight cats. Suburban citizens, dependent on public transit.

For our first year or so in Richmond Hill, I had been writing on-air commercials for a local radio station that had just gone country and western. And in my spare time, I was also working on a novel about a boy who kills his family: *The Last of the Crazy People.* You may find some connection between those two sentences.

Bill was commuting by bus and subway to the CBC in Toronto, serving as science editor on a radio show that later became well known as *Ideas.* He was also just beginning to write for television, mostly on the series *The Nature of Things.*

Apart from greatly expediting the commuting to Toronto, Gulliver lived up to his name and took us on true travels—beginning with one that included a visit with Bill's parents in Regina. It was also my first glimpse of the prairies. Magical. At some point west of Kenora we emerged from the trees to be confronted with a flatter vista and a larger sky than I had ever seen. I have never quite recovered from that magnificence. But that was only part of my introduction to the Canadian west.

After a very pleasant sojourn in Regina, we went farther towards the Pacific. Not all the way, but into a terrain that was another first for me. The Canadian Rockies. Banff. Lake Louise. Then south to the Waterton Lakes. Blue waters, black rocks and an array of arboreal greens that will never fade from my mind.

Farther south, into America's Glacier National Park. Bill had been there as a teenager, and had special memories about the beauties of the Going-to-the-sun Highway—an alpine route that wound its way up a mountain and over the summit. Well. The years had been a lot kinder to Bill than they had to that highway. The stone-wall barriers that separated the roadway from the precipices along which it ran had begun to crumble. So, in places, had the outer edges of the road itself. It was impressive all right—

but it was also terrifying. Somehow, Gulliver got us all the way up—and all the way down again.

That was the voyage on which we learned how to go camping. A tent, sleeping bags, a kerosene stove with two burners, a cooler, and a collapsible table and two chairs became our mobile home for years to come. We established a routine for setting up the camp. We would work together to erect the tent, and then while Bill unrolled the sleeping bags, set up the table and chairs and got the stove ready to work, I would go in search of water. There was one lovely moment in the Rockies when he could hear me coming back up the trail from the lake that lay below us. He wondered why I was not responding to any of his comments about the day's journey, and when he turned to see what was going on, it was a considerable shock to find that what was standing a few feet from him was not Timothy Findley and a pail of water, but a cow moose and her adolescent calf. By the time I arrived, the visitors had proceeded on their way, and Bill had almost recovered.

Gulliver was sadly not immortal, and eventually reached the point of retirement. By then, we had taken advantage of having a car and in 1964 had moved from Richmond Hill to what was to be our home for the next thirty-five years, a farm about a hundred kilometres northeast of Toronto—a property we called Stone Orchard.

Gulliver was released into retirement in 1967 and his place was taken by a brand new Chrysler, purchased in our nearby village of Cannington. We had not even given the new acquisition a name when we received a visit from two glorious friends—the two women who had founded the theatre in which Bill and I had spent our last season as actors. Marigold Charlesworth and Jean Roberts. They arrived at the farm in a gorgeous new Citroën. The French car with the hydraulic suspension system that raised the chassis up every time the engine was turned on. Bill was speechless with envy—and to tell the truth, so was I.

Needless to say, our new unnamed Chrysler was soon traded in—at a considerable loss—for a used 1965 Citroën. Green and grey. We called him the Green Gull—which came from a hybrid French-English concoction: *Le* gull *vert*—in honour of our recently retired Gulliver.

He was the first of three Citroëns that were to grace our lives and fascinate our neighbours. Every time we drove into Cannington, the farming community about a kilometre from our home, people would gather to watch the car sigh down into his resting position when the engine was turned off. Some would stay to watch the magical rise into *ready to move.*

We had countless opportunities to learn how appropriate such a car was to rural living. If the snow was deep, we simply set the hydraulic system on high and blasted through. If the car skidded on winter ice and one wheel ended up in the ditch, we again moved the lever to high and the system would lift the whole car, along with the ditched wheel, into a *go* position.

It was the Green Gull who carried us up into the Northwest Territories in the summer of 1969. We continued to appreciate all its features. Especially the swivelling headlights when we were driving through dense bush at night. And that wonderful suspension system, once we hit the crushed stone highways of the far north. There, it was not uncommon for one or more tires to fall victim to the sharpness of the shards. Once, while crossing the several hundred kilometres to the next town, we had to use the spare to replace our first flat tire—and then we suffered a second flat. By raising the car up to its highest level, we found we could proceed at a stately fifty kilometres an hour, balanced on three wheels. At the same time, we could not help wondering what would happen if we needed mechanical help, once we lost contact with the cities that might contain a Citroën mechanic.

Over the years, we were able to replace the Green Gull with two more of his brothers before we finally moved on to other makes.

We tried a Peugeot station wagon, one that ran on diesel fuel. That was when we learned the difference between liking a car and loving one. We never did get to love the station wagon, although we did come to respect its power and cargo capacity.

Another of the same dealer's products eventually attracted us, and so we spent a few years cruising around in something we came to call The Pod. It was a Pacer, with so much rounded glass it produced an impression of interplanetary space travel. This was the vehicle that in 1977 carried us through our first book tour across Canada, in behalf of a novel called *The Wars*. Given the heady reception that book received from critics and the givers of awards, we did indeed have a strong sense of lift-off.

By then, though, we were each past the age of thirty-five, and so we ended up passing the car to one of our teenage employees at the farm. We had begun to feel the need for something more stately.

Because our service station in Cannington was also a Chrysler dealership, we decided to try another of their products—a burgundy-coloured New Yorker with classic lines and space-age technology. One of its innovations was that it spoke to you. It asked you to do up your seat belts. It told you that your fuel was getting low. It mildly scolded you if you got out of the car without your keys or if you had left your headlights on.

The trouble was, the first one we got scolded us in French. That was before either of us spoke much of anything other than English, and so we asked for a replacement. It duly arrived, but this one had a female voice with which to nag us. Not a good idea for two bachelors. And so we finally ended up with Benchley, named for Robert Benchley, who had once written for *The New Yorker* magazine. If Robert Benchley could have played the role of a butler, that was the impeccably polite but firm voice that guided us through our Chrysler drives.

Once Cannington's Chrysler dealership was abandoned, we

moved on to Ford. We chose a Taurus whose size and amenities suited us perfectly. And we finally gave in to the idea of a personalized licence plate. The only vehicle about which I had written with any significance was Noah's Ark, which can be found in a retelling of the story of the Great Flood—*Not Wanted on the Voyage*. To our sorrow, we found that others had beaten us to plates that proclaimed *The Ark, Noah* and even *Noyes*—the surname I had given to Noah and his family. Finally, we found that one of the novel's characters had a name that was available—and so to this day, our plate announces that we are travelling in "Mottyl." Who else would drive a car named for a blind cat?

Stratford
1999

Wings

I have no idea what time it was when I first noticed that the plane was falling apart. All I know is, it was dark. One of the longest nights I had ever spent, and certainly one of the longest flights. Twenty-two hours to Australia, broken only by a brief stop in Honolulu for as many cigarettes and glasses of wine as time allowed.

I looked to my left and could see that the engines on the port wing were still active. Of course, I knew that keeping the plane airborne was really a matter of willpower. *My* willpower.

As my friend Phyllis Webb had advised me: "on longer flights, Tiffy, just beat your wings more slowly."

I looked to my right and saw that Bill, across the aisle, was finally asleep. I looked up and saw something fall from the ceiling of the cabin, down into the aisle. What in God's name . . .

I took a closer look at the ceiling, and was frozen with horror. As I watched, a screw slowly vibrated out of its hole and plummeted down.

Obviously, we were in trouble.

One of the stewards came down the aisle, saw the look on my face, raised his eyes to the ceiling and then smiled. He nodded reassuringly at me and passed on by.

In a moment, he returned, carrying a full bottle of wine and a glass. As he lowered my table and placed his burden on it, he smiled again and said: "it's all right, but I think you need this." How right he was.

I had my first doubts about the whole process of flying when, in 1955, I was among the passengers on a British airliner carrying the entire cast and crew of a London-based production of Thornton Wilder's *The Matchmaker*. We were on our way to present it at the Berlin Festival of that year.

And we made it. Eventually. But not before we had crash-landed in a potato field.

That's all you need to know about that. We crash-landed in a potato field. It is not something I would recommend.

Another early encounter with flight was in 1959. By then, I had spent three years in the US, first with the Broadway production of *The Matchmaker* and its American tour which, I am relieved to say, was carried out by train because the star, Ruth Gordon, did not like flying any more than I did. The tour ended in California, where I got what might be called a job as a hack writer for CBS in Los Angeles.

By 1959, I was back in Canada, happily working as an actor in and around Toronto, when I was offered another writing stint in Hollywood. Even though the timing of the work would require flying down, it was all too irresistible. A flight was arranged—and off I set, by way of Chicago.

Well, in Chicago, it was discovered that the visa under which I had been working earlier had expired. I had to cancel my ongoing flight and pay visits to the appropriate offices. By some miracle, a new visa was arranged and I made a call to re-book my flight to Los Angeles. That was when I learned what had happened to the plane I was originally supposed to travel in.

It had met another flight, head-on, over the Grand Canyon. There were no survivors.

A combination of willpower, ambition and liquid sedation put me aboard the same flight, a day later. I did not look down as we crossed over the Grand Canyon, nor when we were descending towards our destined landing. I did not look down, in fact, until what I was able to see was the cement-covered Los Angeles soil beneath my feet.

I might have been able to put all this behind me had it not been for the headlines a few days later. An army pilot had taken a detour to get a glimpse of the wreckages in the canyon—and had met that day's same Chicago flight, head-on. There were no survivors.

One of the casualties, for me, was my willingness ever to enter another airplane. I simply swore off. For life.

And then I met Bill.

Our first fifteen years together were spent on or near the ground. We took a lot of trains. We drove a lot. We had to. Our farm, Stone Orchard, was over a hundred kilometres from Toronto. And we would visit Bill's parents in Regina. We even spent a whole summer in the Northwest Territories, wandering around in either our Citroën or our collapsible kayak.

The hardest year was 1977. The book tour for *The Wars* and the fact that I was Chairman of the Writers' Union of Canada. We had to be in Vancouver, twice—once by car, once by train—and in Halifax, twice—both times by car. We were based in Ottawa for a while then, and both times we drove between Ottawa and Halifax non-stop. Over 1500 kilometres.

By then, we were a corporation. I was President, Bill was

Treasurer. The first time there was any conflict between these two offices was in the mid-1980s, when I received an invitation to deliver a prestigious lecture in Vancouver. It was tempting, but there was a problem. Land transportation simply could not get us there and back again in time to meet our other commitments. And then the fee was mentioned. At that point, the Treasurer had a little word with the President. More than one little word. Five, if I remember correctly, all of them very, very firm: *we are flying to Vancouver.*

Of course I rebelled, but Bill was unrelenting—and so were his arguments. We needed the money. Flying machines had changed a lot since 1959. He would hire a limo to take us to an airport hotel the night before, to avoid a morning rush. We would dine well. Wine would flow freely. Extra tranquilizers could be arranged.

And so, after almost thirty years, I boarded an airplane. And I have been flying ever since. Even to Australia . . .

We landed in Sydney and immediately sensed the uniqueness of Australia. The light was different. The colours were brighter. The air smelled fresher. More fragrant. And somehow, there was no sense of the American presence that was so strong in Canada—although we were soon to learn that Australia, like most of the world, had been infected by a growing plague of Golden Arches.

Our voyage would include a visit to Canada Week in Sydney, a holiday up in the tropics and attendance at a Book Festival in Wellington as well as visits to other New Zealand centres. Our first date, however, was the Adelaide Festival—and so we immediately took to the air again.

We were warmly welcomed in Adelaide and to our delight, instead of going to a local hotel, we were driven out of town and up into the vineyard-covered hills, to a gorgeous little resort at MacLaren Vale. This was where all the overseas visitors were being taken to recover from the rigours of long flights.

The main building faced a small artificial lake, while a series of cottages nestled under the canopy of towering gum trees—each one filled with flocks of parrots and parakeets whose colours were as vibrantly loud as their voices.

It was enchanting. By day we were to find the gardens alive with hovering hummingbirds. At night, we could hear the wings of giant moths, quietly vibrating through the flowers in the dark.

Once installed in our cottage, we went into our arrival routine. I headed for the bathroom to depressurize, while Bill began to unpack. In a few moments, I heard a knock at the back door, and then Bill's voice saying *hello*. He later told me that what confronted him at that moment was a very large lady dressed in vivid pink and brandishing a very large mixed bouquet and a very large smile. The next words we heard were followed by a stunned pause.

Hallo, dear! I've just come to do up your flies!

I have no memory of any action, but Bill also told me, later, that the lock on the bathroom door was suddenly snapped into place.

That was our main introduction to the Australian accent. The bouquet of *flies* was ensconced in a vase, and the lady left, very large smile still in place.

Our ears gradually became attuned to the Aussie vowels, but vocal mysteries were to be encountered all through our stay down under. One of the most memorable came in Sydney, as we were relaxing one night in our hotel. There was a television commercial for the Australian Reserve Army, jauntily sung by a military chorus. I can't remember the tune or all the lyrics, but one line seemed to proclaim: *come on, guys! We got the energy, we got the expertise! We got the Anti-Christ!*

It took all evening, but we finally got to listen to the thing again, and were profoundly relieved when our ears finally transformed the Anti-Christ into *the enterprise*.

The Adelaide Festival, for us, was highlighted by a reunion with Alison Summers, a wonderful young Australian we had met while I was writer-in-residence at the University of Toronto. When she sought us out, we arranged to have lunch with her the next day. She said she had just been married, and asked if we would mind if her husband came along, too. Of course not. It wasn't until the couple arrived at the restaurant that we discovered who her husband was. Peter Carey—a wonderful writer, and soon to become a wonderful friend.

Sydney had its moments, too—most of them unfortunate. The cultural attaché at the Canadian Consulate there had insisted we leave the Adelaide Festival early in order to take part in Sydney's Canada Week. When we reached our Sydney hotel, Bill called the Consulate, and asked what our activities were to be. He was assured that details would be delivered to the hotel. Otherwise, we were simply to join in the festivities of Canada Week. What festivities? Well, the Red Rose Boys from Alberta might give a concert, and on Sunday, there was a big church service. A church service? Yes—with a Canadian flag out front. Oh.

Details finally arrived and we discovered that two readings had indeed been arranged—one of them at a suburban university about fifty kilometres from our hotel. We duly took a long taxi ride, and found our way, as instructed, to the offices of the Head of the English Department.

As usual, Bill introduced us both to the secretary and confirmed our purpose in coming. The secretary smiled brightly, welcomed us and disappeared behind a closed door. We could hear a flurry of feminine whispering. *Who? What on earth for? What???!*

The door then opened to reveal a beautiful woman whose smile was as genuinely charming as her manner was gracious. *Mister Findley! I am delighted to meet you! And I'm so sorry to say that I have not had the pleasure of reading any of your poetry!*

And equally sorry to say that no arrangements whatsoever had been made for a Timothy Findley reading. Neither of poetry nor of prose.

There was one reading, however, that did take place, and that made up for everything else. It was held in a huge pub near the dog-racing tracks—and it was quintessentially Australian. Two spacious rooms with sawdust on the floor and an endless flow of beer. Once we made it past the crowd of beer enthusiasts in the outer room, we found an equally large and enthusiastic crowd of book lovers. Young people sitting on the sawdust; old people with dogs; children everywhere. It was wonderful. Noisy. Vibrant. Happy.

The roster of readers that night was equally wonderful. It included Tom Kenneally, who had just published *Schindler's Ark*—and whose name is sadly given little prominence in the credits of its film version, in which the *Ark* becomes a *List*.

Also present was Ken Kesey.

We were to encounter them both again in New Zealand—but that night in a Sydney pub remains vivid in memory. The audience was a writer's dream—eyes sparkling with attention and appreciation, laughter filling the room, cheers as raucous as those pressing in from the drinkers in the outer room.

It was during Ken Kesey's reading that the fight broke out next door. The cheers turned into angry shouts. Ken had to up his volume to be heard. Suddenly, there was the most awful crash. Followed by screams. And followed, ultimately, by sirens. The whispered news came through the connecting doorway and spread around the room. Someone had been thrown through one of the pub's plate-glass windows. Blood. Ambulance. Police!

And Ken? The only time he broke his reading was when the glass was shattered. At that moment, he slowly turned his head towards the sound, paused a moment and then, with a deadpan look at his audience, he carried on with his reading. To the sound of even louder cheers.

Something else was special about Sydney. It was where one of my oldest and dearest friends, the novelist Marian Engel, had spent considerable time, leaving an indelible impression and lasting friends. One of them was the poet Tom Shapcott. He drove us all around—to where Marian had stayed, and to her favourite haunts. He introduced us to some of her other friends—writers, teachers, artists.

And he took us to Ku-Ring-Gai, up in the hills, the site of some of the best-known aboriginal rock carvings in Australia. Marian had loved the place—and so did I. Its memories are inseparable from those of Marian, and I couldn't stop thinking about her as I made my way across the slanting black and grey rock face.

"Look," he said. "Petroglyphs."

And, indeed, there were. Rock carvings—deep incisions—God knew how old, of beasts and fish and birds.

And men.

The patterns were all quite similar . . . the shapes of turtles, birds and sometimes snakes. The "beasts" turned out to be giant platypus. And everywhere, in context with the animals—or totems—there were etchings of stick men and women—the sexes plainly and even grotesquely limned with oversize phalluses and breasts.

There was always a moon—though never full. This moon was always in its quarter phase and it always shone in the sky directly above the figures of the men and women.

That was how I described the place in the first of a series of stories about two writers, Bragg and Minna. Stuart Bragg, who was something like Timothy Findley. And Minna Joyce—something like Marian Engel. A deep love lay between them, in spite of the fact that Bragg's true love was a young man named Col. Some of Marian's Australian friends—including Tom Shapcott—served as seed beds for other characters in that first story. As did a vivaciously sad young Janis Joplin look-alike we encountered on our eventual flight back to Canada.

What else can I tell about Australia? Swimming in the Bight without knowing how popular its waters were to the Great White Shark. The popularity, also, of BYOB restaurants, where people brought their own bottles of wine in elegant leather cases.

Snorkelling over the Great Barrier Reef, feeding galley scraps to clouds of fish whose colours were torrid, tropical—and terrific.

That was during our holiday in Cairns, to the north. It's one of those places you fear to revisit, for fear it might have changed. And sadly, I hear it has—with what Jimmy Durante might have called *a revoltin' development!* When we were there, however, it had all the tropical ambience and charm of a Somerset Maugham setting.

We had rented a small apartment in the Pearl Lugger Hotel on the Esplanade, which meant that right across the street lay a ribbon of sand which led to the tidal mud flats bordering the ocean. Whenever the mud was exposed, it was populated by wading birds of all shapes, sizes and brilliant colours—uncountable—and indescribably beautiful.

The sound and sight of beating wings punctuated our entire stay in Cairns. Our quarters had little balconies both front and back, with no screens on the doors. Whenever we tried to cope with the tropical heat by getting a current of air moving through the place, this opened up a flight path for all the smaller birds who became our constant companions.

Sparrows on the table, looking for edible scraps. Tiny Peaceful Doves doing their mechanical strut around our feet as we sat on the front balcony watching life on the mud flats. Larger doves, wings whistling them through the air, landing on the iron railings, one red eye on the crumbs we had scattered around our outdoor chairs.

Then there were the most astounding wings of all. A cobalt blue, vivid and iridescent. At first, they evaded me entirely. We had taken a narrow-gauge train up into the mountains to one of the market villages there—Kuranda Station. On the way up, Bill kept making excited noises as he gazed out the open window, but every time I looked, all I could see was jungle. "Ulysses butterflies," he explained. "One of the most gorgeous creatures in the world."

Well. All the way up and all the way down, I tried to spot one, but they were too fast for me. It was disappointing and extremely irritating. So Bill told me that the next day we would drive up the same route and he would show me a Ulysses butterfly.

"It's a promise," he said.

In the morning, off we went. The road was a series of hairpin turns flanked by dense tropical rain forest. I was afraid to ask how he could be so confident of a sighting. And what if the expedition failed? What would that do to his entomologist's pride?

About two-thirds of the way up, Bill spotted an opening in the trees, where the road had enough of a shoulder to allow us to pull off from the traffic. We got out and found ourselves looking down a steep gully that ultimately disappeared into darkness, far below.

"Five minutes. I promise." And he smiled.

I said nothing. I didn't even look at my watch.

There was a pause.

Then Bill pointed down. "There!"

I ventured a look.

Nothing.

But then, I caught a glimpse of movement.

Something very small seemed to be winking in the distance. I watched, and gradually became aware of the most intense blue I had ever seen, flashing on and off as it moved erratically up the gully.

Eventually, it got close enough for me to understand the flashing. Only the tops of the wings were blue, so they could be seen only when the wings were open. Every closing, accompanied by a sideways roll, brought the black undersides into view. Blue—black—blue—black. All the way to where we stood.

The butterfly seemed to know of my eagerness to see it. For a few moments, it bobbed and wavered right in front of us—and then, with a salutatory snap of its wings, it flew above our heads and disappeared across the road.

Neither of us said a word.

We got back into the car and drove home in silence.

The word *wonderful* hung in the air all the way back.

*   *   *

On our ultimate return to Canada, one of the first things I did was to have a talk with Marian. I told her all about the voyage—and all about the wings. The planes, the birds, the butterfly. It took about half an hour.

The Toronto sun was warm, but there were still some patches of snow on the ground. Fortunately, the ground was bare and dry around her grave, and so I was able to sit there and tell her about the trip. Just as I had sat by her hospital bed a year or so earlier, and told her about that flight to Vancouver—the first one I had taken for over thirty years. Then, she was in the final coma that was to mark the end of her long struggle with cancer—but the nurses assured me that she might have heard me, since—they said—there's evidence even then of some response to voices and words.

And so, I hope she also heard something of our trip to Australia. Somehow, I feel that she did.

Stone Orchard
1993
Article

> The Very Pineapple of Perfection
> If all you want is sleep, go to bed.
> But if you want to dream, go to Barbados.

Every day at noon, the Pineapple Woman walks along the shore, crying her wares in front of our hotel.
Pine—apple! Pine—apple!
This is almost a song—and it carries up beyond the fences and across the lawns. Five or six of us leave our chairs and, bringing money, cluster in her vicinity.
"Same today as always?" she asks—as if I'd been there all my life.
"Please, Missus, yes."

Holding the pineapple up by its hank of stubby leaves, she produces a knife and proceeds to peel away the skin with a series of downward cuts that leave the fruit naked and dripping, filling the air with the sweetness of its juices. Then, without pause, she makes a second series of cuts in descending spirals, removing the pineapple's "eyes." All this while she is singing beneath her breath—barely audible.

> Jesus leads me where I wander,
> Jesus leads me where I go . . .

"You want it whole or sliced?" she interrupts her song to ask.

"Sliced."

She hands me a clear plastic bag from the woven satchel sitting on the sand by her feet. Inside, besides its load of limes, tomatoes and fresh pineapples, there is also a change purse and a clean white handkerchief. "Hold the bag down under, honey," she says and lifts the pineapple up where her eye can judge it.

Then, with a series of flashing gestures, she drops the whole thing down in pieces into the plastic bag. I am afraid to look for fear her fingers are in there, too.

"That'll be eight dollars, Bajan, honey. Just put it there in the purse."

Roughly five Canadian dollars. Not bad for pineapple brought right to your doorstep, freshly sliced.

The Pineapple Woman must be in her seventies. Her grey hair is cropped short, most of it hidden beneath a soft wool hat. Her legs are bare and bowed. She wears a cotton dress, one day of white and blue, another day of red and yellow. Sandals on her feet, a crucifix at her throat and several beaten silver bracelets on her arms. As she walks away along the beach, she hoists the multi-coloured satchel onto her head and, counting her take, moves on to her next encounter.

Jesus leads me over yonder,
This is all I know . . .

She will have walked all day before she finishes and turns for home.

It's not a large island—roughly twenty by thirty kilometres; the natural underground reservoirs in its limestone bedrock hold the purest fresh water in the Caribbean—excellent for drinking or for making the local Banks beer. The island takes its name from the shaggy fig trees that once lined its shores; in Portuguese—the language of an early visitor—they were known as *los barbados*, the bearded ones.

At the southern tip of Barbados, in the parish of Christ Church, there is a stretch of coral sand that is known as St. Lawrence Gap. To the east, with its historic churches, chattel houses and fish market, the town of Oistins lies in the curve of a wide, green bay. This is where you go when you want to buy fish taken from the sea that morning—or fresh shrimp. Away to the west, beyond the Needham Point Lighthouse, the old city of Bridgetown spreads its narrow streets and alleyways in a maze of charming chaos. Along the roads that run between these towns, there are dozens of hotels and restaurants offering a choice of food and lodging for every taste and pocketbook.

We settle on the Casuarina Beach Club, with its lawns shaded by palm trees, almond trees and, of course, tall, evergreen casuarinas. Everywhere you look, there are flowerbeds filled with hibiscus, orchids and oleander. And beyond them, a gorgeous white-sand beach meets the surf.

Every morning, we sit very early on our balcony, overlooking the gardens, pools, restaurants and tennis courts. We feed bread crumbs to the birds while we breakfast on tea and pineapple.

Small, grey finches and tiny, hand-sized doves walk on the tiles at our feet. They are chased by Carib grackles—small, black brats with vivid yellow eyes. They have a rude, loud voice and a cocky walk that reminds me of Sammy Davis, Jr. and that famous rolling gait he used when he was playing "Here come the Judge!" There is also a black-hooded hummingbird nesting nearby, and a pair of tiny black and yellow sucriers attracted by the sweetness of the cores of our pineapple slices.

For an hour or more we sit and watch the first arrivals of the hotel staff, the maids and cooks and gardeners who stand and chat with one another on the paths between the flowerbeds before they go their various ways to begin the day's work. This is always a pleasant moment, with laughter rising from the gardens—a pause before the serious business of a holidayer's life take over: the sunning—the swimming—the snacking—the shopping—and the snoozing.

Having opted for a small suite with a kitchen, three or four times a week we pass through the gates and walk down a tree-shaded road past other hotels and houses to do our shopping at the local "99." It is much like Becker's, but with character instead of sheen. It is also a general meeting place, and the yard—with its trees and fruit stands, its bicyclists and taxi drivers gathered on the steps with cigarettes and Cokes and its joking, rambunctious kids and sedate, slow-moving elders under their parasols—is a place where a dozen stories could be had for the asking.

All the streets on the island are exceptionally narrow and many of them have no sidewalks. Taking an evening stroll, you can all too easily find yourself staring down a racing driver as if you had wandered onto the track at Indianapolis. Cars are driven on the left-hand side, as in England, and Canadians and Americans make perfect pedestrian targets because they are always forgetting to walk on the correct side. Raised fists and screams will not help you. Run for the nearest tree.

One of the restaurants we always pass is called T.G.I. Boomer's. Boomer's is more or less exactly what its name implies—a wild ride of music, American food and beer, and hundreds of college students. Every time we go past, I think of an incident that happened before our journey began.

Waiting for our departure call in the restaurant at Pearson [airport in Toronto], we were seated near two young men who were talking about the holiday before them. From what was being said, it was obvious they were also on their way to Barbados. "All I want," said one of them, who was dressed entirely in black and who wore a silver earring, "is six square feet of sand all day and a seat at Boomer's all night."

"Boomer's?" said the other man, who favoured hot pink ski clothes and a yellow baseball cap. "What's that?"

"Boomer's," said the Silver Earring, "is this terrific restaurant. Music all night long and women stacked three deep at the bar wearing nothing but bikinis!"

The Yellow Baseball Cap thought about it. "Three deep, eh?" he said. His face was utterly blank. There was a pause. And then he asked: "do they have a satellite dish?"

Passing Boomer's in the flesh, I see that, indeed, they do. I hope it made him happy.

Our favourite restaurant turns out to be one called L'Azure. Its Bajan cuisine is enhanced by a delicious touch of the Mediterranean. Its paella is superb. And if you want—as I always do—one meal that will shoot you down in flames, order the Crevettes Méditerranée, in which the shrimps are sautéed with chilli peppers, white wine and lime juice. It makes a glorious fire and wakens the palate for weeks afterwards. Sort of like feeding the palate amphetamines: *wake up! wake up and smell the chillies!*

But L'Azure is not just about food. It is also one of the loveliest settings we found—set back from the road above the sea and open, in part, to the sky. Waves crash against the rocks and you can watch the moon and the stars while you dine. The proprietor is Monique Hinds, a brightly charming young woman who took her degree in business at the University of Western Ontario in Canada. Her father, Cyril Clarke, owns the Rostrevor Hotel with which the restaurant is associated—and if you are lucky enough to be present some evening when Mister Clarke is dining alone, you may end up, as we did, having some wonderful conversation with him. And any evening, at the waterside tables you can look over the parapet and watch the translucent green of the garfish as they dart through the waves surging against the breakwater at your feet.

Just down the street, you can have equally interesting dining companions—the little geckos gathered around each pillar light, waiting for the next course of invisible flying insects. They are true acrobats, and often venture upside-down onto the ceiling. No— they never fall. Your soup is safe.

This is Josef's—a white-stuccoed house surrounded by tamarind and almond trees. It is European to its fingertips, and although its owners are Swedish, it's the sort of restaurant you dream about when you imagine dining in the hills above Nice. The wine list is excellent—though the variety of reds is limited, as it seems to be everywhere in Barbados. Nevertheless, we found some very good Merlots and Cabernet Sauvignons. At Josef's you will be glad of these, because they serve, bar none, the best filet mignon I have ever had in my life. Tender and thick, it is superbly prepared and cooked.

From where we sit on one of our visits, we can watch the chef—a young European—through a doorless portal leading to the kitchens. All we can see is his back—but the fascination is in watching him exercise control—with perfect timing—over the simultaneous preparation of what seems a multitude of different dishes. He might be Siva, with a myriad of hands and arms—stirring, lifting, shaking and spooning each concoction to its plate with panache and artistry.

The service at Josef's is particularly good—and, along with the glorious food, attracts an international clientele that will keep you counting languages the way kids count licence plates. One night we hear at least eight different languages in less than an hour. This gives the flavour, to some degree, of one of those restaurants in 1940s movies where the European élite sat out the war while waiting for contraband visas that only Humphrey Bogart could secure. I kept expecting Ingrid Bergman and Paul Henreid to come through the door and sit in the corner. All Josef's lacks is Dooley Wilson and "As Time Goes By." But then, you can always hum it to yourself.

We quickly learn that the best way to become further acquainted with the local cuisine is to find a restaurant that features a Bajan buffet—such as Brown Sugar, on the road leading down to the Hilton at the west edge of Bridgetown. Most of what's served comes from the island or the sea nearby, in seafood and meat dishes featuring okra, bananas, curry or lime. We also learn to avoid something called Neptune Night at one of the ritzier hotels—a gargantuan buffet of repetitious and largely tasteless dishes, followed by an equally tasteless show which, apart from the enjoyment of such ubiquitous Caribbean entertainments as limbo dancing, fire-eating and stilt dancing, offers endless bottles of cheap rum (and cheap jokes) to the oldest, youngest, most recently married, etc. of its audience.

We learn to deal with the army of beach vendors who constantly interrupt your sunning and snoozing to offer aloe for your sunburn, handmade jewellery and coral souvenirs for your friends back home—or a full range of delights for your nightlife enjoyment. The interruptions aren't always welcome, but the barter—and the banter—are never dull.

★   ★   ★

While Barbadians can give the impression that life is a laid-back stroll beneath the trees, do not be fooled. The pace of their lives can suddenly shift into high gear.

Yellow buses hurtle through the streets as if their destination were a pit-stop in hell. For a single Barbadian dollar—less than seventy cents, Canadian—you can go just about anywhere on the island. Passengers all sit smiling, rocking back and forth with practised balance, glancing happily at one another—beating time to the endless jumped-up music streaming in the air through the open windows. The streets themselves are twisted and lumpy, carved from the coral in an age when traffic was confined to horse-drawn wagons. The driver pinches his horn at least a dozen times a minute, scattering pedestrians in all directions, the sound of it lilting and disconcertingly Parisian. All the way into town, I have the feeling we've been hijacked by a disaster novel—the kind that always ends with someone saying: "*wow*, for a moment there, I thought we weren't going to make it!" But make it we did—and no crash landing.

You can always find a taxi, if you prefer such a thing, or if it's too late for the buses, you can rent a car or a light, Jeep-like vehicle called a "moke." But for us, by far the best value is the merry-go-round excitement of a bus.

In Bridgetown, we walk through a park beneath some trees and make for the nearby marina. This is the heart of the city, where all the streets converge at the water's edge. On one side is Independence Park and on the other, beyond twin bridges, is Trafalgar Square. We can see the statue of Lord Nelson raised on its pedestal above a mass of green and yellow umbrellas. We call him Horatio at the Bridge.

Everywhere, there is a constant joyous noise. Street vendors cry their wares on every corner; the clock tower, rising over the 17th-century public buildings, tolls each quarter of the hour; music rolls and swaggers from the shoulders of hawkers armed with ghetto blasters; small parades of uniformed schoolchildren march across the bridges, calling out one another's names; and, above all this, the buses and the taxis sing out a descant of horns. As noise, it is enthralling; it has an optimistic edge to it—as if some secret happiness you had not yet found was being celebrated.

We head for the Bridge House, overlooking the careenage. This is a shallow inlet where fishing boats were brought in the past to be *careened*—tipped on their sides in order to have their hulls scraped clean of barnacles.

Upstairs in the Bridge House there is a marvellous restaurant called the Fisherman's Wharf. It has a long, narrow verandah where you can dine looking down at the yachts and launches moored at dockside, and where you can also enjoy the breezes blowing in from the sea.

The menu at the Wharf is mostly fish and seafood. I particularly enjoy the lobster thermidor and the lobster with lime mayonnaise. My favourite accompaniment to almost anything is the piquant cucumber salad served with chilli peppers and lime juice. There's also Lambie Souse—a Bajan concoction of conch meat tenderized in lime juice—and coconut shrimp—deep-fried in a light, coconut-filled batter. The desserts are among the best on the island, ranging from various kinds of mousse to a wide selection of sherbets and pies. Of course, you can always order a richly refreshing piña colada, and call it dessert.

Mostly, we spend our days reading in the shade and swimming in the sun. The sea on the south coast is a wondrous mixture of Atlantic and Caribbean waters—warm, clear and multihued. The Atlantic waters are a dark, rich green and the Caribbean waters are turquoise. When they mingle, they produce a frothy, almost milky indigo. The waves can be three to five metres high and the undertow must be acknowledged. Over on the east coast, the Atlantic pounds in too spectacularly for swimming unless you know the area very well, while on the west coast, where the more expensive hotels and restaurants can be found, the Caribbean is usually glassy calm. We swim for half an hour at least three or four times a day, after which we lie on the coral sand in the sun. The sun can be extremely dangerous—and we are justifiably warned by our Bajan hosts to take it seriously. For the first few days we use a #24 sunscreen—and never less than a #15.

In the evenings, prior to our restaurant forays, we sit with a Banks or a ginger beer on the balcony and watch the sun go down. The air fills up with the sounds of birds, and of parents calling their children in from the lawns. It is also heavy with the smells of soap and Noxema, Nivea Cream and women's perfume—all mingling with the scent of flowers, cut grass and damp earth.

The last time we go to the fence to buy our fruit, the Pineapple Woman gives us a dazzling smile and shakes our hands and thanks us.

"Goodbye to you, boys!" she calls, as she walks away. "Goodbye, and journey well!"

We do.

Cotignac
January 10, 1997
Journal

In 1994 we decided to take the most extensive journey of our lives. We sailed from New York on the *Queen Elizabeth II* (later to fly back on the Concorde) and visited London, Dieppe, Venice, Florence, Athens and the Aegean islands of Santorini and Paros. Then we headed for the south of France. Our friends Marigold Charlesworth and Jean Roberts, from our theatre days, had a house in Provence—so we asked them to find us a relatively nearby house to rent for a couple of months. This they did—and thus we came to the village of Cotignac.

Our first view of the village was from our rented car as we followed our friends' car down the steep switchbacks that would take us into a deep valley. There below us, nestled at the foot of a towering red lava cliff, was a jumble of pastel-façaded houses, each with a terra-cotta tiled roof. We were enchanted, and by the time we reached the rented property, we were in love. Stone-walled terraces cascaded down the valleyside. Under the pines and olive trees the gardens were crammed with flowering shrubs and perennials. The house boasted a view of the valley, a fireplace and two bedrooms, each with its own bathroom. Perfect.

Within a year we managed to buy it, and after another year we had remodelled the garage into a studio for Tiff—complete with running water for his tea. And there, until the end of his life, he did almost all of his writing—free from interruption and distraction. WFW.

In daylight, there is laughter—quite a bit of it. We're both getting very good at being eccentric old men with foibles and problems that are almost fun—me not being able to put on my socks without getting out of breath—falling over trying to put on my trousers and WFW pouring food down his front as if we were doing it on purpose—blind, both of us—going deaf (WHAT????) and having lovely times not quite understanding one another . . . But in the night—in darkness—there is no laughter. Maybe that is the meaning of all this—that I must get about finding it there. And wouldn't it be nice to think so?

The hunters are potting away at everything that moves, because the sun has finally come out. I am learning not to hear them. The valleys roar with their shots—made worse because of all the echoes. I am reminded of something read or heard long ago—of the man

who was born to hunt saying: "it's such a nice day, I think I'll go
out and kill something." He must have been a Frenchman. . . .
   Will write more about New Year's Eve and Day—our visit to
St. Paul de Vence and the [Bruce] Westwoods. Albee [Alberto
Manguel] there and Craig [Stephenson] (Bruce is their agent) and
a French journalist, Edith Sorel—with whom I immediately fell in
love. Perhaps our age or slightly older—covered Eichmann trial—
knows *everyone*—but no pretensions—no airs—just herself in all
her simple splendour. We had, with them all, an enchanted time. I
ate my first raw oyster (oh!), we drank champagne. There was a
fire—a dog—a glorious house and WFW/self were ensconced in a
shepherd's cottage with private bathroom and huge bed and
kitchen—all overlooking the village in a garden soaking wet with
rain. And to think I was so apprehensive of being there, I did not
want to go!!!! What a time we had.
   The play (*Famous Last Words*) has sprouted wings and I am
excited. . . .

Cotignac
January 17, 1997
Journal

The days hurtle by! Good grief! Showered, dressed and off to Brig-
noles . . . to look for old tiles, old doors (in pairs) and pools of the
variety suitable for our proposed foyer. The tiles will be its floor and
the doors will face its three cupboards—one for clothing—one for
brooms, etc.—and one as a pantry . . . We went to the most extraordinary place (Duttus') owned and managed by a heavenly Italian
whose voice has cracked. He sounds like an excited puppet. Wonderful. Basically, what he manages is a wrecking firm which is also a
place for restoration. He showed me a pair of Louis XV doors that
were exquisite—pointing out the brand new wood and carving laid
in beside the old. They were beautiful. A master craftsman. We

found three sets of doors that will be perfect—each set different than the others—but all with the same feeling—simple, elegant and *old*. Also, with beautiful old hardware. Then we found two irresistible chimney pots, quite ornate, of red clay which John [Bertram, our *gardien*] will use to create lamps on the driveway where, at night, it is quite dark. Then, also, we found a beautiful container for our pool in the foyer—originally the surround for large clock on a 17th-century tower.

Then we came home to discover a letter from Alec Guinness, the first I have had in years, although the Christmas cards have always arrived—and am delighted to receive it and will record its contents at a later time, since I must now work. But it was lovely to hear from him—and at some length. Strange, since I had written about him in this journal only two days ago—NO!—*yesterday!* (Time isn't moving *that* fast, Tiff.)

Stratford
2003

A Moveable Feast of Fodder for Fiction

Book signings seem to be an inevitable feature in a writer's life. Sitting at a table, greeting strangers and the occasional friend, checking the length of the line with truly mixed feelings: *the longer it is, the happier the publisher will be; the shorter it is, the sooner I can get back to the hotel and have a nap!*

All that, and more—especially the endless answering of questions.

According to many writers, including me, the most common question is some variation of *where do you get all your ideas?*

The answer, of course, is simple—and perhaps a little dull. *From experience.* Or, at least, from what imagination can take from experience and reshape into something that might be worth communicating.

On reflection, I am struck by how much my fiction owes to travel. Journeys across the face of the earth. Voyages back into the past, triggered by either memory or research. With the occasional leap of the imagination into one or more possible futures. For example, when I embarked on a memory trip back into my World War II childhood, I discovered a whole novel, *You Went Away*—the story of a young wife's attempts to hold her marriage and her family together in the face of her husband's absence in the RCAF. With the exception of a fictional three-year-old girl named Bonnie, all the characters are based on my own family and their friends. And again, almost all the events are versions of things I remember happening—except for Bonnie's death, and for a fictional affair the little girl's mother has with one of her husband's friends.

Then there is Dieppe, which Bill and I have enjoyed visiting several times, as a result of writing two television documentaries about the disastrous Allied raid there in 1942. Using our own Dieppe experiences, plus research and my memories of family friends whose lives were drastically affected by that raid, I found myself writing the title story in a collection called *Stones*.

Place, of course, can play an important role in fiction—but the writer has to be careful. For one thing, it is not a good idea to use an existing address as the precise location for a property that provides the setting for fictional characters and their actions. Street names are no problem; numbers on a street can, however, prove dangerous. The real occupants of the real property may protest— even to the point of legal action. Consequently, Bill and I spend a lot of time driving or walking around various cities, making sure that whatever the fiction, the action takes place in a building bearing a number that does not exist on the named street.

We did a lot of this when I was writing *Spadework*, which is set in the Ontario town we now occupy, Stratford. And on one of our trips to England we spent part of a pleasant afternoon choosing a house on Cheyne Walk that looked as if it could have housed the title figure in the novel *Pilgrim*—and then we assigned it a number that had not been used on the real street. The same thing applies to names—but here, the writer has to gamble. There simply isn't time to spend hours going through telephone directories, checking on names!

In two of my books, however, I was asked to give characters specific names—all for a good cause. In the 1990s, a kind of cottage industry sprang up in the world of literary journals. What became a featured item at their fundraising auctions was the privilege of having the successful bidder's name given to a character in a book by some well-known writer.

Thus, two of the characters in *Pilgrim* were named in this way: Seonaid Eggett and Leslie Meikle. Seonaid became Mrs Eggett in the book—an eccentric Irish woman who accompanied Oscar Wilde on a visit to a famous brothel. It was a lovely shock, during the promotional tour for *Pilgrim*, to meet the real Seonaid—a beautiful, shy young woman whose mother had made the bid as a gift for her daughter.

Leslie Meikle, in the novel, is a Scottish tourist who unwittingly assists Pilgrim's valet, Forster, in his plans to help his master escape from an asylum. In real life, she lives not far from Stratford and kindly allowed me to use her maiden name when I had difficulty fitting her married name into the period and place.

The other book in which I acquired character names in this manner is a collection of short fiction called *Dust to Dust*—a collection whose images and storylines owe much to our travels. The theme of every one of these stories is, in some sense, death. That may offer some idea of how I feel when the flight is too long or the car is going too fast. . . .

Anyway . . .

A title occurred to me one day. "Abracadaver." It was to be a murder mystery involving a magician, and the murder was to be solved by an elderly character I had already found, based on Dorothy Warren, a dear friend we had known at the Atlantic

House Hotel in Maine. She first entered my fiction in a book called *The Telling of Lies*, set in a fictional version of our coastal hotel. She had thus already gained her fictional name: Vanessa Van Horne. But what was I to call the magician? For various reasons, I wanted this character to be a woman. Then, out of an auction arranged by the western journal *Prairie Fire*, came two names I should use. One of them had an irresistible surname. Timushka. The sound of this word—its look on the page—presented me with a whole person. I have rarely had an easier time bringing a character to life than this world-famous female magician. And her assistant, named in the same way, became Erik Kelgard.

"Abracadaver's" setting was one of the most glorious hotels in Paris, the Lutétia. Glorious and grand, but with some dark moments in its history. It had housed Nazi headquarters during World War II, and after the war, was used as a hospice for holocaust survivors. Bill and I had been guests of the hotel in 1996, when the Canadian Embassy in Paris arranged accommodation there for all the English-Canadian writers invited to take part in an annual literary event called Les Belles Etrangères. It featured writers whose work was originally done in a language other than French, with a different nation taking part each year.

At first, we were completely awed by the Lutétia's splendour. The gold, the marble, the red velvet. The perfection of the service. It is all too easy, however, to relax under such expert pampering. This became evident when we were entertaining a friend at lunch in the Brasserie there. Bill leaned over to pick up a fallen napkin and managed to tip both himself and his chair into a sprawl on the floor. Suddenly, three staff members appeared as if by magic (*abracadabra!*) and restored diner and furniture to their proper positions. Embarrassed? Not a bit. We were all laughing too hard. Even the waiters.

There was no laughter in another of the stories about death. It is called "Hilton Agonistes," and its storyline emerged from two other trips we took in the 1980s. The first was to a resort hotel on the island of Sanibel, just off the Gulf coast of Florida. The setting was stunning—but not the experience. For one thing, the other guests all seemed to be malcontents. They would ignore the glorious white sand of the beach and huddle around the swimming pool, complaining loudly that the water was a full two degrees cooler than the tepid temperature proclaimed on the bulletin board. The ringleader was a rake-thin woman in gold pumps and a lime-green bikini with matching robe. A true harridan. Unkind thoughts about *all those Americans* began to occur when, to our intense embarrassment, we noticed that her Cadillac bore an Ontario licence plate.

What really bothered us, however, was the discovery not only that all the more menial positions on the staff were black but also that every one of those employees was bused in daily from the sordid shanty town we had passed just before driving across the causeway that led to the island.

We experienced this same unnerving contrast between white visitors and black natives in Barbados. The tourism industry had created big, flashy resort hotels with a fairly wealthy foreign clientele, while at the same time reducing much of the native population to lackeys, beggars—or worse.

What would happen, I began to wonder, if this unbalance ever became absolutely and disastrously intolerable. My fictional answer lies in the horrendous slaughter that takes place in "Hilton Agonistes."

I deeply hope that answer remains only fictional.

We had much better experiences in the Greek islands in 1994— more enjoyable and, in terms of resulting fiction, more useful— especially in some of the stories in *Dust to Dust*. Still, the travelling itself was a bizarre mixture of luxury and torture.

The whole journey began immediately after we had endured a disastrous US tour for the novel *Headhunter*. (Disastrous because the publisher's promise of meeting journalists in San Francisco, Chicago and New York turned out to be completely unfulfilled.)

Fortunately, our spirits were to be lifted by the fact that we had decided to sail to Europe—on the *Queen Elizabeth II*. The crossing was a dream. Our cabin was huge and luxurious, as was the bathroom (once we found it—the door was so cleverly camouflaged that I panicked totally when we first entered the cabin). Our dining room was heaven—as were our waiters. One of them, when I commented on the incredible pace and posture used by one of his confreres in carrying a tray, leaned over and muttered: *"they don't call us the Queens of the Sea for nothing, dear."* Anyway, great food, much resting and strolling of decks (even did our laundry twice in a pleasant little laundromat) and much keeping of me out of Harrods (I escaped once, and almost drove us to bankruptcy).

Then, after a lovely old-fashioned hotel in Hove/Brighton, on to Dieppe, where our favourite restaurant, Le Sully, is even better—and a terrific three days of more resting, walking and eating.

Then—the nightmare—struggling with all our luggage (roughly ninety pounds each) through four sets of trains on one day, in order to get from Dieppe to Rouen, Rouen to Paris and then, Paris to Marseilles and on to San Raphael. The cry for that whole journey was: *"l'ascenseur ne marche pas, Monsieur!"* We didn't find a single elevator or escalator in any station that was in working order—so, much heaving up and down stairs. And our last train broke down just out of Toulon, while our friends Jean Roberts and Marigold Charlesworth waited for us in San Raphael. Panic! But, after forty-five minutes, it started again, and we finally arrived.

After that—everything went superbly. We left half our luggage with Jean and Marigold, headed off to Venice, were met as we had been told, had a marvellous Canadian Studies Conference—they love my work in Italy, it turns out, and the speech I was to give was, in fact, the keynote address of the conference, and received with wild enthusiasm—even by the twenty or thirty Québécois delegates, who (thanks to federal blandishments for the upcoming Quebec election, I guess) outnumbered us Anglos roughly four to one.

As for Venice, all I can say is—we fell in love with every inch of the place. Can't wait to go back. One of the graduate students wanted to interview me for her dissertation, so we made a deal: I will give the interview if you'll guide us for a day. It worked out beautifully—we even got over to the island where Ezra Pound is buried—and just as we got to his grave, a huge lizard ran across it. I whooped with joy.

Then, a flight via Rome to Athens and on to the Aegean islands. That brought two weeks of paradise. First on Santorini, that incredible island whose centre was exploded away in a volcanic eruption centuries ago, and which now exists as a ring of islands with cliffs almost a thousand feet high on their inner edges. We visited Fira, the capital, up on one of the cliffs, and had dinner watching the sun set over the volcano—which last erupted in the 1950s, and still smokes and heats the sea.

It was in Fira that I caught sight of something irresistible to a writer. In the late afternoon, we slipped into a small Greek Orthodox church to see its icons. There, we found three elderly women, each one of them tiny, each one of them wearing huge furry dusters on her feet. They were skating back and forth across the floor, dusting and polishing the marble—darting around like water beetles on the surface of a pond.

You will find these glorious creatures in a story called "The Madonna of the Cherry Trees," where they are transplanted from Greece to France.

From Santorini, we took a ferry to the island of Paros. There, a wealthy South African family had just opened a new seaside resort within walking distance of the fishing village of Naoussa. The place was so new that accommodation was being offered at a tremendous discount, which meant that for a week, we lived like kings, at a distinctly unroyal cost, in our detached white stucco apartment with its marble floors and its magnificent hand-woven drapes and bedspreads. The menus were as glorious as the dining-room, which included poolside tables, outdoors. The pool, surrounded by potted palms, had its own bar and looked out across a sandy beach to an Aegean bay.

Bliss.

And so were the other guests. Several were reincarnated in the story "Dust," each with a fictional storyline—the French couple with their maddening little boy; the elegant older woman and her entourage; the old man who always swam with his yellow ball. (It was great fun to find a fictional reason for this particular pairing!)

Another story in *Dust to Dust* was "Kellerman's Windows." Some of its characters grew out of what we had witnessed from our hotel windows as we travelled in Europe. On our way to Florence after the stay in Paros, for example, we stopped for a couple of nights in Athens. And there, I indulged in one of my most passionate pastimes: people-watching. Our small hotel faced two apartment buildings, and I spent about an hour watching windows and a balcony belonging to one of them. What appeared to be a couple of gay men were having an argument. An argument? A tirade. A war. A *never-want-to-set-eyes-on-you-again* explosion. Great fodder, for a writer.

In Florence, the view from our balcony was calmer. For one thing, it lay at the back of our building. For another, our balcony time always seemed to be in the early evening, when the only sound was the chirping of clouds of swallows that swooped past. Totally in tune with the atmosphere was the sight of an old woman passing back and forth across the windows of her apartment just across the way—arranging, rearranging and polishing her treasured bits and pieces.

It was an earlier trip that gave me the setting for "Kellerman's Windows," which was one of those quiet Parisian backstreets lined with charming five-storey hotels. Like Kellerman, I was a writer visiting one of the most evocative cities in the world—a city that scintillates with a sense of the past and of how writing can come alive there—even though a writer may die there.

And so, like Kellerman, I stood gazing out my window under

the eaves and watched a young couple through two windows across the street. And like Kellerman, I imagined that the young man was a writer who had come to Paris for inspiration, but that his young woman remained totally uninspired by the experience. When I fed all these witnessed images into the mill, the story almost wrote itself.

That doesn't often happen.

Stratford
2003

Driven to Distraction

Limousines—particularly the "stretch" variety—have never been our choice of transport. This stems in part from our visits to New York, when we would see literally hundreds of these status symbols, some of them obscenely and comically long. As we would watch them gliding past a cluster of tattered street people, the stretch limousine, to us, also became a symbol of the tragically widening gap between America's rich and poor.

One image in particular said it all. We were standing on a street corner waiting for the traffic lights to change, when something long, dark and shiny silently pulled up in front of us. The tinted glass of the back window was slowly lowered just enough to allow a mink-encased arm to reach out. A gloved hand daintily dropped a half-eaten bagel into the gutter, and the window rolled back up.

We didn't wait to see if anyone picked up the bagel.

Bill and I had a more personal reason for being reluctant to ride in such ostentatious automobiles. I wrote a novel called *Headhunter*, in which I "borrowed" characters and images from a number of famous literary sources. One of the characters was a high-class call girl who conducted all of her business in a pale, chauffeur-driven limousine—an echo of Emma Bovary in her *calèche*. In my book, the limo had become a familiar sight on Toronto's streets, and had come to be known as the Great White Whale.

All well and good, but shortly after the book appeared, I took on the task of giving a creative writing workshop for Humber College. As always, Bill accompanied me and took part in the discussions I was able to have with my students. Along with other well-known writers who were similarly engaged, we were staying at the Royal York Hotel in downtown Toronto. The workshops were taking place at Humber's northern campus, to the northeast of the airport.

So—what transportation was arranged to get us all to the campus and back again? A snow-white stretch limousine. Bill and I had to explain to the others why we were not anxious to be seen—why we scurried inside so nervously, and crouched in our seats, regardless of the protection of tinted glass.

One useful thing did emerge from our week of such daily trips. Once, as a few of us waited for the others outside the workshop building, the driver—at the request of one of my female colleagues—gave us all lessons in getting in and getting out, gracefully.

It's easy. To get in, stand with your back to the car and gently lower yourself onto the seat. Swing both legs, together, into the car as you swivel to face the front. To get out, simply reverse the procedure, and hope there is a waiting hand to help you stand up.

We have found there usually is, but we don't wear mink or eat bagels on the move. And we still prefer taxis if we don't have access to a car of our own.

Toronto taxi drivers have always treated us well—even though we've noticed an increased aggression in driving styles in the western and northern reaches of the city—which includes getting to the airport. However they drive, they all seem to have remarkably little to say.

In New York, on the other hand, our cabbies always seem to act as would-be tour guides, relentlessy pointing out the city's landmarks. One of them, however, became my guardian angel, when I arrived in Manhattan alone to deliver the manuscript of *The*

Butterfly Plague—my second novel—and managed to get roaring drunk on the way down. When the manuscript's pages blew all over the street, the driver not only helped me retrieve them and get them up into the publisher's offices, he also took me out and bought me a drink while I recovered from my publisher's fury.

Taxis in Paris are not for the faint-hearted. There seems to be a code among their drivers that they not only exemplify the expert recklessness of French driving—they epitomize it. Being driven in Paris is a high-speed adventure involving passion, invective, near misses and resourcefulness, all combined with an incredible knowledge of the city's streets.

In our experience, to take a taxi is to ensure that there will be at least one *manifestation* blocking our way—one of those frequent mass demonstrations when Parisians take to the streets in protest against almost anything. At first, with precise time commitments to meet, we despaired of ever reaching our destination, let alone reaching it on time. Somehow, though, every driver seemed to have a combination of instinct and secret knowledge about where the demonstration was taking place, how far it had progressed and how best to circumnavigate it. We have never been late in Paris.

This used to become most urgent when it was a matter of getting from Charles DeGaulle airport to the Gare de Lyon, the departure point for trains heading south to Provence. Now, one can simply take a shuttle bus to another area of the airport, and step onto the appropriate T G V—*le train à grand vitesse*. And these days, the "*vitesse*" sometimes exceeds three hundred kilometres an hour!

Before the transfer from plane to train was so easy, however, we had one taxi ride that seemed destined for failure. Our plane from Canada had landed late—so that we had less than thirty minutes to battle the morning rush hour and reach the Gare de Lyon on time. To our horror, immediately on leaving the airport, we found the roads completely blocked with honking cars and fist-waving drivers. Rush hour had been exacerbated, we assumed, by some complex accident or another of those frequent *manifestations*.

Our driver was a young Vietnamese, and we had told him our time pressures. With a reassuring wave to the back seat, he executed a smart U-turn and upped his speed. Neither Bill nor I uttered a word after that, nor do we have any idea what route he used to reach the central area of Paris. We know it involved other satellite towns and the kind of driving usually reserved for the Paris–Dakar Rally. We also discovered that the trip from airport to station was done in what for us was record time. Once we recovered some degree of composure, we found ourselves getting out of the cab at the station—ten minutes before the train was to leave.

Then, the fight broke out. What we assumed to be a porter approached us with his wagon, but as we loaded our luggage onto it, another porter rushed over and rammed his wagon into ours. We gathered, from the furious shouts, that the first man was not an accredited porter, but simply someone who had come to the station to collect what fees and tips he could. Blows were exchanged. And as we stood there, still dazed with jet lag, we knew that time was rapidly running out.

Our driver had stayed to watch the fun. When he saw us looking at our watches he waded into the combat. He and the real porter overpowered the interloper, and handed him over to two members of the station police who had suddenly appeared. The driver smiled, waved us on and drove away, while the porter ran us to our train.

Bienvenue à la France!

Athens, in 1994, presented us with a new taxi problem. That spring, for whatever reason, cabbies simply refused to accept any passengers whose native tongue was English. The only exceptions, it seems, were drivers waiting to carry you from the airport or the ferry docks to your hotel—or who had been summoned by your hotel, in Greek.

On the day we set out to visit the Acropolis, we had no difficulty in getting a cab. The reception desk at our hotel was happy to call one for us. Two hours later, glassy-eyed from what a Sondheim lyric refers to as "all that lovely debris" and reeling from heat and thirst, we walked down from those famous heights to find a cab and return to the hotel.

Finding a cab was relatively easy. There were ranks of them all along the major streets. *Taking* a cab was another matter.

Every time we approached one and gave an English intonation to the name of our hotel, we were scornfully waved away. We tried hailing passing taxis—with the same result. Nobody would accept us—and it was a long way home.

Finally, having been refused at the third taxi rank we had found, help arrived in the form of another English-speaking tourist. He kindly told us of his own strategy—and it worked.

We went to yet another rank, but instead of approaching the first cab in line, we headed for the third. The moment we spoke to its driver, we heard shouting from the head of the line. The driver there was furious that anyone try to hijack passengers that were rightfully his. After forcefully expressing himself to "our" driver, he escorted us, still muttering, to his vehicle and installed us in the back seat. Not even our accent gave him pause—and we roared off in the direction of home.

I am happy to share this strategy with all. It works, I've found, in almost any country—including our own. If you are in a hurry, but the driver at the front of the line is engaged in a long conversation with his mates—or in lighting up another cigarette—just make for one of the cabs behind his and watch what happens.

Bingo!

Stone Orchard
1997
Article

Home

As I write, robins' nests are tucked on the corners of our porch. Every bit of grass and mud so carefully selected—every laying in and every tamping down exquisitely precise: not just any old straw—not just any spill of wetted earth—but, bit by bit, exactly what was required. A Monet—a Cézanne—a robin's nest—a crucifix. This and this and this and this.

What is home?

It is where we are.

Not just anywhere—but where we survive. And, if we're lucky, where we will die. This is the circle described by *home*. Name one who does not hope that life will end *at home*. Where else? *Down in the woods*—my second choice. *In a hospice*—my third. But first and foremost: *at home*.

Home.

No one ever comes home. Everyone goes home. Where are you going?

Home.

I have an unbearably persistent sequence of images in my head. Sounds and pictures that will not go away. They depict an April night over twenty years ago when a barn down the road caught fire. Everyone went hell-bent for leather, but to no avail. All the beasts, with their young, were inside. I wish I didn't have to write this, but it tells us something about the meaning of *home*. They would not come out, no matter what was done. In the morning, all were dead.

There are theories explaining why this happens—telling us why the beasts will not come out and why they trample one another, despite the flames, to get inside. That *animals know a fire is borne upon the wind* is one theory. They go towards the flames because beyond the flames is a place already burnt. This well may be. But also, there is the thought that *home* is all there is of safety. Even on fire.

As it is with barns and houses, so it is with countries. Now, my country is on fire—threatening to be razed, brought down, and nothing left of it but a shell, a shape that will bear the tragic image of who we were. Lost, because we played with matches. Lost in the turmoil of the Troubles—just as so much of Ireland has been lost. The home where once we sat together, sharing with one another, laughing together, trying for survival and continuity with one another—that house is smouldering already. Smouldering— and the wind is rising.

Our governments are withdrawing from us—leaving us as refugees are left—abandoned. Homeless. The very young and the greatly old—the sick and the needy have been the first to suffer. This is always so in desperate times. A person might imagine, here, that our governments have declared war on the people. The stringencies are all the same—loss of place and loss of hope; loss of security, loss of dignity. The roof that once was safely set above our heads has been blown away. Gone. Our home is not what it was—not what we intended—not what we created and shared. The arsonists have come, and—God knows why—we seem to be powerless to prevent their fires.

Home is the centre of our lives. Only a fool—a determined, not a true, pessimist—would tell you otherwise. *Home* is not just people. *Home* is what people dream: a bed—a window—food—a blanket. Something—anything—kindly to remember. For horses, the smell of hay and other horses. For cows, the mother-smell of milk. For us, for humankind—a photograph of someone loved—the taste of marmalade, curry, wild rice—the scent of snow. In a trunk or in a suitcase, in a mind or in a memory—something carried everywhere. The permanence of nowhere—nowhere made somewhere, because you have it in your hand. I am here—and, with me, who I am.

The Banff Centre
August 20, 2001
Journal

In the late 1990s, Tiff received a National Arts Award, which provided not only cash but an opportunity to spend a free month in one of the studios at the centre's Leighton colony. Other commitments prevented him from staying in Banff until the summer of 2001. Following that stay, we moved into Calgary where Tiff spent a month as writer-in-residence at the University of Calgary. WFW.

We arrived from Stratford on the 15th (Wednesday) and spent Thursday–Sunday recovering from everything that preceded— publishing *Spadework*, the Italian tour (loss of wallet)—leaving France—arriving Canada—moving back into 72 Ontario Street— a month's rehearsal of *The Trials of Ezra Pound*—opening the play and a brief collapse before leaving . . .

Jesus! There have been seven years of this. We're both in our seventies. We've both been ill—me with pleurisy/pneumonia and WFW, following cystoscopy, falling prey to a *terrible* virus he picked up in hospital.

Anyway—somehow, we have survived thus far. And here we are, ensconced in an absolutely splendid suite at the Banff Centre and in the Evamy Studio at the Leighton Colony. The studio is utterly charming—practical—beautifully designed specifically for writers . . . Every studio was designed by a different architect— geared to writers, composer-musicians and visual artists. A stunning collection set deep in the woods—quiet—protected—with views of sky—heights—gullies, etc. and with other visiting residents, elk, bear, squirrels, deer, crows, ravens—an occasional cougar—and mice. Heaven on earth.

This afternoon, I began the first draft of *Shadows*, the one-act play for the new Studio Theatre at Stratford, which will open in

2002 with a season of one-acters, including five new plays by Canadian playwrights, using a company of extraordinary actors. I have Brent Carver, my God!!! And I'm hoping for Dennis Garnhum (*Ezra*) as director. I'm the luckiest man in the world. Period.

The Banff Centre
August 29, 2001
Journal

Yesterday evening, after our lovely Pernod, WFW gave us a superb shrimp curry over raisin rice. Best ever.

We're having a terrific time. Beautiful location. The mountains. Occasional deer. Many squirrels, magpies, crows. Today, halfway to Evamy, there was a sudden burst of pine scent—fir trees—the unmistakable absolute identity of the forest world. Every childhood, every lifetime experience of the woods—the trees and lakes of my earliest memories and of later summers in the mountains. The NWT and the Yukon. Also that glorious long drive into the hotel at Atlantic House under those massed, massive pines and cedars and firs. I almost wept. But, oh, the wonders I've experienced—going down into the woods at Stone Orchard that final time with Casey and Minnie and sitting on the fallen cedar at the heart of all my visits there over the years with all the dogs— Maggie, Hooker, Belle, Birdie-Berton, Casey and Minnie. Even with Moth, that adventurous spirit and the only cat outside of Graylag who ever came on my walks. Graylag loved the snow walks best and Moth the spring and summer. It was Moth who brought the groundhog up from the hill in a summer of drought to share the cats' waterbowl.

Well.

Gone. Yes. But not. Never.

The Banff Centre
September 1, 2001
Journal

There is one squirrel I've become friendly with, who lives under the last hut on the right. I talk to him as I pass and I lower my head three times to assure him I mean no harm. He seems to understand by this that I'm benign. I've made the same gesture with dogs, cats, horses, cattle, sheep, goats—wild birds, deer, raccoons, moose, rabbits and porcupines. For whatever reason—and I'm sure there is one—they all appear to receive the signal and behave accordingly, continuing to go about their business as if I wasn't there.

Two days ago, there was a squirrel squabble going on in one of the trees behind me. I was fascinated. What a carry-on! Loud, contentious, almost violent. Intrigued, I got down from the bridge and went to locate the source—expecting to see two squirrels chewing each other's ears—pulling each other's tails—fur flying and blood squirting. But, no.

It was a single magpie—entertaining himself and anyone else who happened to be present with a mock battle in the trees. Quite remarkable and wonderfully entertaining, with overtones of "doesn't anything exciting ever happen around here?"

I was enchanted. It reminded me of Alec (Guinness) and Merry's parrot, Percy—who used to get Vesta and Tilly and the two Siamese cats into battle-royals by imitating dog and cat insults and challenges and then sitting on his perch cheering them on. These wars raged up and down stairs—in and out of every room in the house—with the cats climbing up the curtains and the dogs knocking over the dining-room chairs sometimes. The only way to get it to stop was to pull the hood over Percy's cage until they'd all wound down and collapsed.

The Banff Centre
September 11, 2001
Journal

Towards the end of our stay at the Banff Centre, the morning news shattered the peace and productivity of our sojourn there. The date—9/11—remains a dreadful symbol that international terrorism has reached unthinkable levels.

As soon as I realized that the TV images were not fictional, I woke Tiff. We sat and watched, wordless. Ironically, through the windows beyond the television set, we could see the majesty of the Bow Valley, framed by the ramparts of the Rockies. It all looked so serene and so safe, but serenity and safety, that morning, took on a new fragility.

Needless to say, very little writing got done over the following days. What was to become Tiff's final piece of work—a one-act play called *Shadows*—was set aside. WFW.

This morning, at roughly 8:45 EST, in New York City, a giant airliner, which had been hijacked between Boston and Los Angeles, plunged into one of the towers of the World Trade Centre. Twenty-odd minutes later, a second hijacked airliner plunged into the second tower. Within two hours, both towers had collapsed to the ground.

This is not the scenario of a sensational film. It is all too appallingly and unbelievably real. America is in shock. The world is in shock. This attack has already been described not as a terrorist attack, but as an act of war—the worst America has suffered since the Japanese bombing of Pearl Harbor in December of 1941.

Calgary
September 19, 2001
Journal

One week later—the dead still uncounted, unidentified, though over five thousand are reported missing. John Allemang in *The Globe and Mail* wrote that *reality will never be the same.* And it won't. *Everything* has been changed, yet again, forever.

In our lifetime and the lifetimes of our parents, at the beginning of the 20th century—it started . . . with World War I, the '29 crash, the Depression, the Dust Bowl, World War II, Hiroshima, Nagasaki, McCarthyism, the Korean War, Vietnam, the Kennedy assassinations, Martin Luther King, earlier Suez crisis, Cuban missiles, etc. Then the rise of terrorism . . . the AIDS epidemic . . . And now this. All these events crowding closer and closer on one another's heels.

How does one proceed—move forward without sinking back or settling in the uncomfortable present? We must join the living with determination, while never forgetting the dead, who perished in all these dreadful landmark events. There is no avoiding reality—whatever it may be, whatever it might entail, however it might present itself.

I think it unlikely that anyone who *does* fly can be more fearful of it than I am—but it must be faced. It is now a standard part of our lives. Yet, I am not brave—though I would not be happy with the thought that I am cowardly. I have done too much of what I dreaded to be called that, I think—but still . . . the very thought of sitting belted in another aeroplane is terrorism enough for me. . . . Yet it isn't solace enough to sit back and say: "well—I'm now in the hands of fate." Of late, the hands of fate have been covered too often with blood.

Calgary
September 27, 2001
Journal

Afternoon—at fivers—spoke with Mary Lou (Finlay) on the phone. She is going to New York, to show defiance. A brave act—of which I am, alas, incapable. . . . *But*—WFW is right when he says: "if we cancel the Canadian tour (for *Spadework*)—eight flights—we would be admitting and acknowledging that they've won." That we must not do.

Calgary
September 2001
Article

Shortly after September 11, 2001, Toronto's *Globe and Mail* asked a few people to write for their Thanksgiving issue. What, in the light of what had just happened, could anyone be thankful for? What follows was Tiff's answer. WFW.

A Thanksgiving Prayer

If you can read this, you're alive, and are more than likely aware of what life means to you.

If we know what life means to us, one by one by one, then it is possible we have the beginning of a collective will to go on living—in the face of a new danger.

Yet again, a form of fascism threatens us. Yet again, there are those who have appropriated the idea of God and are making use of it to achieve their own ends—in what they call a holy war. No. It is the unholiest of wars.

What do we have to use against this insidious enemy?

Us. That is what we have now. Us. And in whatever condition we may be—however endangered, however vulnerable—that is all we have—us. And our regard, our respect and our concern for one another.

What terrorists want of us is despair, and if we do despair, we will have offered them an unparalleled victory. This we must deny them.

We are here. We are, for however long, alive. Be thankful.

*From Past Imperfect
to Future Tense*

Time Waits

Stone Orchard
1979
Play (John A.—Himself)

In the mid-seventies, Tiff and I were commissioned by the CBC to write a television series based on two books by Pierre Berton. The series, called *The National Dream*, used a variety of styles to tell the story of the building of the Canadian Pacific Railway. I wrote most of the documentary sections while Tiff wrote most of the dramatic scenes. Pierre was the on-camera host and the leading role of Sir John A. Macdonald, our first prime minister, was played by one of Tiff's oldest friends, William Hutt.

A few years later, when Hutt was artistic director of the Grand Theatre in London, Ontario, he asked Tiff to write a play about Macdonald. The result was *John A.—Himself*, with Hutt in the title role. The play was conceived as Victorian theatre, with John A. as a great actor giving his farewell performance.

The first act told the story of Macdonald's public life, presented as Victorian music hall. Parliament was a troupe of acrobats trying to form a human pyramid; the press consisted of a ventriloquist who could make his John A. puppet say whatever was wanted; Van Horne, the engineering mastermind of the great railway, was seen as a magician; and Louis Riel performed as a pea-shooting acrobat whose trapeze became a hanging rope.

Act Two was Macdonald's private life presented as melodrama—
his drinking, the death of his first wife, the birth of their deformed
daughter. The following speech opens the act as Macdonald muses
aloud to a young parliamentary page. WFW.

JAM: My whole life is in this watch. (*He opens its back and touches
the locks of hair.*) My mother's golden hair . . . my first wife
. . . my dead son, John . . . and my brother Jamie. He was six
. . . and I was seven. My mother and my father . . . *our*
mother, *our* father . . . *went* somewhere. I don't recall. They
went somewhere. And my sisters . . . *our* sisters, went with
them. We were left in the charge of a man called Soldier
Kennedy. "Soldier" Kennedy. He was a soldier. Once. And
he carried a stick. I don't know why he carried the stick. But
he did. Jamie was a *playful* boy. Noisy. And active. I was not.
I read a lot. I guess, about that time, I was learning *how* to
read. "Rain, rain, go away—come again some other day.
Rain, rain, go away. Brother Jamie wants to play." I don't
know what happened. There was a noise—and something
got broken. Jamie came running. Soldier Kennedy was chasing him. Brandishing the stick. They ran around the table.
Bang! Bang! All the chairs fell over. And the stick came down
on the tabletop—over and over. Bang! Bang! Bang! And I
kept saying . . . "don't." I just kept saying: "don't. Please
don't." Then they ran out the door. And I ran after them.
Jamie fell down. Soldier Kennedy hit him. With the stick.
Jamie stood up. Bleeding. I said: "don't." Jamie went on running. Into the woodshed. Why did he go in the woodshed? I
said, "don't." But he did. There weren't any windows in the
woodshed. No windows. One door. Kennedy went in after
him. I said: "don't." "Don't," I said. "Don't." He was six.
And I was seven. Kennedy was drunk. (*He looks at the
watch.*) Almost seventy years ago, now. (*Holds the watch up.*)

Real time. *Real.* I jumped on Kennedy's back. I tried to stop
him. But I couldn't. I was just a child. So all he had to do was
. . . shrug me off. (*He shrugs.*) Like that. Just . . . (*He shrugs
again.*) And then he killed my brother. With his stick. While I
watched. (*He holds the watch in the palm of his hand, then he
slowly lets it dangle from its chain.*) Time . . . is like a spider.
See? Just like a spider. Waiting for us all . . .

(*The* LIGHTS *slowly fade as the watch swings from side to side.*)

Stone Orchard
April 1968
Journal

I am afraid of death. But in saying so, I think I am saying, at heart,
that I am afraid of pain—and I am afraid of "stopping." Nothing
else frightens me in death but whatever is inherent in those two
facets of it. I have absolutely no fear of the so-called unknown,
basically because I have no formal concept about what people can
possibly be talking about when they talk of "heaven"—or "the
hereafter" or "what-have-you?" All that is merely comfort and
consolation and so meaningless to the dead—although the living
may draw some brief solace from it. What I fear is what I *know*—
not what I do not know.

Ancestors Reinvented

Toronto
May 31, 1962
Journal

Gran Bull [E. Maude Bull, known as Maudie], who fell down last Saturday and broke her hip, is somewhere over ninety years old and now is down there in the Toronto General Hospital, probably dying . . . I went down last night . . . Granny was holding onto the sheets with one hand and onto the iron bars of her bed with the other . . . She told me that there had been a terrible, terrible earthquake and that we were in a trap and that Father had been missing for days and days and that people kept on looking for him. She kept praying, she told me, that he would come and get us all away safely. . . .

We talked a little more and I was able, gradually, to tell her where she was and what had really happened and then she began to remember it bit by bit but she still had a lot of it wrong and she said: "yes, something terrible happened to me . . ." Then she looked at me for a moment and tears came into her eyes and she said, so quietly that I could only just manage to hear it: "I went in somewhere and they took something lovely away from Maudie and I don't know what I'm going to do." And the one hand still held mine and the other held the iron bars by her side and I am quite sure that I will never forget that as long as I live:

"I went in somewhere and they took something lovely away from Maudie and I don't know what I'm going to do."

Stone Orchard
1992
Speech

As a writer, what informs you?

Your own experience, of course.

The age you live in. Where—and when.

Culture: your own—and the cultures of others, as the case may be.

Other writings by those you admire.

Mythologies.

Another way to express reality.

But there is a difference between reality and our perception of it. Something vital is always lost in the translation.

Let me give you an example of what I mean:

The mundane truth about Helen and Paris, for instance, is told in every discarded condom in the gutters of every city. Homer was able to elevate this truth to mythic heights. A myth is not a lie, as such, but only the truth in size twelve shoes. Its gestures are wider—its voice is projected farther—its face has bolder features than reality would dare contrive. When Paris discarded his condom, its contents drowned the citizens of Troy.

Is this not true?

If myths are the truth in size twelve shoes, then what is fiction— fiction as in novels, stories, plays?

One of the definitions provided by the *Oxford Dictionary* tells us that fiction is an *invented statement or narrative*. I suppose that's sort of right—except that it leaves the door wide open to the idea that fiction is pretty well made up of alibis and fabrications that wouldn't pass a lie detector test. Another of the *Oxford* definitions goes like this: fiction is *a conventionally accepted falsehood.*

So polite, the *Oxford Dictionary.* Why not come right out with it and say: *the bugger's lying!*

Well, not in my books, he ain't!

Try these on for size: *fiction is truths told by liars.*

Fiction is lies told by experts.

Fiction never bears false witness.

Fiction is truth disguised as lies.

Did Shakespeare ever lie?

You bet he did! Take a peek at *Richard III.* But while he may have winked at history, he never lied about human nature. He always told the truth about being alive.

All of my life I have been fascinated by the mythology of here and now—by the largeness of the gestures which have defined the 20th century. The vastness of the landscape of these times was created for monsters—and monsters is what we got. Where did they come from? Where?

They came from us.

We made them. You made them. I made them. *Me.*

I am a hiding place for monsters. If I were not, I should not be able to articulate half the human race.

Here is an informing moment that stems from both mythology and culture:

I am five years old. My mother's father has died. There has been a schism in her family for many years. My grandfather's death is loaded with other sorrows besides the sorrow of loss: the sorrow of reconciliations never to be completed—the sorrow of many questions never, now, to be answered.

What I remember of that time is this:

I am standing looking down a long, dark hallway—dark, but not sinister. This happens in a house I love.

Way off down this hallway I can see a place in sunlight. Standing in the sunlight I see three women, dressed in white. They are standing in a circle, arms extended to embrace one another. All three heads are bowed and all three women weep.

Held in their hands are large bouquets of flowers—the flowers all white—the whole scene vivid in sunlight. My mother is being comforted by her sisters-in-law.

How am I to know, at such an age, that what I am seeing has been lifted from mythology—a view of grief as old as time?

And this:

I am looking at a photograph. In the photograph, my mother is the very same age as I am, gazing down at her. She is standing looking up at her father. Also in the photograph are her sister, her brother and her mother. It is a pleasing photograph. Happy. Everyone is smiling. One of them is laughing. The long, dark shadow of the photographer is on the grass before them. They are standing in a garden. It is 1916.

Think how much I have already told you. Parents. Children. Smiling. Laughter. Brothers. Sisters. Sunlight. Gardens. Grass.

And yet there is no colour in the photograph. It is black and white, turned sepia with age.

1916. It is not a happy time, yet all of them are smiling. People do that. Interesting.

Looking down at them, I rehearse their fates. The parents divorced. The brother and the father tragically dead. The sister in an institution. *Mad.* Their word for it—not mine. And the girl in the long, white sailor's blouse called a "middy"—her hair tied back with a large black bow—her face turned up to her father—and the sun? This, of course, is my mother. All unsuspecting . . . that shadow on the lawn might well be the future, for all she knows. Or just some gentle friend who is calling out: *smile!* And she does. They all do.

How wonderful it is—this token from the past. And as I look at it, aged thirteen, I see my mother's hand lying in against the skirts of her middy. Her hand—her left hand. This is important. Something is being said. Something that, later, will inform me in part of who I am. It is this:

My mother's left index finger is pressed against its neighbour—the knuckles bent—the nail perhaps in the process of scratching an itch. Though, I think not. I look down over the hand that lies on the table beside the photograph—my own left hand. The index finger is pressed against its neighbour—the knuckles bent—the nail absolutely not in the process of scratching. It is worrying its neighbour—rising and falling—pressing hard against the skin as if to reach the bones in there . . .

How far back in time does this gesture reach? Or the smiles on those faces, echoed today in mine and my brother's? All the way back to the caves, I'll venture. All the way up from there—to here, in my own fingers.

This is not habit.

And there is no perennial itch.

It is a sign. A signal. That I am who I am—and not by accident, but by design. The design of genes, drawn in bloodlines—the informant—*the teller*. The shadow on the grass is time; the shades of everyone—conglomerate. A congregation of ancestors gathered to remind me: no one is himself, alone.

Stone Orchard
1984
Speech

The Mind of Ontario

My love for Canada was a feeling very nearly allied to that which the condemned criminal feels for his cell—his only hope of escape being through the portals of the grave.

When Susannah Moodie wrote those words, she was recalling her reaction to life in the backwoods of Upper Canada in the early 1830s.

In those days, there were many settlers living here who must have shared her sentiments. Trapped in their own private cells in the bush, these people were also caught in the larger prisons of distance and of climate; held at bay by intransigent mud and snow; stunned and exhausted by the labours that were needed to get through a single day. The grave, though never entirely welcome, held out, at least, the idea of deliverance from what must have seemed incomprehensible torments. It was also a place whose name you recognized. You knew where it was and you didn't need to find it on the map.

We take too much for granted, those of us who can now escape on the wings of Air Canada and the wheels of our Toyotas. We forget what it meant to have the escape routes confined to death and the imagination; the grave and the mind.

Indeed, we now take escape itself for granted, almost as part of our birthright. *We don't have to stay here, you know,* we say to one another. *We're perfectly free to leave anytime we like.*

And we do. Physically, there's nothing to it. Distance, once our foul-weather enemy, is now our foul-weather friend. A place in the tropic sun is only a matter of hours away.

There are other kinds of modern escape.

Of course, these other kinds of escape don't bring you home with a tan, but they're cheaper and more accessible—available to those who cannot, whether because of time or money, afford the costs of physical distancing. Tranquilizers, for instance, and television sets; the shut doors and the drawn shades of the 20th century; the escape routes of failed imaginations. But these are the subject matter of another story altogether, and not what I'm here to talk about.

What I'm here to talk about is imaginations that didn't fail. I'm here to talk about . . . perhaps a little madness . . . and about the mind—the collective mind—of my people. I was born in this province of Ontario—of Upper Canada—and when I say *my people,* I mean the people who fed my life with their spirit and their standards and their stories; the people who surrounded me from birth. Not just my family, but my society.

For a writer, every person is a gift.

Take my Uncle Frank, for instance.

Uncle Frank was really my mother's uncle—but I have long since claimed him as my own. His name was Frank Bull and he was one of a clutch of brothers, another of whom was my mother's father. I have a photograph of all these brothers, the five of them together, sitting in their wicker chairs on their mother's lawn. *Brighton, Ontario—1912.* Here is a scene rampant with the signs and symbols of our past: the house, the chairs, the shutters and the clematis vine, the men in their suits and their high starched collars, their elegant legs and their tight-laced highly polished boots . . . And all their familiar faces, familiar both to me and to anyone who has seen the face of Ontario; their serious, slightly squinting eyes, their bemused and private mouths. *Oh, what is not being said in this photograph!* And their hands, rather shyly displayed—beautiful, but not yet quite to their liking—not yet matching the hands of the aristocracy across the water. And, hovering in the background, beyond the open door that leads to the house, the thought—almost the very smell of the Sunday dinner even then being laid upon the cloth—and all their wives and their children and their mother, so patently absent from this photograph, still humming the morning's hymns as they set the table . . .

> Lord of the living harvest,
> That whitens o'er the plain,
> Where angels soon shall gather in
> Their sheaves of golden grain . . .

And here are the men, the brothers, seated on the lawn. Their names are Claude and Harry, Clarence and Fred—and Frank; the very quintessence of Southern Ontario names, whose female counterparts are Maude and Aurethia, Margaret, Emily and Caroline.

> Accept these hands to labour,
> These hearts to trust and love,
> And deign with them to hasten
> Thy Kingdom from above.

It is almost any Sunday in Methodist Upper Canada and everyone is behaving precisely according to the code set down by tradition.

And so, besides the implacable terrain on which they had landed or from which they had sprung, there was more—much more—that held them, or wanted to hold them in place, singing their hymns and folding their hands. There was always the dreaded God—whose vengeance was so clearly visible in every plague and every storm that struck and in every buried child. And there was Society, the social order, held together by ten thousand ears and eyes and by gossip and the endless dispensation of moral precepts. And all of this created a need, an appalling need sometimes, to escape. And sometimes, as with my Uncle Frank, this appalling need became unbearable. But luckily, he had the will and the daring and a sense of fun that allowed him to imagine breaking away. Uncle Frank thrived on the wonder of throwing open the doors and of flying full tilt on the wings of his imagination out into the forbidden world beyond the lawns of Brighton and far away from the pews of the Methodist Church.

All these brothers seated on the lawn had a love of music. In fact, their lives were devoted to it. My grandfather, Fred Bull, owned a piano factory, and each of the brothers played some part in its bureaucracy. Uncle Frank was the family inventor, turning over bits and pieces of pianos in his mind to see how they might be improved. He also loved to sing—and had a voice.

Now I can tell you how it was that Uncle Frank made his escape.

To begin with, you have to see him very clearly as the handsome one, the one with the hair that was slightly too long—because it touched the back of his collar. And the one who wore a cape in the wintertime, instead of a great coat. And now you have to see him younger than he was in the photograph. You have to see him, now, at the century's turn—unmarried and violently in love; the epitome of all young men who sigh.

The woman he'd fallen in love with was another epitome—Caroline, the romantic Edwardian beauty, who fell in love the way she had seen women fall in love on the stage and in books. It was the kind of love that says: *I will die without you* . . . and thrives on pressed roses; the kind of love that dreams—but only dreams—of patricide. If she had been French and had lived in the 1850s, caught in the eye of a great French writer, her name would not have been Caroline—but Emma.

Aunt Carrie's father is the last of this story's epitomes to fit into place—the late-Victorian Gothic father who carried a walking stick and who used it to strike the tops of tables in order to emphasize his demands and his pronouncements, and who raged against my Uncle Frank as the worst of the candidates for his daughter's hand and the one man absolutely forbidden to enter his house.

And so, adopting the mode of melodrama and romantic novels, Uncle Frank and Aunt Carrie ran away; eloped—by train. They took the farthest destination their money could buy and this, it so happened, was Minneapolis, Minnesota. Here, both in order to establish anonymity and safety and in order to give himself an edge in the marketplace, my uncle changed his name. Plain Frank Bull from Brighton, Ontario, became the eminent vocal coach from God-knows-where in Europe, whose elegant cards proclaimed *Maestro François von Buell,* with all the usual flourishes of royal connections and the names of dead or fictitious opera stars. My Uncle Frank was not alone in his deception. There was also little Maisie Roach of Southern Ontario, who decided people who wrote bestsellers also had to give themselves an edge in the market-place, and called herself Mazo de la Roche.

It was, in many ways, a schizophrenic society.

Let me explain graphically what I mean by schizophrenia—because I may not mean quite what you think I do.

I have a schizophrenic friend, and, very often, we talk on the telephone. She lives some distance away and her voice is always filtered through that distance just as you might imagine: making its way into my ear past intermittent clouds of static and fadings in and out of clarity. But, because she is schizophrenic and because sometimes she is drugged and sometimes she is not—because of these things, she has to find her way to where I am by means of what she has told me herself is a journey passing through ten or a dozen universes. I live very far away from her, indeed. So far away, I cannot tell. And the distance has nothing to do with miles.

When she is drugged, which is to say when she is most coherent and can reach me through the static and the fadings alone, she is wonderfully articulate and tells of her daily life in the world of shopping malls and taxis and walks in the park. But when she is off her medication and the journey to my ear is made through all those universes of which she speaks, then the voice I hear and the tales I hear take on an edge of panic and confusion. She will tell of not being able to find her way down the street. She will tell of buildings she cannot recognize. She will tell of people she last met a hundred years ago, who are still walking out the door. She will tell of what she thinks the world is about—and then she will tell of what it *is* about. And they are not, they are very definitely not the same thing. And yet, she sees them both—both worlds—and her mind is living in one and her body is living in the other.

And when I think of my people, my family, myself and my society, I think of them very much as I think of my schizophrenic friend—as I know my schizophrenic friend. Our bodies, too, are living in one world, while our minds are living in another. Not that our minds are living in a dream world. Very much the opposite.

Our minds are living in a world we have been told exists. They are living in a world we have been promised but have never seen. Not a dream world—not unreal—but a world not present in the world we see.

As we move our bodies up and down the streets of our cities, in and out of our houses, and as we lay them down in our beds at night, that other world—through which our minds are travelling—is parallel to this one. It contains the same rooms, the same chairs, the same bodies—but the voices are different, the lights are different—and the shadows.

One or the other of these worlds must surely be a lie. The world outside the mind is tangible; we pluck our food from its trees; we sit beneath its sun; we are washed by its rains; we are bruised by its corners. It is full of dangers and pleasures. Most of what is got there we pay for or steal. In the mind, the world is also full of dangers and pleasures, but the dangers and pleasures there are free. They are based on promises meant to have been fulfilled in the tangible world. But the promises are broken over and over again and fulfillment is consigned to the imagination.

And so, while we move through the physical world, we are mourning the absence of the other, though the other never dies. It is just that it has never fully lived, never been fully realized. The world in our mind is our constant companion and the source of nearly all our hope. But looking outward from that world of hope, the mask we are watching through has been made for the tangible world of apple trees and corners.

Masks. We all wear them. And we pass them down through time.

This brings me back to photographs.

Photographs are the masks through which we must decipher the dead—our ancestors.

This is not easy.

They were very good at hiding. And—why, I wonder? We, after all, are their children and their grandchildren. Didn't they want us to see them? Was it that? Was it themselves they were hiding, or was it something else?

I suspect a little of both.

The thing, of course, being hidden in either case, was the truth. The truth, if I may put it this way, about lies.

If you have enough photographs, you can watch the mask being made.

Let me show you one, the making of one mask—the mask of a woman. The mask of my mother's sister.

She was born in 1893.

The baby photographs are charming. A baby is always charming. Sometimes they make you laugh out loud. Always, they make you smile. But sometimes you find yourself saying: "how serious this baby is." Of course, this also makes you smile. But still, you have said it. And it can be said, to some degree, about this baby here—the one I am showing you.

You can see by the length of the face and the width of the eyes that this is going to be a beautiful child. And more than likely intelligent. There is lots of curiosity showing; one hand is already reaching out, and the lips are already pursed as if in waiting for the first question. And serious. Whatever mind there is, however deeply it functions, however profound its ability to contemplate—it is certainly already saying: "something is going on out there—and I wonder what it is."

This is not a baby saying: "me."

This is a baby saying: "are you there?"

Through babyhood, through early childhood, her photographs

clearly show she is exposed to and grasps what we like to call *the wonder of it all.*

She is healthy. Her parents love her. She is secure. Her parents are second-generation Ontarians who have survived—and whose parents have survived—assimilation. Let us not be fooled too deeply by what has been called the cultural mosaic of our country. It is there, of course, but within that mosaic, there are accepted and acceptable community standards and, in each community, those who wish to survive and succeed accept assimilation. This entails artful use of the mask.

By the time our baby, born in 1893, is an adolescent, the country has changed. Her family has changed, and so has her mask.

The beauty we have noted earlier is now well established. But with it an almost alarming poise. No one so young should be able to sit so straight, so still, so wondrously in control of herself. Not a hair is out of place.

The hand that once reached out has now drawn back, and it lies held down beneath its companion in the girl's lap.

Further examination reveals an alarming expression, just at the corners of the mouth. I know something, she is telling us. You have lied to me—and I know it. I will never forgive you . . ." But: "I will pretend to forgive you. I will lie to you."

The eyes know something, too. They have not quite worked it out. But the mask is taking shape now. And the mind, with its burden of lies and its thwarted sense of wonder, is going in behind a wall.

This girl, this child, was only thirteen years old—too young by far to feel compelled to hide. But, hide she did.

Let us posit what the lies she complained of were, or might have been.

Let us simply make a few statements, say a few words. Hearing them, we will all have our own reactions. Hearing them, we will make our own assumptions. Hearing them, we may even remember precisely how we reacted to these same words and statements when we heard them first as children.

God is everywhere.

God sees everything.

God is watching you.

There, in the photograph with her, are two other children. A fourth—a dead child—is missing.

God is love.

So it goes.

Then, there is this picture here—1917.

The mask is slipping. The mind wants out.

By 1919 it is firmly back in place.

There are only two in the photograph now, and soon there will only be one: one, as there was at the beginning.

But now, that one has two distinct faces: her own, which we recognize by its shape and its features, and the mask, which we also recognize—if not by its shape and features, then certainly by its firmness, by the way it has set. By the way the eyes are not and never will be happy, staring through the mask.

There is something else to know here, now, about the child, the girl, the young woman—the person behind the mask.

In around the time when the war was claiming lives in a way that even God could not keep track of—in around 1916–1918—the girl in the photograph started using another name. Her mind declared its separation from her body by uttering this name. First, only to the girl—and then, through the girl to pieces of paper. The name of her own great-grandfather.

"I am Nicholas Fagan," it said—the mind said—the hand wrote. "And I have waited long enough for what I have known and what I have seen to be matched by what I have been told."

It was more than a declaration of separation; it was, as it turned out, a declaration of purpose. Nicholas Fagan was not to be silenced, as the girl had been by the lies surrounding her. Nicholas Fagan wanted articulation—and gained it through the pen. When the girl, and then the woman wrote, she used this name in her desperate bid to match the world she saw and the world in her mind. But the world she saw and the world in her mind had been pushed too far apart and there could not be—and there never was—a reconciliation. At best, there were moments of riveting lucidity in which the truths she spoke had the sound of breaking glass.

That child, that girl, that woman and Nicholas Fagan, died last week after almost seventy years of sharing a cell whose bars, while not beyond her understanding, were far beyond her comprehension. Those of us who loved her will miss her. But memory is good to us and death is not always death.

Some years ago I decided that Nicholas Fagan wasn't going to die without having said a few words aloud, beyond the secrecy of her notebooks and letters. So I wrote a play about a woman who could not accept the acceptable realities and who could not, above all, accept our placid acceptance of them.

This woman—in the play called *Can You See Me Yet?*—enters an asylum for the the insane. It is 1938. Her only possession is a photograph album.

Her name is Cassandra and she perceives not only the figures in her photographs but the other patients as well, as being her own family. A family, perhaps remembered—perhaps imagined. Cassandra herself, as might be guessed by her name, is a missionary who has failed her mission. No one believes a word she says.

Well—the play was written and performed, but I cannot tell you the end of this story. It hasn't been written yet. And maybe it never will be written. I think that, if ever it is, I would rather have it written by Nicholas Fagan—or someone not unlike her—who will not be content to reconcile the world she sees with a world she is told to see. For I fear that we are raised on lies: more lies than truths—and I fear that, in order to escape these lies, we are returning to our

cells: our locked doors, our drawn covers—call it what you will—
our mass migration from imagination.

Now we are—what? Two hundred years old? And the mind
more than ever locked in its singular cell? If you find that thought
alarming and out of touch with reality, given the wondrous prosperity on every side—the glory of our cities and the bounty on our
shelves—then I ask you: "whose are these children walking the
streets and riding the subways, hiding behind their expressionless
faces—watching us through darkened glasses?" Where are their
questions? Why are they silent? Can it be that, for all our prosperity and progress, we are their wilderness?

Stone Orchard
1995
A letter to readers

The Piano Man's Daughter is a novel that celebrates the imagination, that celebrates the power to see the world as it actually is—
and that celebrates being alive. Of course, being mine, it sets out
to do all this by plunging the reader into the life of a woman who is
burdened with mental illness, trauma and violence!

Take heart. There is not only light at the end of this tunnel,
there is light all the way through.

Some of this light is reproduced in the photographs you will
find in the book, a few of which show members of my own family.
Their lives share some, mostly superficial, aspects of the fictional
lives presented here. Photographs, for me, act as "kickers"—not
just as kickers that move me into fiction, but that make me understand how important it is to be absolutely alive in the time we are
given. Not to slough it off and not to miss it as we pass. There is
always something wonderfully telling about the vivacity of people
captured by a camera. *Look at me! Here I am—forever.*

The people in the book grew out of stories and memories of my own family around the end of the 19th century and the beginning of the 20th. *The Wars,* for example, relied on the story of my father's people. Thomas Ross, Robert's father in the novel, is a greatly fictionalized portrait of my grandfather, Thomas Findley, who was the president of Massey Harris, the farm machinery manufacturers.

In *The Piano Man's Daughter,* there is an echo of those same times in my mother's family, whose fortunes rose and fell in much the same time-frame. They were involved in the music business— first of all in the selling of pianos, then in the making of them. My grandfather, Frederick Bull, ultimately became the president of the Williams Piano Factory in Oshawa, Ontario. Earlier, when he was on the road as a salesman for another company, he met my grand-mother—then, Edith Fagan—in Collingwood, Ontario. They fell in love, married and had three children: a son, who died in the flu epidemic after the war, and two daughters: my mother and my aunt.

Aunt Ruth was the elder. She was schizophrenic. My early encounters with her were, for me, magical. Her version of reality cut through a lot of the veneer that most people place on reality in order to survive. I was deeply taken with her and her way of seeing things, and she is the "seed" from which Lily Kilworth grew.

Lily's father, Tom, was a salesman-entertainer who travelled Ontario demonstrating pianos; my grandfather had also travelled in order to sell them, and otherwise, he was somewhat like Tom— a dapper man with a lot of style. I remember him—his blazer, his straw boater and his snappy walk.

The glory of it is that you can take such people and in the fictional writing, use details of their daily life, their houses, costume and other incidental similarities. Also the reality of incidents that come through the voices of aunts and uncles and, in my case, grandmothers—or through the letters that were saved or all the wonderful photographs that families accumulate. There they are—all the details verified. Then, you transform them, extrapolating fiction from reality.

For all the confusion and all the problems she inherits as a result of her illness, Lily Kilworth lives a magical life. Her version of reality is to be completely alive. This, she tries to share with her son, Charlie. She brings him to life inside her magical world and she passes it on to him with passionate urgency. Lily's motto is: *pass it on*—which is what I have tried to do with her life in this novel.

My mother's sister was schizophrenic. She spent almost fifty years in institutions or living in halfway houses under institutional care. She was a wonder.

When I was a child, my aunt was still in the world-at-large, and I adored her. I was in awe of her. Her stories, her explanations of the world that children inhabit and her versions of reality were mesmerizing. By "versions of reality," I mean her readings of events and relationships—and of who I was and where I'd come from—and of animals, trees and birds. She was, I am certain, a shaman, a medium, a mystic.

She was also damaged, betrayed, abandoned and, in some ways, destructive. As the disease increased its hold on my aunt, it drove her to fight back in sometimes alarming ways: disappearances, violent gestures, silences. But I loved her. So did her children, so did her mother—and so did my mother, her sister. Her increasing separation from reality, however, made all relationships difficult.

Sometimes, though rarely, I was taken to see her in the asylum. Green lawns, trees and park benches—buildings that had been created as army barracks. Gates—walls—many people wearing white. These are seminal images for me of those visits. And of my aunt: tall, somnambulistic, reticent—and beautiful.

This is the stuff from which Lily Kilworth was born. Lily, however, is not a portrait of my Aunt Ruth. Though Lily suffers a kind of mental illness, it is closer to autism than schizophrenia. And, although she sees things differently than most people, it's not the same way of seeing that possessed Ruth. Actually, I guess Lily is the closest I've ever come to attempting a self-portrait. The problem with fiction—and the privilege—is that you get to give the person you're describing more victories than happen in real life. So I don't come away from my own life with the same sense of victory that Lily had. But to whatever degree Lily's life is unique, my own sometimes despairing sense of uniqueness has finally hit the page as bluntly as it can through the exploration of a character such as Lily. In essence. Lily and I are both saying: "this is me." And to some degree: "take it, or leave it."

Fiction *is* fiction—distilled realities, the articulated diffusion—and confusion—of what reality offers.

Munsterfield, the Kilworth farm, is very roughly based on Stone Orchard, where Bill Whitehead and I live. It's in precisely the same position, south of the town of Cannington, Ontario, which was originally called McCaskill's Mills—the name I've given it in the book. The landscape is absolutely the same. The corner of the field in which Lily is born is directly across the road from our own house. We can't see it from our windows, because it's over the rise of a hill and down into the corner. The house itself is not the same as ours. Munsterfield is a large white wooden mid-Victorian creation that is more or less based on a beautiful clapboard house about twenty kilometres from us. It's on a side road running out of Leaskdale, where Lucy Maud Montgomery lived and wrote. Still, Munsterfield, like its fictional inhabitants, is basically itself. It's named for Munster—the county in Ireland from which some of the Fagans emigrated in my own family past. It's in the south, and it's from there that I seized on a town named Kilworth, to give the name of the fictional family living in Munsterfield.

The Queen's Hotel in the book, however, is the very Queen's Hotel in Cannington. Alas, in 1994, it was torn down—an architectural wonder for which the town, for some reason, found no use. And that's very sad. But there is a photograph of that hotel in the 1800s, published in a history of Cannington written by a great, dear friend—now dead—Islay Lambert. I used that photograph as the basis of a photograph in the book, and I used some of the people shown there as characters in the book. I also put Islay in as herself. And so here, I seized absolutely on the actuality of place and appearance and history.

The name Wyatt in this book is taken quite deliberately from the name of the man who built Stone Orchard in the 1840s. This was Alfie Wyatt, a pharmacist who had come to Canada from England. Because, in so many diverse ways, Stone Orchard had served as a kicker for various elements in this book, I wanted to do him the honour of being present. At first, Frederick Wyatt was called Alfred—but that simply wasn't right. The character, in fact, refused the name. So I kept the family name—and trust that Alfie, wherever he may be, doesn't mind.

The ants in the book came from France. Bill and I were living in Provence in the summer of 1994. I became intrigued with the lives of the different kinds of ants who were resident in our garden there, with all its many different aspects, different topographies and terrains and conditions. There were huge black ants and tiny little red ones—also some almost invisible, translucent ants. And, because Bill had been a biologist and was familiar with the world of entomology and insects, he had introduced me to the figure of Jean Henri Fabre. At home we have all of Fabre's wondrous, magical books about insects, and I had read enough of them to have fallen in love with his uniquely insightful and revealing essays about insect life, including the lives of ants. So—there we were in France, just a few kilometres from the area in which Fabre had lived and made his fascinating observations at the turn of the century. And it was a gift, because the fact is that one of the signals of autism is a fixed attention on some aspect of reality that catches the whole of an autistic person's focus. This is particularly true with autistic children. And in Lily's case, the focus was ants. She passes through a period when they are her only contact with reality and with survival. Simply watching the ants in Lily's behalf and then transcribing what I saw into the novel—the whole process of ant life—was wonderful! You don't have to be autistic to become mesmerized. The fascination of simply observing these intricate, meticulously structured societies is splendid.

One last thing. Taking her cue from Fabre, Lily creates entire civilizations with the ants. With the black ants, she fashions a version of ancient Egypt. While exploring this aspect of Lily, I began to do somewhat the same thing in France. Ramses II, for instance. I discovered him one day, lying dead on my doorstep—a very large black ant—clearly a royal personage. And I preserved him and he's now entombed, appropriately, in one of the workbooks I used while writing *The Piano Man's Daughter.*

If you want to know even one aspect of what it might be like to be Lily Kilworth, you could do no better than to go, some summer afternoon, and watch the activities around an anthill. I'd be willing to bet—unless, of course, you hate insects—that you won't be able to tear yourself away. Some people call that *fascination.* I call it *paying attention.*

For years, I have wanted to write this book—write about someone like Lily, someone like Ede, someone like Charlie. All of the people here in *The Piano Man's Daughter* are figures I have longed to draw on the page, but I couldn't find a way of gathering their stories into one book. Then it happened—and here it is.

If Lily's autism and my aunt's schizophrenia touch base at all, they do so in the same fashion that realities I remember—or have been told about—touch base and create fiction. I have heard many times and many versions of the Toronto you will discover in this book. That, too, is something I have dealt with only once before—in *The Wars.* I mean the Toronto of late-Victorian, Edwardian and Georgian times. It was a beloved but muddled city, sometimes lovely and sometimes cruel. I was very glad of the opportunity to explore it further in fiction.

Lastly, about the music in this book. I grew up with pianos and with singing all around me. My father played, my mother played and my grandmother sang. It was the sound of this music that wafted up the stairs as I drifted off to sleep in childhood times. And the sound of that music remains with me in the only way I can describe such vital memories: it is in my blood and it is me and I am it. And I am grateful.

Personal Past

Stone Orchard
1985
Article

Other People's Houses: Other People's Rooms

War is a time of leave-taking: this is accepted as one of the standard expectations once the uniforms are donned and the ration cards are issued. Vestibules and front steps, sidewalks and curbs take on a whole new meaning and significance. They become those mysterious places where a man is last seen before he disappears: scenes of the crime. *X marks the spot!* Railway stations, once so immensely exciting, are newly haunted by ghosts of the departed; they echo with last words and promises and there is always someone singing, so it seems, way up through the tunnels where the trains are. The streets are a blur of Navy blue and Air Force blue and Army khaki and all these colours have a single drab meaning: goodbye.

This was the world in which I spent the last years of childhood and the first years of adolescence. It was a world through which my father, then in the Air Force, was always passing on his way to some new posting, each of them more distant, until at last, he went overseas. It was also the world in which I remember my mother most clearly—in which I first perceived, with any real consciousness, the essence of her character. Up until then, she had been that necessary, central figure who stands centre stage in the life of every child: a mother, whose being was perceived exclusively in terms of her relationship to me. But, during the war, I began to see her as herself: as a person independent of her husband and her children: as one who had a life of her own and whose resources, hitherto a mystery, slowly came into focus.

Shortly after the Depression began, we lost our house and all through the thirties and early forties, we lived in rented houses. Briefly, we also lived with one of my grandmothers. The particular house we lived in through the war had almost everything a child could want: a garden to play in, a wall at the back, over which you climbed to enter a deep ravine that was like a park. The rooms in the house had leaded windows, plastered ceilings with ornate medallions, fireplaces, window seats and one of the rooms even had a skylight. Sometime around the middle of the war, my mother decided this was the house where we would end our days—all of us—the whole family, once my father had returned. If this was where we had said goodbye, then this must be where we would say hello.

A child may not always be aware of adult determination. I certainly wasn't. "Ambition" is an adult word and children full of longing don't always know how to make things happen—certainly they don't know how to make things happen the way an adult does. My mother wanted to buy that house and she worked towards its purchase with wonderful resourcefulness. There had been a time when the card table only came out for cards or for the dwarf, Miss Murphy, who set up her Singer on its surface and then would sit on top of several telephone books to make my mother's clothes. But now the card table came out so that a secretary could sit there, typing on a great black Underwood that had appeared like magic. *What*, I wanted to know, *is going on?* But my mother wouldn't tell me. "Just some things to be typed," she would say enigmatically. I asked my brother, but he was as much in the dark as me. Some nights, we used to sit at the bend in the stairs, and watch the typist typing, while my mother hovered near her, reading to her from a series of five-cent scribblers of the kind we used at school. It was all very mysterious and, for all we knew, our mother was planning to rob a bank or to kill someone in order to raise the money to buy the house. We came to such conclusions with some justification, because the few words we could make out in what seemed to us like the middle of the night as my mother read and the typist typed, all had to do with something deadly that either was going to happen or already had. In the long run, of course, we discovered that what our mother was doing was writing a book: a murder mystery. This came as something of a shock—to learn that our mother was capable of plotting such a thing, a killing in black and white.

Alas, her hopes for the book and the money it would make were dashed when, all at once, the landlord put our house on the market. Whatever money was needed was needed now—not later when the book would be finished. It was sad when the typist went away and the card table fell back under the exclusive purview of little Miss Murphy and the card players. My mother flew in all directions to find the money—but all to no avail. The house was sold to a waitress from Simpson's. Our lives, after that, became alarmingly bound in with slide bolts and door chains. The waitress wanted to move in with us, but mother said: "over my dead body!"

The thing was, we hadn't anywhere to go. My father, by now, was in England—so he couldn't help. It was dreadful. Especially dreadful to see my mother trying to keep us together in the face of what could become real separation if we had to move out. One night, at dinner time, we were seated at the dining-room table when out beyond the living-room windows, we saw a large moving van pull up in front of the house. Mother told me to stay where I was and not to pay attention. She sent my brother to check all the locks and chains on the doors and, when he returned, she said to us both: "no matter what happens, do not answer the door—just go on eating. We must pretend we don't hear them." And so, while the waitress, who wore a carrot red wig and carried a lot of coats over her arm, rang doorbells and pounded on the glass, we went on with our eating and pretended to be lost in a deep conversation. So long as she couldn't cross the threshold, the waitress could not take possession.

In the long run, of course, she did take possession, and for the briefest while we all lived there together—never saying more than *good morning* and *good night.* Tersely, to say the least. My mother was wonderful. She never growled, she never cursed, she never complained. She simply played it through as if the woman wasn't there—as if, in fact, she did not inhabit the earth, let alone our house. When my father came home from the war, we said our last goodbye and left the waitress to live with our ghosts.

For a while, we lived in other people's houses like refugees. But, it was an age of refugees and somehow it only seemed fitting. The families who took us in were pleasant and thoughtful and, I'm sure—looking back from here—they pretty much lived as we had lived with the waitress: as if there was no one else there. In the end, after much cajoling of my reluctant father, who didn't want to buy a house, and after conducting an infinite search that lasted for three or four years, my mother came home one day and said: "there's a house—a perfect house—and we're going to buy it."

And we did. The time of goodbyes was over.

Stone Orchard
1990

The Kitchen Table

. . . Sitting alone at the kitchen table . . .

The image conjures every season and every time of night and day. Of course, I would never be absolutely alone; one of the cats would sit with me—especially Mottle, who loved to lie up close to me, curled on her chair, the chair pulled over near my leg.

In the winter, steam would cloud the window in front of which the table sat. In summer, other cats would sit and doze on the outer windowsill. In spring, the fir tree filled with birds and in the fall, the fields across the road were awash with cattle moving through the waist-high grass.

The table was round and made of oak. It stood on a pedestal, the pedestal itself having curved supports whose patina had been polished over time by the many feet that had used them as footrests. Its surface was hand-rubbed, polished with floor wax and buffed with flannel rags. The feel of it was the same as old, worn velvet. We'd found it somewhere near Markham and bought it just before we moved up here in 1964. Later on, we bought six pressed-back chairs for seventy-five cents apiece. They were covered with paint and old shellac. We stripped them and set four of them around the table, with the two spares standing ready, if needed. And once the cushions went on them all, the guests began to arrive. . . .

Sitting at this table, whether alone or with our friends, has acquired, for me, an almost ritualistic appeal. I suppose this has something to do, perhaps, with the fact that its place is in the kitchen, so there is always one kind of food and drink or another involved with being there. All the way back to the very first days, when Mrs Mortson, Bill and I, and the Burseys would sit there drinking beer and tea and coffee during the time the first kitchen renovations were in hand. There are photographs of this: Doug Bursey, our handyman, with his wife, Edna, and their boys, all looking young again—and Agnes Mortson, our friend and housekeeper from Richmond Hill, looking like the prairie farm wife that once she was, smiling and squinny-eyed—and Bill looking ten, and me looking twelve, and Maggie, the dog from the Humane Society, pregnant with the litter that would give us Hooker.

Thank God we had those times—and all those people in our lives. They were the early infusions of spirit the house acquired when, after standing empty all that time—five years—its doors cracked open and we walked in. Trailing dogs and cats and cardboard boxes—with hardly any possessions. Bill and Agnes and I were the first of a parade that, through the years, has included both our families and most of our friends—walking out across the lawns and swimming in the pool, lying by the fire and standing in the greenhouse, running up the hill from the woods and sitting at the kitchen table—all the families within the family. Twenty-six years of continuity.

Ghosts. Both the dead and living.

Part of the mystique of the kitchen table must have to do with the rituals of food and drink. Also, I guess, with the fact that kitchens have always been centres of family life. Go where the fire is—go where the food is.

And the light. If only one light burns, it is almost certain to be the light above the kitchen table. Someone is hungry at midnight—someone is ill at 3:00 a.m. Someone is waiting for someone else to arrive with good or bad news—the kind of news that must be told before you can go to bed.

My father's brother died on a kitchen table—victim of a tumour on the brain. That was in 1909, and the surgeons performed a good many kitchen-table operations then. My mother's appendix was removed while she lay in a cloud of ether on her family's kitchen table.

I spent much time when I was a child, sitting with the maid at the kitchen table. This was not because I had been banished to the kitchen, but because I had chosen it as being the most likely place where the world beyond my world might be explained. Food for thought, served up on plates.

"Here's how you butter toast," my Aunt Dode told me—Uncle Tif's wife. "Take little dabs of butter, like this, and make sure you spread them all the way to the edge . . ."

"When Jesus comes," said one of the maids I loved with a passion, "He will come here riding on a cloud of glory . . ."

And my father said, one midnight: "in the morning, I'll be gone. We may not see each other again, but I really don't think that anything bad is going to happen. The most dangerous part of this is getting across the Atlantic. . . ." 1943.

"Now, boys, I'm not dictatin' to ya! Not trine to tell you what to do . . ." said Leonard Griffin, the farmer who ploughed our land and mended our fences for almost twenty years. "Not trine to tell you how to vote. No, sir! But you vote Libral!"

"Oh, my," said Islay Lambert, the local historian, "I do be tired, I do . . ."

The language of individualists.

Voices passing into time.

One whole winter the voices around the table, spoken voices and written ones, fought for and argued over the contents of a television series that had, as its subject, the present state and the ultimate fate of Planet Earth.

This was a volatile time, stimulating and exciting—but I was only a witness, not a participant in these discussions. They were among the most vital and fascinating conversations I have encountered and I will not soon forget them.

The participants were John Livingston and Bill, both of whom had been engaged by the CBC's *Nature of Things* unit to take part in the writing of this new series of eight programs. The title of this series was *A Planet for the Taking* and all the while Bill and John Livingston were exploring how to articulate its various segments, I was writing at the same kitchen table—the antediluvian chapters of *Not Wanted on the Voyage*, in which Noah and his contemporaries lay the world around them to waste.

It was not, I guess, a coincidence, given the subject at hand and our collective concerns. Nonetheless, there were often moments when it seemed there was a single voice to which each one of us was listening—and, comparing notes, our jaws very often fell because of the similarities in what each one of us had just discovered.

When *A Planet for the Taking* aired, in 1985, I thought what a pity it was that the scenes at our kitchen table were not a physical part of it. What got said at the table was sometimes even more effective than what got said on the screen. Granted, the series was a much needed and superbly articulated exposé of how and to what extent we have destroyed the integrity of the planet. But there was more to be said—and there's the great pity. I heard people saying it—around our kitchen table. But somewhere beyond that place, it was silenced, as being too harsh for the viewer to bear and, perhaps, too great an indictment to voice.

Every Wednesday, Nora Joyce provides the workforce at Stone Orchard with the greatest egg salad sandwiches ever contrived by anyone, anywhere. Oozing over wedges of lettuce, the salad itself is crisp with celery and onion. Nora layers it inches deep between slices of homemade bread and hands us all table napkins to catch the drippings before they reach the floor. Nothing I can think of compares with these sandwiches—and I dare say, half the ghosts around the table in some future time will be dropping bits of delicious egg salad onto bewildered diners who have been condemned to plastic food.

Nora Joyce is one of those people for whom you get down on your knees and thank the powers that be. She is a housewife, mother, grandmother, artist, baker, housekeeper, bicyclist and daredevil driver who has made it her objective in life—or so it seems—to see how many lives she can improve with caring. I am in awe of her. And I cherish her. If Nora Joyce is in your life, you are lucky.

She has, of course, flaws.

She mangles the language. Al, her husband, suffered many years from *very close veins*. Nora herself fears *Old Timer's Disease*. And she loses things. Many of us, including every member of her family and every member of ours, fear the day of her death not only for our permanent loss of Nora, but of everything she has misplaced over time. We have a rendezvous, which she knows about already, at her graveside. I am going to stand at its edge and scream down into the coffin: "NORA! NOR . . . A! WHERE DID YOU LEAVE THE . . . !!"

The ghosts at the table range through every state of being and every age. Babies are seated there and also the ancient of ancients. Somewhere, all in a row, there are a dozen lads or more who have worked the summers here—mowed our grass and hoed our gardens—cleaned our eavestroughs and fed our animals. Every one of them has been different from every other—which creates sure hope for the future in which they will live out their lives. All but one, who was killed in a tragic accident, years after working here.

I once said to Bill: "if I hear just one more breaking voice I will scream!" But it passes, all things pass, and all boys come to manhood through an often tortuous route, far harder for them to bear than for those who share their lives. Not being parents—and therefore lacking parental responsibilities—Bill and I have nonetheless taken some parental pride in watching these young men take up their lives and walk, so to speak.

Some, of course, are bound to be remembered more vividly than others, if for no better reason than that some were with us through more interesting and more exciting times than others. David and Charlie, for instance, who were here when major changes were being made to the house, and who helped us create the first formal gardens. Charlie was fearful of food and David, so it seemed, was fearful of words. If vegetable were served, poor Charlie would turn pale and push them aside. Bill once gave him mushrooms and told him, jokingly, when Charlie asked, that they were snails. Charlie's nose began to bleed!

David favoured very short words such as *yes* and *no*. That was it for quite a long while. We worried. *Why had he nothing more to say?*

In time, David's studies led him to computers and thus to the languages of a programmer. He came, one day, and covered the living-room floor with a computer print-out—and he started to talk. He had found his language and he has been talking ever since.

Charlie gave up his fear of food in time and became six feet tall and the father of giants.

Jimmy is the only lad we've lost. He was David's brother and was killed out west—in Alberta—driving his car. He was just beginning to find out who he was, having had, in his way, a rebellious and difficult start. Bill was good for Jim—good with him and good to him. Jimmy knew who he was, but finding out how to articulate who he was had been hard on him. He expressed himself with great, long rushes of speech—and he walked, sloped forward, as if he was always bucking the wind. I regret his death—but Bill regrets it more. He never speaks of him. And that is special.

None of our lads was perfect; flaws abounded. I have none, of course, but those I observe in the people close to me can fair drive me mad. I've already spoken of Nora's flaw—and hinted at others—but one of the worst is Len Collins's habit of banging his spoon.

Let me explain.

Len Collins came to Stone Orchard in 1979. We had, by then, decided that it was time—if we could find such a person and afford such a person—to take on a permanent employee who would both replace the lads we had been hiring for so long and also begin the series of major renovations and additions the house now required.

We could not, it happens, even begin to find such a person—for the simple reason that, as soon as we had decided to start our search, he found us. The doorbell rang—and there he was. Because he was of Jimmy's generation—and one of Jimmy's closer friends—Len had heard about Stone Orchard. Having heard a rumour—I think we may have breathed a word or two—he said: "I gather you may be looking for someone like me . . ."

An electrician.

A plumber.

A carpenter. (A superb carpenter!)

A gardener.

Skilled in animal care.

And wouldn't touch Toronto with a ten-foot pole!

After five minutes or so, we decided we could say yes—and Len Collins has been here ever since. He has put—single-handed—a tall, two-storey addition on the house, created a combination kitchen-study for Bill that is the envy of all who see it, established a workshop from which tables, desks, bookshelves and assorted boxes have appeared as if by magic—but it isn't magic, it is discipline, skill and wondrous talent. Len is an artist. Period.

In 1980, he married Anne Brandon, whom we have come to love and admire, and they have given birth to three children: the beautiful and deeply serious Maureen, the all-singing, all-dancing, Technicolor Caileigh and the future king of hockey, Brandon. (Gretzky is already a has-been.)

However, I mentioned Len's "flaw"—namely, his banging spoon.

It happens at the table. At the table, this is Len's voice. His ghost—for all its other wonders—is inevitably announced as follows:

"Coffee?"

"Love it."

"Sugar?"

"Love it."

"Milk, Len?"

"Love it."

And then: *banga—banga—banga—banga—BANGA!*
Silver spoon. China mug.
I could kill him.

The table, now, is gone from Stone Orchard, like much of the kitchen it sat in. Having been remodelled, that room no longer affords the round oak table a place to stand. We have given it to Scott, another of our lads who has gone to university and who, I suspect, will come back to haunt us either as a prime minister or king.

Perhaps the ghosts of those who sat at the table have departed with it, though I think what we inherit is the table's spirit—and with that, all the others.

In some ways, I am always at that table—or I can be, when I close my eyes and think of it. I can sit there any time I choose, with Willy Hutt or Nora Joyce—with Mottle resting against my thigh and Maggie lying, dreaming, down on the floor. The laughter and the conversation never end—and the voices will go on forever. The table, after all, is sitting in my mind—a fiction, made of the best realities—the ones we keep alive by fixing them with love.

Historical Research

Klondike Days and Nights

In 1974, having completed work on *The National Dream*—a television series based on Pierre Berton's two books about the building of the Canadian Pacific Railway—Bill and I were invited to start writing another series based on a Berton book. This time, it was *Klondike*, the story of the Yukon gold rush of 1898.

The project would require a considerable voyage into the past, through the reading of Berton's vast assemblage of research, which included copies of diaries and accounts, written by those who had taken part in this great northern adventure.

The work would also take us far from home, as we were to join the producer, designer and production manager in retracing one of the several routes used by the gold seekers to reach Dawson City— by train to Prince Rupert, by ship to Skagway, Alaska, on horseback and on foot to the foot of the Chilkoot Pass, backpacking across the Pass to Bennett Lake and finally getting into an inflated Zodiac that would take us down the Yukon River to Whitehorse, where we would rent the car that would take us to Dawson.

So much has been written about the Klondike gold rush that I don't want to tell much about that history—or of what remains to be seen of that history. Yes, there are wonderful old buildings and recreations of period hotels and saloons to be found. And graveyards where the ages carved on the markers are almost all tragically young. And superb photographic archives that bring that time back to life (including, in Whitehorse, a shot we found of a young couple standing outside the cabin they had built—an eerie replica, in face, stature and costume, of our old friends Margaret Atwood and Graeme Gibson as they looked in the 1970s.)

Instead, I want to tell just a bit about what happened to us as we made our way to where it all took place so long ago.

First, we were to retrace part of the journey we had made as part of our research for *The National Dream*—with the difference that, at Winnipeg, we would leave the CPR tracks and head northwest.

We bought down-filled, hooded jackets, high-topped boots and filled our new backpacks with such essentials as packets of freeze-dried food, blocks of sweetened chocolate and, for me, my travelling mascot, Sebastian—a somewhat battered teddy bear. Possibly the only teddy bear in history to have had his photograph taken on Midnight Dome, high above Dawson—in the midnight sunlight of June 21.

As the train clicked and swayed us across the continent, we spent much of the journey reading some of the research material we had crammed into our suitcases, along with a generous supply of sweaters and thermal underwear. Just before reaching Prince Rupert, we put on our hiking outfits—including our bulging backpacks—in order to impress our television colleagues, who, having sailed north from Vancouver, were to meet us at the docks.

When we met, our friends took one look at us and, fortunately, decided to be kind. They gently informed us that our brand new rubber boots—the kind we used in trudging through the spring muds at Stone Orchard—were totally inappropriate. We needed hard-toed, lace-up hiking boots. They also looked at our suitcases and asked us—equally gently—how we planned to get them up the trails to the Chilkoot Pass, across the Pass and overland to Bennett Lake.

Fortunately, Prince Rupert came to the rescue—in the form of an outfitter who sold us the right kind of footwear and provided the huge cardboard cartons in which we were able to send home our inappropriate boots and our suitcases with their excess clothing and research papers.

During the offshore voyage north to Skagway, we entered a dream world, bathed in the silver light of the midnight sun. We spent hours on the deck, watching the British Columbia coast slowly become Alaskan, as mammoth glaciers dropped icy calves into the Pacific, while killer whales escorted our stately passage.

Two moments remain indelible in memory—each one convincing us that we had left our own world—and our own time—to make an unforgettable visit to the past.

The first came one evening as our ship was inching its way through a shallow narrows that separated two offshore islands. Our progress was painstakingly slow, guided by the ship's pilot who was taking soundings off the port bow. With his weighted line hanging down into the calm water, he called his readings out into the silver air—and to our amazement, we heard the same calls that had been used in Mississippi traffic of the previous century. One of them, signifying a depth of two fathoms, resonated with wonderful significance—since it had given a nom de plume to someone who had once worked on a Mississippi steamer: *mark twain!*

The second manifestation of the past visited us one morning, when we saw a young couple struggle up from below to deposit on the deck what turned out to be a beehive. As we watched, they appeared to be releasing the bees into the air. At that moment, the ship was at anchor, just offshore one of the smaller Alaskan settlements. A small trawler had come out to take on supplies for the villagers.

I spoke to the young couple, who turned out to be from

Vermont. Their names were Beth and Eric, and when I asked why they had bees, and why they were releasing them, they replied: "we're going to homestead in Alaska, and these are part of our stock. We let them out whenever we're close enough to land, so they can feed." In response to the concern and puzzlement on our faces, they explained that the bees could fly ashore, collect pollen and nectar from the spring blossoms there, and make it back to the ship before we would get underway again.

I used the image of the beehive on the deck in a later novel about the great flood—*Not Wanted on the Voyage*. The release of the bees was one of the signs that the Ark had finally come within sight of land.

The couple then invited us below to see the rest of their menagerie. It was housed in an old van which had been converted to a travelling barn, with two horses—Kit and Lottie—three Nubian goats, a young boar and an old sow, four hens and a rooster and four ducklings. Piled around the animals were sacks of feed and seed grains—and suspended in the atmosphere of the assemblage were the invisible hopes that had once been carried west as our country slowly became populated with the first European settlers.

There were to be many reminders of the past in the next few days, as we stayed in the older section of Skagway before setting off inland. Old hotels with Victorian furnishings—saloons rebuilt long after more modern gold seekers had panned around the original bars, which had been outlined in a faint but profitable powdering of the gold that once used to pay for the drinks.

And finally, one morning, we had to face the reality of the present. Our producer, in honour of his younger days in Britain, had decided we would begin our inland journey on horseback. As it turned out, this presented a number of problems. For one thing, neither Bill nor I had been on a horse since childhood. For another, there were no pack animals available, which meant we had to wear our backpacks in the saddle—a situation which considerably alters one's centre of gravity—to say nothing of one's ability to remain mounted. In fact, there weren't even enough mounts for the entire party. The wrangler, himself, was somehow unavailable, but had sent his wife and young son to accompany us—on foot.

Then, there was the fact that ours was to be the horses' first trek of the season, when all they wanted was to get back to the comforts of the stable.

We gathered near the point where the Dyea River flows into the Pacific, and immediately had evidence of some equine reluctance. Bill's horse, Bandit, obviously had an aversion to inexperienced riders, as well as to the party's large coffee pot, slung behind Bill, jangling and rattling against the saddle. Before any of us realized it, Bandit had taken off at a brisk pace, heading for home. Bill finally managed to bring him under control, and we tried to keep everything calm while receiving final orders from our guide.

By then, we were beside the river itself, swollen with raging currents fed by the spring runoff. The guide assured us that the horses were used to crossing such tempestuous waters, and all we had to do was to trust our mount and let him find his own way to the other side. The final bit of advice was as chilling as the icy waters. "If your horse loses his footing, just hang on and he will manage to scramble to safety . . ."

Well. Somehow, Bill and I—and our horses—achieved the far bank, watching in horror as one of our party was indeed washed downstream. Miraculously, he clung to his horse and they both ultimately got across and rejoined us.

Then came an unbelievable comment. "So, that wasn't too bad, was it? Now, this island is only a few hundred feet wide, so all we have to do . . .

Island?

Island???

Yes, we had to plunge into the river again. And again—somehow—we all got across. With more than our spirits dampened, I can tell you. Still, once we got going, the trek through the Pacific rain forest was a gorgeous experience.

Once we started climbing the lower slopes of the coastal range, however, the going got tough.

Bill, whose life had provided even less "saddle time" than mine, finally solved the ongoing problems of Bandit's skittishness. At one of our rest stops, Bill "kindly" offered his mount to the wrangler's wife, and with great relief, trudged forward on foot, managing to keep in sight of the rest of us.

As it turned out, I was soon to join him.

The terrain worsened—dense forests with trees so close to each other the horses could barely get through—shallow riverbeds either in full flood or, for some unexplained reason, perfectly dry. Oddly enough, the flowing water was easier to deal with than the rock-encrusted dry beds. As we went along one of them, the horses were spooked by something (the smell of a bear?) and began to stampede. As we raced along, the metal bar on my backpack caught on an overhanging branch. I was pulled backwards from the saddle, directly into the path of the pounding hooves behind me. Fortunately, as an ex-dancer and actor, I knew how to fall (relax!) and, equally fortunately, the horses were able to avoid my stunned body.

Nonetheless, I decided that Bill had made a very good decision, and once all the horses were calmed down and reassembled, I relinquished my mount to the wrangler's young son. Bill and I carried on together, on foot—which provided another minor disaster of quite a different kind.

The mention of the smell of a bear was both serious and accurate. Although we didn't lay eyes on one through the whole journey, we frequently encountered the unmistakable aroma. Musky . . . wild . . . dangerous. And since two humans and their backpacks could slip through gaps between trees that were too narrow for a mounted horse, we got considerably ahead of the rest of the party. We managed to keep going past two of the "bear smell" incidents, but when we encountered a pile of huge droppings, green and steaming, it seemed like a good idea to wait for the others to catch up.

Gratefully, we slipped off our backpacks and sank to the ground for a rest. To my amazement, Bill immediately gave a howl and struggled to his feet. Terrified, I look around to see where the charging bear might be. Nothing. Just moans from Bill. He finally explained. He had sat on something sharp, which had penetrated both his clothing and some of the tenderest of his flesh.

It turned out to be a porcupine quill—one that, years later, I still have in a box on my desk.

"Please, Tiff—you've got to get this thing out!"

As he gingerly lowered his trousers and then his underwear, I eased the thing through the fabrics until it was as exposed as Bill was. He painfully bent over as I began to work it, as gently as I could, through the flesh of his right buttock.

Well, you can guess what happened then.

The rest of the party caught up to us.

First came: "hi! How are . . ."

Then: "oh . . ."

When I looked around, half of them had averted their eyes while the rest stared in disbelief.

After a brief explanation and much laughter, the operation was completed and we all continued on our way.

Fortunately, it wasn't far to the first campsite, where we would eat supper and sleep in two small log cabins. This is where our first guide, the wrangler's wife and her son would leave us, taking the horses with them, while three young guides would take over for the rest of the journey: Kris, the water expert, Wayne, the mountain expert and Mike, the ice and snow expert.

The next day was one of the hardest. The trails grew steeper and rockier—and then we were shuffling through snow. We were

(*left to right*) Timothy Findley's grandfather Fred Bull, Ruth Bull Carlyle (upon whom the character Lily Kilworth in *The Piano Man's Daughter* was based) and Margie Maude Bull Findley, at Brighton Bull House.

Edith Maude Fagan Bull, 1908, who inspired the character of Ede Kilworth in *The Piano Man's Daughter*.

Timothy Findley with Judy Spearman and Gerald Flood, outside their hotel in Moscow, circa 1955.

Timothy Findley in England, 1955.

Bill sends love.

January 25. 81

Dear Mother,

Julie gave me this paper for Christmas. Every sheet has a different pair of butterflies on it. I thought these red ones would be suitable for the corner where you sit — since there are so many variations of red there. This morning, there were two mourning doves outside my window, as well as all the sparrows, chickadees, blue jays and evening grosbeaks. Quite a sight. We also have a lot of snow which here, of course, is different than the city — the snow stays white. All along the front porch there are icicles. And the paths through the snow for us to get to the cats and dogs are quite deep. Hope you can visit us in February or March. So proud of you. Love, Tiff.

Tiff and his mother, Margaret Findley, in 1951, on board the ship that would take them from Quebec to Europe for a recuperative holiday in Switzerland.

Timothy Findley relaxes with his parents, 1960.

Stratford Shakespearean Festival

of Canada Foundation
STRATFORD, ONTARIO

1 Market Place, Stratford, Ont.
April 8, 1953.

Mr. Timothy Findley,
c/o New Play Society,
782 Yonge Street,
Toronto, Ontario.

Dear Mr. Findley:

This is to confirm your engagement to play the parts of _____
SIR WILLIAM CATESBY
in "Richard III" and SECOND GENTLEMAN
in "All's Well That Ends Well" at the Shakespearean Festival Theatre,
Stratford, Ontario, for five weeks from Monday, July 13, 1953. The management reserves the right to extend the length of the playing period to six
weeks or more and to inform you of any such extension not later than June
31, 1953.

Rehearsals will start on June 1, 1953 and you will be required to
attend all rehearsals arranged by the Director unless prevented by illness
or your absence from rehearsals is approved by the Director.

You will receive the sum of_ Seven Hundred and Fifty- - - - - - -
- - - - Dollars ($750.00) for the season, to include the rehearsal period
and 5 playing weeks. Payment will be made in four equal installments on
June 1, 1953, June 20, 1953, July 11, 1953 and August 1, 1953. If the
playing period is extended to six weeks, you will receive payment pro rata.
The number of performances in any playing week will not exceed eight.

You will be required to supply such modern clothes and footwear
for "All's Well That Ends Well" as may be requested by the management, but
all costumes, footwear and wigs for "Richard III" will be supplied by the
management.

Please sign and return the enclosed duplicate letter to signify
your acceptance of the terms contained herein.

I accept the terms contained
in the above letter

Stratford Shakespearean Festival
of Canada Foundation

Date May 8th 1953

Signature _Tim Findley_

H. T. Patterson
H. T. Patterson,
General Manager.

HTP/vm

The only time Tiff and Bill appeared on stage together: when Bill, as co-producer, had to take over a role in Sheridan's play *The Rivals*, at The Central Library Theatre in Toronto, 1962.

The cast, and director Marigold Charlesworth (*centre, arms raised*), of Findley's play *Can You See Me Yet?*, 1976.

Timothy Findley in England, circa 1953.

cautioned to be quiet. Snowy overhangs on the heights above could easily become avalanches. The backpacks somehow grew heavier. And the rest stops never long enough.

Then, without warning, there it was. The Chilkoot Pass.

A steep, almost four-hundred-metre incline over which most of the gold seekers had had to haul every ounce of their equipment. We had to make the ascent just once, carrying only twenty kilograms. Some of them did it over a dozen times, with loads of over fifty kilograms.

The slope was covered on the left with snow, while on the right, the spring sun had exposed an uneven cascade of huge boulders. Mike explained that the snow was too deep and too soft for us—and we could see for ourselves that the size of the boulders was daunting. So how were we to get to the top?

In single file, moving just along the border between white and black, where the snow was thin enough to allow a careful passage, while the boulders offered something to cling to.

It took over an hour. An hour of pain, gasping and aching muscles. Even the guides, twenty years younger than any of us, found it hard going. Not as hard as Bill, though—whose prairie upbringing had never equipped him to deal with heights. He never once looked back down, but just kept his eyes fixed on the crest of the slope.

When we got there, the view was spectacular. So was the look on Wayne's face when Bill asked if he could cling to the young man for one brief glance back down the slope.

We were all quite pleased with the timing of our arrival at the top of the Pass, since a helicopter was to come from Whitehorse to take our CBC colleagues off on a broader survey of sites, while the guides led Bill and me to where we would reassemble and drive to Dawson.

Sure enough, right on the hour, we heard the sound of a rotor. The helicopter—as orange as the guide's parkas—came into view. As it approached, we all waved. We could see the pilot waving back.

And then he stopped waving.

And the helicopter kept right on going.

Down the slope and out of sight.

It was almost half an hour before we heard the 'copter sound coming back up. This time, we stood—solemn and quiet—while it landed and a laughing pilot emerged. He explained. His instructions had been to meet us at the foot of the Pass. He had spotted another party, just about to make their ascent—and had caused some amazement when he landed beside them and invited them to "hop in."

So—off went our colleagues while we picked up our packs and started off, single file, through the snow. Deep snow. Soft snow. Melting snow. Sometimes icy snow, lying across slopes that slanted down at angles so impossible we found ourselves wishing that one of our legs could be shorter than the other.

Nonetheless, we reached the next log cabin—and collapsed. There was barely enough energy to boil water and rehydrate some of our freeze-dried food. Then—blessed sleep.

In the morning, we heard the guides trying to get out of bed. Moans and groans. Like the horses, this was their first trek of the season, and the terrain had taken its toll, even on their young muscles. We two middle-aged, sedentary writers were in much worse shape—but it became a matter of some pride that soon we were moving more briskly than any of our companions.

That third day would see us gradually make our way down the inland slopes of the mountains—where the snow was even deeper and softer. We could hear it melting far beneath our feet, as small buried streams of ice water flowed away to feed rivers. We could occasionally see "snow bridges," formed when the flow was strong enough to carve away the bottom surface of the winter's fall.

Rest stops became more frequent—and so did our consumption of energy-giving chocolate. To our surprise, we were advised to eat the chocolate only when we were on the move. Otherwise, we were told, it would tend to slow us down, rather than energize us.

We were also given a variation on the classic advice of the north: *don't eat the yellow snow*. For us, whenever we became thirsty, it was: *don't eat the red snow*. The powdering of red we could see every so often was apparently a poisonous red algae—a slightly less deadly relative of the organism that created the "red tides" of the south.

There's just one more snow story to tell.

Every so often, one of us would plunge thigh-deep into the snow, and would have to be helped out again. I was second-last in line, and at one moment saw Mike, the snow expert, suddenly sink right up to his armpits. Bill stepped forward to help him out, but as far as I could tell, Mike stopped him, signalled a halt for all of us, and very slowly eased himself up until he was lying on the surface. He motioned us to move over to our right, and rolled himself in the same direction.

When he got to his feet, he signalled a move forward.

I saw him say something to Bill, who, after a minute or two, dropped back and told me what he had heard. When Mike had gone down into the snow, he had found that his feet were dangling in space. That was when he realized we were all on a snow bridge—a bridge that could easily collapse.

It was around that time that the guides suggested we lighten our backpacks as much as possible—discarding whatever wasn't absolutely essential. Nothing was said, but I did notice a couple of odd looks being exchanged when I opted to abandon my complete supply of chocolate rather than Sebastian, my teddy bear. I didn't mind. I had very clear ideas about "essential."

In truth, the whole trek seems more difficult in retrospect than it was at the moment. It was simply what we were doing—so we kept on doing it. And we all reached our various destinations, by our various means. On the water, on trains, in cars—and sometimes, still, on foot.

Sadly, the television series never got made. As soon as we had written the first two scripts, CBC budget cuts hit the project, and it was cancelled. But we still have the photograph that shows us all resting at the top of the Chilkoot Pass—just as we hold one more special memory from our trek into our country's history.

After we had spent a few days in Dawson, soaking up the atmosphere of the place, we decided to take a hike—partly because there were no roads leading to our destination. It was a tiny abandoned mining settlement called Forty-Mile—for reasons I now cannot remember. Fortunately, it wasn't forty miles from Dawson—but only about ten. So, armed with a detailed map, a compass, some sandwiches and drinks, we set off.

It was a flat and desolate landscape that managed to be breathtakingly beautiful. Lots of shallow ponds, some still with traces of ice, a few stunted and gnarled trees that gave an almost Japanese look to the place, distant horizons and clear skies.

And suddenly a river that, according to the map, did not exist. Perhaps it was only a temporary one, a short-lived artifact of the spring runoff. Temporary or not, it was too deep to cross—as we soon found out with a few tentative steps into the water.

And yet, we had to get to the other side.

As we stood, talking about this unexpected barrier, Bill noticed a set of tracks in the mud beside the water. He followed them for a few metres—to where they entered the water, came out again and continued along.

He called back: "a wolf . . ."

I thought: "so??"

And then it dawned. Perhaps the wolf had faced the same problem we were now pondering—and perhaps he had been much better at solving it than we could be.

We followed the tracks for almost a kilometre—until they entered the water and disappeared.

And there was our crossing.

I don't remember much about Forty-Mile—just a few collaps-ing shacks—but the unseen wolf remains alive and beautiful in my memory—trotting along beside the river, and then, with a toss of his head, wading across.

I wonder what that means.

Stone Orchard
1986
Article

A Small Town in Normandy

I was eleven years old when word hit the headlines of Canada's "triumph" at Dieppe. We learned soon enough what a dreadful lie that was. The survivors told us. One of our neighbours had made it back from the raid. He had no visible scars—the scars were inside him. At the dinner table, we would see him suddenly grow pale, fall silent and begin to sweat. The horror of what he'd endured would never leave him.

I was in my fifties when I first visited Dieppe, and stood beneath its cliffs. No amount of holiday laughter can ever hope to drown out the echoes of that battle. Wherever I walked in the town, I walked with the dead from that August morning—ghosts who joined all the rest who had put Dieppe into the history books. The notorious and fashionable who had once strolled on the prome-nade—Oscar Wilde and Sarah Bernhardt, Camille Saint-Saëns and Edward VII.

Above all, we are reminded that this historic port was the embarkation point for many of the families of France who came to settle along the St. Lawrence River. Almost four hundred years later, some of their descendants returned to die on the beaches of Dieppe. The town is a monument to all this history—a monument

and a wonder. The gothic splendour of St. Jacques Cathedral—
the cobbled marketplace—the restaurants—the incomparable
Norman cuisine . . . But August 1942 is never out of mind.

For a Canadian of my age, the journey from Newhaven to
Normandy is haunted by echoes of war. It was from this gentle place
on the south coast of England that the doomed raid on Dieppe was
launched in August of 1942. Ignorant of the horror that lay before
them, the men went singing to the ships. At the end of their journey,
they would be slaughtered. They hadn't a hope in hell. Later, it was
said by someone in my parents' generation that, as a nation, Canada
grew up on the bloody beaches of Dieppe. The ghosts of those who
died there will cling to us—and to Dieppe—forever.

Today, as we set sail, there is singing yet again—and I revel in
it. The ferry is alive with Shakespeare's "golden lads and girls,"
roaring songs and waving down to the people on the jetties. In a
world of relentless North American pretensions, British youth has
about it a kind of natural attractiveness and unaffected integrity
that is wonderfully refreshing. Carrying haversacks and eating
cheese-and-chutney sandwiches out of brown-paper bags, they
wear non-designer jeans (remember them?) and oversized
sweaters that can act as changing rooms or snoozing dens when
needed. Wherever they are present on the ship there is an endless
chain of laughter, whether they are playing cards or drinking
pints of ale or rushing out "to see the sky" as one girl does, pur-
sued by half a dozen others.

It is an impulse I cannot resist—and I go with them.

On that August evening fifty years ago, when the ships went out
from Newhaven into the English Channel, the sun had barely set.
A haze that was partly heat and partly mist lay over the horizon. It
was described, in one account, as a perfect summer's night.

Crowded onto every inch of decking, wearing battle gear and
bearing arms so newly issued they had not been fired, five thousand

men—three thousand of them Canadian—stood in the twilight, each one privately trying to cope with the sudden news that France was their destination. The Allied High Command had all at once decided to proceed with the assault on Dieppe that, weeks before, it had cancelled. As the men were being assembled, they were under the impression they were merely being prepared for one more training exercise. None of the Canadians had ever been in battle. Now, as the ships pressed forward, their true destination had been announced—though it would not be seen. Sixty miles of distance hid Dieppe, at first—and after the distance, darkness.

Of the five thousand troops who were crowded onto the decks of that small armada, only eighteen hundred would return. The rest would be wounded, taken prisoner or killed on the beaches. Among these casualties were two thousand Canadians—two-thirds of those who set sail. All along, their leaders knew—or at least suspected—they were doomed. It was a callous, brutal waste of youth—a kind of massacre—and it must never be forgotten—or forgiven.

At Dieppe, the town sits down along a kilometre of stony beach in the gap between two flights of cliff that curve along the coast between Calais and Le Havre. It is an ancient town, first used as a harbour by raiding Vikings. For hundreds of years it has been among the most important fishing ports of Northern Europe. Early in the 19th century, it became the favoured playground of the French and then the English aristocracy.

Getting down from the ferry, I am swept along by the young who cannot wait to put their feet on foreign soil. Customs is a merry chase through bags and pockets for misplaced papers and passports—and the long, covered alley is soon a blur of racing, jumping bodies, hurrying through the barricades to the streets. Hanging back with my heavy bags and sixty-year-old lungs, I can only smile at the thought that I will never race like that again towards adventure. I will walk, I decide.

Strolling through the evening on the way to your hotel or your café, you go with the ghost of Oscar Wilde as your guide. He went over directly to Dieppe when he was released from prison. *The Ballad of Reading Gaol* was penned while Oscar sat at the Café Suisse, being tantalized by the sailors strolling along the quays. He chose Dieppe because it had always been a haven for artists and mavericks of every kind.

The Prince of Wales of Oscar's time had a house on the Esplanade. You can still see it today, near the north end—a great brick beauty whose windows and whose balconies and terraces look at England and shut it out. Edward VII had brought his dogs and his mistresses to Dieppe—and there were rumours, very well founded, that he had a bastard daughter living at the other end of town, who gave extraordinary parties and whose love life echoed her father's.

All this is what you join, in part, as you take your table in the open and settle back to enjoy the view.

Now, on this first French evening, I am sitting on the sidewalk in front of Les Tribunaux Café, on Place du Puits where Rue de la Barre and Grande Rue meet. This is the true heart of Dieppe.

The Tribunaux was Oscar's favourite café. He sat here in better times with laughing friends and admirers—and in the bitter times of exile, enduring the snide remarks and rebuffs of visiting Englishmen who, walking with their mistresses and tarts, made sure he was thoroughly aware of their moral superiority. Others were tolerant and kind and made a point of crossing the place to stand by Oscar's table for all to see, inviting him into their houses to dine—as one English hostess put it: "absolutely *en famille*, Mister Wilde. My children adore your stories!"

My Ricard arrives—a splendid aperitif that clouds in my glass at the touch of water, and that sends up a delicious scent of aniseed. Eventually, I make my way up the angled arm of Rue de la Barre to Rue du 19th Août 1942, named in memory of the day's battle. I pass l'église St. Remy, around the corner from where I will take my dinner at Les Tourelles. In every street, the ancient houses lean above me with their iron balconies and window boxes spilling lobelia and geraniums into the twilight. From behind the open windows I can hear the laughter of children sitting down at kitchen tables to their supper—the barking of every family's dog—and the sound of running taps. Passing open doorways, I can see the narrow curvature of worn wooden steps leading upwards. In one of these doorways, a cat is sitting washing its ears with meticulous care.

I pause to see the long-necked gargoyles leaning from the eaves of l'église St. Remy. Poised as they are, so starkly above the cobblestones and grass, I realize that they have seen me pass before—and all the others who have gone this way through time. The Huguenots who fled through these streets towards the beaches and the barges that would ferry them out to the waiting ships and the safety of England. The splendid silver-plated Prussian Hussars whose horses were tethered in the churchyard during the occupation of the 1870s and the Wehrmacht of the 1940s, whose parades and posturings were performed in emptied streets. Here, too, the deaths of two Canadian soldiers trapped up close against the walls of the church, shot down by snipers—the place of their dying marked now by a tablet bearing witness through time to their sacrifice . . . All these persons, one by one, have passed beneath the gargoyles of St. Remy, stone blind, unperturbed and spewing rain.

I go up past the corner where the soldiers died and turn towards the brighter lights of the café where I will dine. Les Tourelles is named for the nearby towers that stand as the last remaining vestige of Dieppe's 16th-century ramparts.

There is a moment in the evening when the whole town fills with music, an accordion playing or someone singing beyond an open window, and all the people walk together through the streets towards some entertainment that has not been named. Cigarette smoke and women's perfume, the mingled smells of food and wine and coffee, the Channel breeze and the scent of night-blooming flowers combine to make the very air you breathe a kind of drug. Somehow, Dieppe is a collective enterprise that does not exist until you are there to complete the picture. Like every beloved place of which we dream, it is nothing without the dreamer.

From my hotel window, I watch the day wind down. The promenade between the sea and me is emptying its cars and motorbikes back into the dark. A few late walkers amble arm in arm or drag along behind an anxious dog who cannot wait to cross the boulevard and seek the trees. A man retreats into the bushes to relieve himself. His wife stands patiently, waiting her turn. Then she, too, moves into the hedges, while the man inspects his fingernails and lights a cigarette. I had forgotten this—that in France, the hedges, the trees, the bushes of a park are there as much for people as for dogs.

And the dogs are everywhere—as well behaved in the cafés as they are on the streets. Some drink from the water trough provided by Edward VII; it still stands—across the street from Les Tourelles—another reminder that this is France.

Earlier, looking out across the beach of stones while leaning on the seawall, I saw a young man, very well made, helping his children out of their swimsuits. Then, quite casually, he removed his own. Facing the seawall, he accepted a towel from his wife and proceeded to dry his hair while his wife towelled down the children. Meanwhile, two elderly women sat nearby and barely glanced in his direction.

Times have changed. At the turn of the century, when Oscar had his downfall and British mores ruled the waves along *la plage* at Dieppe, the actress Marie Tempest was arrested there for walking up from the beach to her hotel in her bathing costume. Bearing in mind that such a bathing costume would have covered her from neck to ankle, it is wonderful to think of what indecent exposure must have meant to the Victorians.

★ ★ ★

In the mornings, sharp at eight o'clock, a young girl knocks at my door with the sort of brisk authority you expect from the police. *Bang! Bang! Bang!* Every day, I leap from my bed and stand, still dreaming, wavering with indecision in the middle of the floor. Where am I? *Bang! Bang! Bang!* It is the one free service I would beg the hotel to abandon. Perhaps I should remind them that, at Versailles, if a person wanted to enter Louis XIV's bedroom in the morning, he was required to scratch on the door with his fingernail and speak his name in a low, considerate tone. Sometimes, royals do make sensible demands. . . .

I open the door and there is a flurry of silver trays and flying white napkins, accompanied by a singsong *bonjour, M'sieur!* Then, having deposited my breakfast on the desk, the child—who might be fourteen—departs with another show of athletic spins and turns and sings from the doorway: *bonne journée, M'sieur!* I half expect her to leap into the corridor doing somersaults—instead of which she gives me a dazzling smile and closes the door with a firm but gentle click.

What she has brought me is a pair of Thermos bottles, one with scalded milk and the other filled with incomparable coffee; a glass of grapefruit juice; a brioche, a croissant and a hard-crusted roll; butter, two kinds of jam and marmalade. The aroma as I pour my first cup of café au lait is France personified. The day cannot fail to go well.

I throw the windows open, scattering pigeons in all directions from the sill, and look across the esplanade towards the Channel. The fishing fleet has already left the harbour and shrimp boats and trawlers prowl the horizon.

To my left are the gardens of memory where floral tributes and a plaque commemorate the 19th of August 1942. A woman wearing a hat is already seated on one of the benches, making lace. Two large beds of wax begonias, red and white, have been designed to show twin maple leaves in honour of the Canadian dead. From time to time, the woman—whose back is ramrod stiff and straight—glances up into the air and sights the birds that are flying there. She makes her lace all morning in this quiet place—and will be there still, when I return from the market four hours later. I have not the courage to speak to her. Whatever her allegiance is, in that garden for the dead, I sense it is not a subject one should broach. Her stillness tells me much. Her patience, too, and her periodic glances at the sky. Her privacy, I know from having witnessed other silences and practised some of my own, is inviolate. She sits there every day.

Once a week, farmers and flea-market vendors descend on Dieppe from the neighbouring countryside. They set up their stalls along Grande Rue and Rue de la Barre and remain there from dawn to dusk. Years ago, these streets were declared pedestrian malls and de la Barre angles off towards the Market Square beside l'église St. Jacques—the church that gave its name to Dieppe's way of serving scallops. Moving from stall to stall, you follow an elliptical path with the church and its tower as the fulcrum.

I have already decided I will take one meal alfresco, so the first thing I do is buy myself a string bag to carry my picnic's ingredients. I want to buy some part of my menu on impulse. All I know as I set out is that wine, bread and cheese will be part of it. At the wine merchant's I pick up a bottle of Merlot which at home would cost me seven dollars. In Dieppe, it costs me two. Then I go looking for the cheese.

The market at Dieppe is happy chaos in slow motion. People by the hundreds crowd the narrow passages that run either side of the vendors' stalls, the stalls being set out down the centre of each street. A brilliant river of painted canvas flows above them from end to end. As with all public markets the world over, more is going on than buying and selling. Greetings and gossip stutter and stammer on every side. Children ride laughing through the horde on their fathers' shoulders. Knots of mothers and aunts and grandmothers form to exchange the news of the week—a tally of minor events and major crises: a child has fallen; a birthday cake has refused to rise; a husband has been unfaithful; a friend has died; a neighbour has given birth to twins . . . And all the while they tell the news, a circle of children hovers impatiently, satellites held in orbit with promises of ice-cream cones and chocolate bars.

Other younger families make their way through the crowds, pushing strollers filled with bread and babies. Not a dozen steps are taken between two dozen reunions. Everyone, it seems, knows someone coming the other way and their gossip extends through time in a pattern of encounters old as the town itself.

I have become so rapt in all these lives that, for half an hour or more, I forget why I am there. Finally, I remember. It is not history I am seeking, but cheese.

I buy a piece of Camembert and a small, heart-shaped portion of Neufchâtel. The Camembert is creamy and ripe and has begun to run in its bed of straw. If I eat it before the afternoon is over, it will be perfect. The Neufchatel is ripe but not so runny. It has a vein of salt that will make it the perfect complement to whatever vegetables I buy. I also pick out a chunk of farmer's butter—pale and unsalted, wrapped in wax paper. As I slip these purchases down into the bag beside my bottle of wine, some Camembert squeezes onto my fingers. I lick them. I think that I have died and gone to heaven.

The tomatoes are irresistible. Large and unblemished, they are displayed in wide wooden trays with stems of basil leaves set out beside them. I purchase two and, from the same vendor, a bunch of small, pale radishes—cream-coloured, delicate as asparagus tips. Later, I choose six apricots and two brown pears and a two-franc bunch of anemones. I will put the latter in a bathroom glass and set them on the windowsill in my hotel room. Finally, having paused to sit with my purchases at Les Tribunaux, where I drink a glass of pale German beer that bites my tongue with its sharpness, I buy a small serrated knife from a gypsy in the flea market and a crisp baguette from the baker. Then I make my way home. With every step, I fantasize about a miraculous Norman market that suddenly appears one summer Saturday morning along the main street of the small Ontario town where I live. And there would also be, besides the market, a venue for Ricard and two-dollar bottles of Merlot, Côtes du Rhône and lethal Normandy cider—the kind of cider that kills with pleasure.

I take my picnic to the grassy little park that sits above the town, halfway up to the top of the cliffs. The climb is arduous, but rewarding. Sitting there, I can see all the way along the esplanade and the beaches spread out below me. In the distance, the ferry from Newhaven is coming into the harbour, making its way past fishing boats and pleasure craft. I remember an anecdote told by a German soldier who had been stationed at Dieppe during the war. That morning in August of 1942, he had been awakened by the sound of engines out beyond the seawalls and when he looked, he could not believe his eyes. *Boats!* he had said to his comrades. *Boats!* Boats where no boats should be. It was dawn and already scorching hot. The evening before, the German soldiers had been swimming in the Channel—young men splashing and horsing around in their underwear—throwing a red rubber ball. Now, they would surely all die because of these boats. He knew it because his sergeant had said so: *they are English boats and they have come to kill us!*

But that, of course, is not what happened.

More happily, I think of another story that had to do with Dieppe and the war. Looking along the esplanade towards King Edward's house with its stone caryatids turning their faces away from England, I am reminded of Edward's mistress, Alice Keppel. Mrs Keppel had been with the King since the latter years of his time as Prince of Wales and she had been in that house on several occasions.

Edward died in 1910, but Alice went on forever. She was, in fact, in France when World War II broke out. She would then have been greatly old—but had retained the strength and the energies of someone half her age. As news arrived in England of the German advances, Mrs Keppel's friends worried more and more about her safety. When the subject was broached in the salon of the famous London hostess Emerald Cunard, Emerald said: "stuff and nonsense! If the Germans arrive, Alice will simply jump into the Channel and swim home!" "And . . ." Emerald added, "I won't be surprised if she arrives carrying her maid between her teeth!"

This is better. I don't want to leave Dieppe with the worst of what had happened there uppermost in my mind. The raid and its dreadful consequences will never be forgotten—but the charm of the town, the colour of its past and the pleasures it continues to provide are what we are given to take the place of horror and to ride it down.

Pouring the end of the wine, I nod towards the town spread out below—at its churches and hotels, its winding narrow streets, its harbours and its beaches, its visitors and residents alike. Raising my glass, I say: "to you; to all your stones and all your people; to all who have come here in the past and to all who will come here in the future. Like Oscar, may we continue our friendship . . . *en famille.*"

"Hail," I say, "but not farewell."

I also say, looking around at the world we have both inherited and created: "what have we done? What have we done . . . ?"

Future Tense

Stone Orchard
September 27, 1973
Journal

Went to Toronto yesterday—and find it really does destroy me. Afterwards I can't work—or organize my mind—or function. I can't go to the bathroom—I can't concentrate—I can't write—and I hate everyone. I dread, for instance, the prospect of people contact. All day long I knew what I must face in the evening: supper with Mother and Father—and somehow, I knew I wasn't going to be able to summon myself to be there. I didn't want to answer questions: *how are you? what are you doing now? how is everything going?* Etc. I just didn't want to have to say the answers or summon the thoughts that would make the answers understandable. There is a real need to be left alone, I think, when your mind is producing—or attempting to produce. And I said to Wolf [Bill]: "the thing is, I can talk to you in shorthand—but I can't do that with other people when I am confident the shorthand will be misinterpreted. I could talk, for instance, to any other writer of my own kind of mind—or to Marigold [Charlesworth] or to people like that ... Graeme [Gibson], Peggy [Atwood], Margaret [Laurence] ... etc. ... but I cannot *face* or talk to or even bear *thinking* about facing and talking to anyone else." And I couldn't face the streets, where the eternal double fascination claws and catches at me—my hatred and despair of the ruins everywhere—and of the people—all dead and ugly—totally self-concerned and always turning away—the noise and the garbage—the sense of everything on view being refuse: that all of it—in windows for sale, or lying in the gutter newly bought—everything is plastic and mean and a cheat—that nothing anywhere displayed (including the people) is real or has depth. It is a civilization entirely of surface—with nothing below it or behind its face—and its face is so ugly that one is simply *repelled* at every turn. And yet (and this is the doubling back aspect—the aspect of desire) there are more and more men and women whose surface beauty is more and more troubling to me every time I go there. And there seem to be, also, more and more superficial things one *wants*. The pictures of naked men in the magazines—the brightly coloured pseudo-Mexican shirts—little glass bottles made to look so appealing—but which there is no real use for (or place at home to put)—images, in other words, to buy—instead of the real thing. And the sexual images are so strong now—I guess my eye is part of that—that I see more, because there is less fulfillment—more desire—but, really, sometimes I can hardly believe the marvellous physiques and the sexual display. Yesterday, for instance, there being a whole series of young men whose shirts were open to the navel—sometimes lower—whose behinds had more "shape" and whose legs were more like flesh without clothes of cover than I have ever been aware of before. And I regretted, to the point of wanting to run away, my whole responsibility to be responsible—creative—and in pain. All I wanted was to go away and fuck and fondle for hours and days and weeks: not to have to *not* to. Which, for all the *seeming* masochistic overlay, is not in the least masochistic. I truly do believe I must not, so to speak, escape into a world where only one aspect of my desire is explored—to a world where I could only buy a lot of paper hats—in which I look and feel ridiculous.

So that I came home—exhausted by frustration on the one hand

and a sense of forlorn and despairing disgust on the other. It's begun—I'm afraid—to be too much Los Angeles—New York—where, even if one had the time and the (courage?) to follow through on the trail of some desire—the young man, after all, would be unclean and in the end, would ask you for his twenty-dollar fee, because nothing now—not even the beauty of the flesh—is given away (except to the eye—and that is merely provocative)—not even for the "price" of a satisfied desire, but must be sold—like the picture of it in the magazines and the skin of it in the plastic trousers, shirts and paper hats with which they clothe themselves. There is nothing at large any more in the midst of the crowd of even the sense of a human presence. There is only the sexual trapping and the copy of a face and beyond, behind and down inside there is less and less of anything lovely to cover.

Stone Orchard
1994
Journal

Q: If you cut the wings from angels, what are you left with then?
A: Same as would cut the wings of songbirds: *men.*

Ottawa
February 3/4, 1975
Journal

In early 1975, after a three-month playwright-in-residency at the National Arts Centre in Ottawa, Tiff moved back to Stone Orchard to finalize his play *Can You See Me Yet?* and to work on a novel that ultimately was published as *Headhunter.* Just before he left, I moved to Ottawa to spend more than two years as assistant to the NAC Director of Theatre, Jean Roberts. WFW.

Bill had a talk with Jean Roberts and settled a few matters. . . . The apartment worked out well. I would leave and he would move right in. We were hoping for a parking space inside. He had an awful lot to wrap up at home and came back here to do it—income tax—television work . . .

He got to Ottawa Saturday (Feb. 1st) and I had already done a lot of packing—cardboard boxes everywhere—etc., etc. A state I *hate* to live in—transitions are the bane of my existence. I don't mind *being* anywhere—but in between one thing and another— one place and another—is hell. I had finished the play—was tired—excited—empty. Bill arrived in the same state—both of us overextended.

Late at night (about 2:00 a.m.) we had returned from a lovely small party . . . when a knock came at the door.

People do not knock on doors in apartment buildings. They ring bells and talk on the telephone and intercom systems—but they don't knock on doors. We should have known better. But I answered it. It was someone I had met while drinking in November. He had three "friends" with him. *Hoods.* I said: "I can't see you. It's late. I have a guest . . ." and closed the door. My inner voice immediately told me to call the police—but I thought Bill would think I was crazy—so I didn't.

We waited—praying they'd take no for an answer—and go away. But they didn't. They were drunk—and wanted company. They kept on knocking at the door. Finally, Willy got angry and went to the door and opened it. He told them to go away and let us sleep. All of a sudden, there was a terrible noise—of pushing and scrabbling and fighting. Bill started saying—over and over again: "phone the police. Phone the police . . ." I went to try to help him get them back out the door and to get the door closed. I knew I couldn't get the police—since the young men were between me and the phone. Bill's elbow hit one of them in the nose. The nose started to bleed. *Fury.* They were going to "punch" Willy out for having so "viciously" attacked them. By now—all four of them were in—and six of us all crowded into the tiny hallway, with this man bleeding—and those others threatening us both.

I was nearly being sick with fear. Bill was already undressed for bed—and I had no pants on. We couldn't get out the door and we couldn't get to the phone. The men starting eating the pears and apples out of the fruit bowl—and looking for liquor. There was one bottle of wine—and, of course, they found it. Then they sat around giggling—drinking the wine and eating the pears and apples and being obviously childish—the nose-bleeder going on and on and on about just having had a very serious operation and Bill had undone all the work and injured him for life—and he ought to kill Bill for doing that to him. (My God—and *he* had just broken into *our* apartment!) Anyway—it all became slowly *very* sinister. The one I had drunk with in November had obviously surmised I was a homosexual, and had brought his friends about for some "fun." I knew, for the next half hour, what James Dickey meant when he wrote of the rape scene in *Deliverance* that he had never experienced other people who were so careless of the flesh and humanity of his person. They treated us like objects without personality. It was extraordinary. Nothing *happened*—but the insinuations of danger were very high and the sense of mindless menace was unbearable. Bill sat on the bed and I was sitting in a chair *near* the phone—but knew I could never get halfway through reaching for it, let alone get to use it—so I didn't try. The men started joking—about sex. I *did* get up, said I was cold, and put on my pants. I didn't like the feeling of being exposed. Nakedness is very important in a situation where you are afraid. You feel help-less, naked—and yet it's senseless. Putting your pants on doesn't make you any stronger—and they aren't a weapon—and they're pretty flimsy "armour"—but you feel better, being covered. So I put them on. One of the men said: "oh—what a shame! Look at him! He's just putting his pants on—and I'm just taking mine off!"

My stomach turned. The man undid his pants and exposed himself. Then he said: "I'm going to the bathroom to relieve myself . . ." (and the others laughed. The man made a "jerking off" gesture). "Anyone want to help me?"

He went into the bathroom—undoing his shirt. I couldn't look at Bill. I was afraid to. It was all so frightening and, for some mad reason, I knew we would be embarrassed to see each other's eyes. They were terrifying us—*but they were also embarrassing.* It was an extraordinary feeling.

I got up. I was in my bare feet. I started to walk towards the bathroom—and just kept on walking. I got to the front door—pulled it open and ran into the hall. I just ran, thinking: I'll go right into the street and get a policeman—or yell "help!"

I got down all five flights of stairs—with one of the others chasing me partway—but thank God—for some reason he turned back. On the bottom floor, I thought of Robin Marshall, who lived at the end of the hall. Nothing concrete or planned went through my mind. Just panic—and "Robin is right there. Get him!" Knocked on the door and, of course, he was sound asleep. Finally came. Had to unchain the door, etc. I could hear footsteps and elevators—hordes of descending murderers. I wondered if they hurt Bill—or killed him—and what, if they could, they would do to me if they caught me. Robin opened the door. I had meanwhile hidden in the stairwell . . . I ran out and into Robin's apartment. Poor man—half asleep . . . me out of breath—senselessly saying: "call the police—I've been marauded . . ." etc. Marshall telephoned. I explained. The police came—very nice—understanding, etc. Very, very calm. We went up and I was expecting blood, etc.—and a dead or dying Willy with a knife in his back. *He* opened the door—"hello!"—all smartly dressed in blue shirt, etc., looking like morning—smiling—and saying: "they've gone."

I told the police the whole thing—and they were terrific. Didn't bat an eye when I told them about the homosexual overtones—and just said: "never answer your door in the night. *Never.*" (I thought of Robin and thought thank God he'd opened *his* door—but that was different. He could *see* it was me while the chain was still on.) Anyway, they said: "don't answer your door. You're in the city now—and if they bother you again, phone us at once and we'll deal with it. Don't try to deal with it yourself."

Very quietly, they left. . . . Later, I asked Willy what had happened when I just walked out the door the way I had. By then, I was aware of how sorry I was not to have warned him and felt he might think I'd "deserted" him—but he said: no, he immediately realized what I was doing and said a quiet *thanks* as he saw me get out. He heard me begin to run—then silence.

The man in the bathroom came out and said: "what's happening?" Someone else said: "I don't know." Bill said: "I think my friend has gone for the building superintendent." He then explained that I was *tired*—and was upset with the way they'd broken in. (I don't know how he got away with saying that—but quite rightly, he treated them like *bad children*, instead of like adults—and, of course, that's really what they were—dumb, thoughtless, bad kids who didn't give a damn about other people at all.) He said one of them hadn't been able to understand why I should get the superintendent and Bill said: "you frightened him" and the man just said: "so? I frightened him. Why's he hafta get the superintendent . . . ?"

Finally, one of them was clever enough to realize I might even be getting the police (I think, from Bill's description, this is the one who followed me partway and turned back) and he said: "come on, boys! We're leaving." And they did. So that was the end of it. I asked Bill if he'd been afraid—and he said: "yes—at first. But I think they were misguided, not evil. Just stupid—not sadistic. Once I realized that—I wasn't afraid."

I guess he's right—but I will never forget the initial sense of menace—as unpleasant and discomforting as knowing you're in the dark with a nest of rattlesnakes. I hope it never happens again. If it does—I will run. No waiting, next time. Just *speed*.

Calgary,
October 2001
Speech

The Bob Edwards award is named for an early Calgary newspaper
editor renowned for his outspoken and controversial journalism.
Recipients of the award are invited to emulate Bob Edwards' style in
their acceptance speeches. At a luncheon just a few weeks after
September 11, 2001, Tiff was the recipient speaker. For days after-
ward, local and national newspapers detailed the outrage of members of the petroleum industry who had been present. None of the
accounts, however, mentioned the fact that with the exception of the
petroleum industrialists, the audience greeted the talk with a standing ovation. WFW.

Remember that disagreement over the price and availability of oil
that Alberta had with the East, some years ago? Well . . . I'm one
of the bastards who *didn't* freeze in the dark . . . I had a wood
stove. When it comes to survival, foresight is everything.

Mind you, believe it or not, I had a certain amount of sympathy
for Alberta's stance. Shortly before that East–West disagreement
occurred, my friend Bill Whitehead and I were on a train heading
from Toronto to Regina—Bill's hometown—and I started talking
to a woman across the aisle. It turned out that she was from
Alberta, heading home after visiting family in the East. When she
found out I was from Toronto, she nodded and said something
about *two different worlds*. This was my first visit to the prairies—
my first sight of that magnificent horizon and that incredible sky—
so I said: "yes, but two beautiful worlds." The woman looked out
her window for a moment, watching the land roll by—and without
turning, she said: "not always." Then she turned to me and told
me what it had been like, trying to survive the "dirty thirties"—the
Depression, the drought and Bennett-buggies. And then she said:

"that was when we would send you a cowhide—and all you'd pay for it was twenty-five cents. Then you would send back a pair of shoes, and expect us to pay almost five dollars for them—and we couldn't."

And I began to understand more about the *two different worlds*—more than what was beautiful about them.

So . . . it's been suggested, given such splendid surroundings, and such conservative company, that I avoid any subjects that could be seen as "sensitive." Therefore, I have chosen to say a few words about a totally neutral topic: *energy and the environment.* . . .

It has been revealed that the two Canadian provinces who contribute most to air pollution are . . . Alberta and Ontario. That's right—in one sense—I am as guilty as you when it comes to energy and the environment. And it's quite true—our Ontario premier has given new meaning to the word "*harris*ment." In addition to all his other sins, Premier Harris has closed so many hospitals that cancer patients in Toronto now have to travel to Buffalo, New York, in order to receive treatment. Shameful!

Now, I understand that your premier . . . forgive me, I always have trouble with his name . . . oh, yes . . . he's so much like so many right-wing leaders today . . . Premier Clone . . . Well, I understand that Premier Clone sides with George W. on the subject of global warming and what to do about it. George W.'s reply to the "what to do about it" question was: *absolutely nothing!* He refused to sign the Kyoto Accord, because that, he said, would be bad for the US economy. And darned if there wasn't a faint echo of that statement coming from the northwest of the continent: if Canada agreed to the Kyoto terms, that would cost Alberta too much. *I beg your pardon?* Does that mean that the rest of the world can still freeze in the dark, as long as Alberta stays rich? Or—as they used to say in England: *screw you, Jack—I'm all right!*

How long will it take before people who think that way wake up to the fact that it's not the rest of the world that's going to freeze in the dark—it's the whole world!

Okay . . . Okay . . .

I don't want to be all *doom and gloom*. When I sat down to think about what to say this afternoon, I told myself: *make it positive, Tiff. For God's sake, make it positive!*

Hah! That ain't easy. Not these days.

Maybe it's not that terrorist hell awaits us all. *Yet.*

But reality does.

And, face it, some of reality *is* hell.

The French philosopher/playwright, Jean Paul Sartre, said—in one of his plays: *hell is other people.*

And he's right.

But why?

Why must it be that hell is other people?

It's simple.

There are other people who don't want other people to survive. There are other people who don't want other people to do what they prefer to do alone. There are other people who don't want other people to "get there first"—or to point out that "it might not be worth getting there at all." There are other people who don't want what you have to offer, if what you have to offer competes with what they have to offer.

Let me give you an example.

We're all too aware of what happened in the States on September 11. Well, in March and April of this year—2001—there was another event in the United States that can now happen anywhere—including here. It is not an event exclusive to America—or to American culture.

A young man, in his thirties—not a great deal younger than me—*what's forty years here or there?*—a young man, whose profession is cartography, put a map on the Internet.

So?

Did he claim the world is flat?

The world is square?

Of course not.

So—this map was not in any sense revolutionary.

In fact, it was so completely ordinary that it should have been destined simply to take its place in the mapping of a single site: the state of Alaska.

The young man, whose name is Ian Thomas, was an employee of the American government. He had delineated—with extraordinary exactness—the territory where Alaskan caribou go to calve each spring. That was his assignment. His job.

The designated area lies within the boundaries of Alaska's Arctic National Wildlife Refuge.

Sacrosanct?

No way.

George W. Bush had designated the area as the site of one of his major oil explorations. Forget the *Wildlife Refuge.*

Well—George W. Bush is the President of the United States.

And so, young Ian Thomas was fired—and the Alaska Caribou Calving Map was eradicated from the Internet. Done. Over. *Gone.* Forever. It was now against the law to publish it.

As Ian Thomas himself put it: "you don't have to burn books now. You just have to press the delete key."

Why have I told you this?

And why is it *positive,* as I believe it is?

I have told you because it is my own most fervent wish that such things should not happen. That some things should not exist— such as censorship and a refusal to look reality in its face and admit it is there.

Positive?

Absolutely.

Do not let *any*one—any organization—any political party, religion or corporation tell you who you are.

You *are.* We *are.* No one can define or classify you but your own integrity—a word increasingly losing its coinage in the modern lexicography of *ifs, buts, maybes* and *not-unless-we-say-sos.* Are we really prepared to let "them" press the delete button on the future? Well—it seems all too apparent that some of us *are*. Now—there is a new world. And a new reality. John Allemang, a columnist published in Toronto's *Globe and Mail*, wrote on the 12th of September that *the face of reality has changed forever*. Nothing we experience from here on until the day we die can ever be imagined as we might have imagined it prior to those dreadful moments on September 11.

But I wonder if there are other acts of terrorism—and other kinds of terrorists, in this new reality, besides those who hijack planes and fly them into buildings.

Go back to the larger picture of the world—and of the future.

Think of the consequences if the corporate world continues to rush headlong and heedless of danger into the continued exploitation of global gas and petroleum reserves. What's already happening to the planet's atmosphere is bad enough. What's going to happen in the future, if we allow corporate profits to prevail above all other concerns? Talk about suicide bombers—and all the innocent others who die along with them. Think about that—and consider the future of our children, our country and our civilization. Just remember—all the multibillion-dollar space exploration in the world ain't gonna find us *all* another place to live. Only the privileged few—if any—will be offered that. And who will they be? The ones who did it here, first, will be allowed to go and do it there, too. Wherever *there* may be. Mars—Venus—the Moon? I think not. They're *already* dead.

On the other hand, there's always the sun—and I doubt that anyone can imagine a greater source of energy than that. And I wonder—who and how many—are preparing and submitting bids for the rights to sunlight. After all, the bargaining for our water is already underway.

The buying and selling of nature is at present creating a muted disaster—a wrecked environment obscured by the tasteful corporate logos that decorate its demise. What will we do when there's nothing left?

We will die.

But . . . who cares?

No one—so it seems.

And yet . . . And yet *what?*

What would Bob Edwards have said to that?

Perhaps—that only those of us now alive can answer that—one by one by one. Thank you.

Stone Orchard
1998
Fable

The Ark in the Garden
(With a bow to James Thurber)

Once upon a sunny morning a man sitting in a breakfast nook looked up from his plate to see an ark at the bottom of the garden. He was eating lemon pancakes smothered in maple syrup and melted butter. Rising from the table, he went upstairs to the bedroom, where the drapes had not yet been opened, and spoke to his wife.

"There's an ark in the garden," he said. His napkin was still around his neck.

"Don't be ridiculous," she said. "We burned the last of the ark in the fireplace at New Year's."

"Well, there's another ark."

"Did you make it?"

"No."

"Is your name Noah?"

"Yes."

"Then, unless you made it, there can't be another ark in the garden. Go back down and finish your breakfast."

"But . . ."

"Go back down and finish your breakfast! I'm going to sleep for another hour."

"Yes, dear."

Noah returned to the breakfast nook, but his heart was sinking. He had lost his appetite. The last ark had landed over twenty centuries before and he himself had been its captain. (People in fables live for a very long time.) On that occasion, Noah had received precise instructions from the Lord regarding the ark's construction and who was to be let on board. But this time . . .

Had the Lord found someone else more trusted and more beloved than Noah?

Well, apparently.

And yet, there the ark sat—in Noah's garden.

The next thing he saw, of course, was a welter of animals trampling his flowers and vegetables. Noah went out beyond the screen porch and approached an elephant who had walked up from the ark and was now standing on the lawn. Noah asked him: "what on earth do you think you're doing?"

The elephant, who was somewhat confused and very sad, said: "I'm doing what all of us are doing. I'm trying to get on board the ark."

"But *why* . . . ?" said Noah, with a vague gesture. He meant: *why is the ark in my garden?* And he also wanted to know: *why are you walking away from it?*

The elephant thought he meant something else entirely. "Well, he said, "it is what we always do. Whenever things go wrong."

"But nothing's gone wrong!" said Noah, indignant. "I have just begun to eat the most wonderful stack of lemon pancakes and maple syrup! The sun is shining! Look—you can see it for yourself!"

At that moment, a cloud appeared and blotted out the sun.

Noah wished that his wife had not decided to sleep for another hour. She had a practical side to her reasoning that Noah lacked. He was extremely prone to panic.

"I don't understand," he said to the elephant. "If something's the matter, why aren't you getting on board the ark?"

"I'm not allowed," the elephant said. "And if I were you, I'd go down there at once and apply for admission." The elephant was now on the move again—heading up the hill. "I'm sorry," he called back, "but I don't think I can stay down here any longer."

"Oh, dear," said Noah. "Oh, oh dear . . ." And he began to panic.

Noah stared down the hill, where a great many more animals had begun to congregate.

Some years before, Noah had made a rustic lane where the cowpaths had been. It ran between the road up top and the road below, giving Noah access to Sodom, on the one hand, and Gomorrah on the other. Not that Noah ever went to visit these cities—but he did have goods delivered which could be ordered by phone: birdseed and cow bran, binder-twine and calf-pullers. Now, he could see that the gates at either end of his lane had apparently been opened and a stream of animals, motor cars and even excursion buses was pouring through from each direction.

Still with his napkin tied round his neck, he loped halfway down the hill. But so many animals were coming up—animals, trucks and even busloads of people, that he could not make his way.

"What's happening?" he called out several times and, at last, a gnu who had bruised her knees took time to pause and tell him.

"There's a man down there," she said, "who has a List. And only those on The List are allowed on board."

"What man? What man?"

"I couldn't make out his name," said the gnu, "but his List includes a great many jaguars and . . . and . . . like that. No gnus at all. In fact, the only animals I've seen going aboard are fatted calves and guinea fowl. It has to make a person very suspicious."

"Indeed," said Noah.

"I must make for higher ground," said the gnu. "I hope you will forgive me, but I'm lame."

"Go right ahead," said Noah. "Dear, dear. Oh, dear, dear!"

From behind him, and passing to his left, a large flotilla of motor cars appeared. The first in line were the Jaguars.

"Jaguars," Noah muttered. "The gnu said Jaguars were allowed on board."

And behind them came all the other motor cars—two by two.

"Millionaires!" Noah sputtered. "In their millionaire cars!"

Mercedes, Daimlers and Rolls-Royces—Cadillacs, Buicks and Lincolns rolled through the dust down the lane. All had tinted windows. The passengers could not be seen.

At the lower gate, beyond which the ark loomed up as if from memory, Noah found and accosted the man with The List. He wore sunglasses.

"Is my name on there?" Noah asked.

"Depends what it is."

Noah told him.

The man, who also wore gloves, ran his fingers through the N's. "Nope," he said. "Not here."

"But . . . ! I'm *Noah!*"

"Do you have a Jaguar?"

"No. I have farm animals—horses . . . sheep . . ."

"Not good enough. Go back."

Taking one last look at the chaotic scene before him, Noah sighed and joined the growing crowd of refugees moving up the hill away from the ark—and, where the path diverged to his side door, returned to his kitchen.

There sat his wife, finishing his pancakes.

"Well?" she said. "What's going on out there?"

Noah told about the ark and all the millionaires' cars, the elephant and the gnu. Then he took off his napkin and wiped his brow.

"I suppose in that case we'd best get going," said his wife with a dab at her lips and a final mouthful of coffee.

"No," said Noah. "No need to hurry. We aren't going anywhere."

"Not going anywhere? But we have to get on board the ark!"

"No," said Noah—and sat down. "Not this time." Then he said: "there's a man with a List—and we're not on it."

"But this is Canada! Our home and native land! We're on every list there is! Old-age pensions—after all, nobody's older than we are! And what about—health care—ark privileges . . . They can't sail without us!"

"Well, they're going to," said Noah. "And there's nothing we can do about it. Are there any more pancakes?"

"No."

It began to rain.

MORAL: No gnus is bad gnus.

In other words, if you want to survive, today—you had best get on the right list.

Pen Power

Protest

Stone Orchard
1991
Playlets

Martha and the Minder

To the artist, freedom of expression is vital.

And yet, such freedom is being denied by censorship—even by imprisonment.

What follows is dedicated to those whose freedom is yet to be won, and to those who help them win it by adopting prisoners of conscience. This process begins with letters written to and in behalf of the prisoner. Those who write these letters are known as minders. Making and maintaining contact is often painfully frustrating, since there is not always evidence the letters are being received.

This dramatization is based on my experience as minder for the writer Kuwee Kumsa, whose English name was Martha and who was imprisoned for seven years in Addis Ababa. It was written especially for presentation at a gala for PEN International, produced in December 1991 at the Winter Garden Theatre in Toronto. Judith Thompson performed Martha, with Timothy Findley as Minder.

The four episodes were presented at intervals throughout the evening. The final episode was the culmination of the whole gala.

Episode One

(There are two lecterns, one on either side of the stage, each with a microphone and each capable of being lit by a spotlight. MARTHA *is stage right;* MINDER *is stage left. Both begin in darkness.)*

MARTHA: Someone? *(Pause.)* Someone? *(Pause.)* Please? Someone?

*(*LIGHT *begins to rise on* MARTHA *stage right.)*

Hello? Hello? Hello! *(Pause.)* Isn't there someone there? Anyone? Anywhere?

MINDER: Yes?

MARTHA: Oh . . .

MINDER: Did someone speak?

MARTHA: Yes. I did.

MINDER: Who are you? Where are you?

MARTHA: I'm in prison. My name is Martha. *(Silence.)* Hello?

*(*LIGHT *begins to rise on* MINDER *stage left.)*

MINDER: Yes? What?

MARTHA: Who are you? Tell me your name.

MINDER: Minder.

MARTHA: How do you do, Mister Minder?

MINDER: I'm well—but please don't call me Mister. Call me Minder. (*Beat.*) May I call you . . . ?

MARTHA: Martha. That's the only name I have that I can give you.

MINDER: I see. (*Pause.*) Why are you in prison?

MARTHA: I don't really know. Something I said—or something I wrote. Well—no. It was definitely something I wrote.

MINDER: You mean it was censored?

MARTHA: Yes. Well—no. Not what I wrote—but me. *I'm* in prison. Not my words. (*Laughs.*) And I'd like not to be. (*Sober.*) Trouble is, there's no one out there who knows I'm in here. Except you—whoever you are. And—now that you know, do you think you could help me? (*Silence.*) Do you? Hello? (*Angry.*) Hello, for God's sake!

MINDER: Yes? What?

MARTHA: Where did you go?

MINDER: Nowhere. I'm standing right here.

MARTHA: Well—you might have answered.

MINDER: Answered what?

MARTHA: My question. I asked you a question.

MINDER: I didn't hear you. What did you want to know?

MARTHA: I wanted to know . . . (*Beat.*) How do I know I can trust you?

MINDER: You don't. But you'd better.

MARTHA: What makes you say that?

MINDER: Well—you said yourself I was the only one who knew you were in there. . . .

MARTHA: Yes.

MINDER: So. What was your question? (*Silence.*) Martha? Please answer. (*Silence.*)

MARTHA: Minder? Are you there? (*Silence.*) No. So it's true. You can't trust anyone. Oh, God—why did he even bother to answer? (*Shouts.*) Why did you bother? You son of a bitch! It isn't fair!

MINDER: (*Not hearing her.*) Well. The only thing to do, I guess, is to go on speaking. . . .

MARTHA: (*Can't hear. Shouts.*) How dare you do this to me . . . !

MINDER: She is there. I know that . . .

MARTHA: . . . Raise my hopes and dash me down again!

MINDER: . . . I heard her . . .

MARTHA: You bastard, Minder!

MINDER: . . . at least once. (*Pause.*)

MARTHA: (*Quiet.*) All right. The only thing to do . . . is to go on speaking. . . .

MINDER: (*Formal.*) "Excellency—I join with International PEN in appealing to Your Honour . . ."

(LIGHTS *begin to fade on* MARTHA *stage right.*)

MARTHA: (*As before.*) Someone . . . ?

MINDER: . . . to reconsider the situation . . .

MARTHA: . . . please . . . ?

MINDER: . . . of the imprisoned writer, Martha . . .

MARTHA: . . . Someone . . . ?

MINDER: . . . We wish for her to be . . .

MARTHA: . . . Hello . . . ?

MINDER: . . . reunited with her children . . .

MARTHA: (*Now in ghost-light.*) . . . Hello! Hello! . . .

MINDER: . . . and to be granted . . . (*He waits.*) . . . her freedom.
(LIGHTS *begin to fade on* MINDER *stage left.*) It's so ironic . . .

MARTHA: Minder . . . ?

MINDER: . . . just when she finally catches someone's attention . . .

MARTHA: Minder?

MINDER: . . . she disappears.

MARTHA: HELP!!

(*Total blackout.*)

Episode Two

(LIGHTS *up.*)

MINDER: Well, Martha, we have waited now two years with no further word of you. We think perhaps you have been moved to another prison, but we have no way of knowing. At any rate, I will go on writing and so will others. Because it seems the only sane thing to do.

MARTHA: Not a word. And, of course, I have no way of communicating with the outside world. The only money I have, I must spend on food. No one out there understands that. Prisons here don't feed you. Or clothe you. Or anything. All they do is keep you. And if I could afford some writing paper, I couldn't afford the postage. And even if I could afford the postage—they wouldn't pass it through the system. Two whole years in silence. They want the world to think I'm dead—and they want me, too, to think the world is dead. And I—right now, I'm quite prepared to believe it.

MINDER: When we were children, my brother and I would write our names on pieces of paper—and we would write the word "hello" and put the pieces of paper into bottles and seal the bottles and throw them into the sea. Well—here comes another bottle with another note. Hello, Martha. Hello.

MARTHA: (*Has not heard him.*) I need a bottle of aspirin. I need a bar of soap. I need a package of toilet paper. I need disinfectant. I need vitamins. I need bread. I need tea. I need a lemon—one lemon. I need clean underwear. I need a pair of shoes. I need a box of tampons. I need a ball of string. I need money. I need news. I need my children . . . please.

MINDER: (*Has not heard her.*) It is winter here, now—and coming on to Christmas. Snow—have you ever seen snow? Martha?

MARTHA: (*Has not heard him. Putting her other needs aside.*) I need one card—one stamp—an envelope. Thank you. Now—I will see if the world is still there. And if it remembers me.

MINDER: Oh—my— (*Opens envelope.*) Oh—my—God! (*Holds up card.*)

MARTHA: Merry Christmas. Love. Martha.

MINDER: She's alive.

(*Blackout.*)

Episode Three

(MARTHA *and* MINDER *share microphone, stage left.* LIGHTS *up.*)

MINDER: This morning, I went shopping with my friend. The store clerk didn't know what to make of us, though it began innocently enough.

MARTHA: (STORE CLERK) Good morning, gentlemen.

MINDER: Good morning.

MARTHA: Is there something I can do for you?

MINDER: Yes. We want to buy some clothing.

MARTHA: I see. You realize, of course, you're in the wrong department. Men's clothing is . . .

MINDER: No, no. It's women's clothing we're looking for.

MARTHA: Oh, I see. Yes. Well. What did you have in mind?

MINDER: Bottoms.

MARTHA: Bottoms.

MINDER: Yes. And tops.

MARTHA: Tops . . . and bottoms?

MINDER: Yes.

MARTHA: What of?

MINDER: Well . . .

MARTHA: (*Staring at him.*) I know you, don't I?

MINDER: No. I don't think so.

MARTHA: Yes. I do. I know you. I've seen you on television . . .

MINDER: Well . . .

MARTHA: And in the papers.

MINDER: I . . .

MARTHA: You're that gay writer, aren't you.

MINDER: Well . . .

MARTHA: The one with all the opinions.

MINDER: Could we get the tops and bottoms, please?

MARTHA: I suppose this gentlemen with you is your . . . friend.

MINDER: Yes. He is my friend. Now . . .

MARTHA: What sort of tops and bottoms had you in mind? We never did get to that, did we?

MINDER: No—we didn't.

MARTHA: Are they for him—or for you?

MINDER: Please, madame, we just want . . .

MARTHA: I suppose you'll want to try them on.

MINDER: No . . .

MARTHA: I can't, of course, let you anywhere near the lingerie. That's not allowed.

MINDER: We don't . . .

MARTHA: Even in the men's department, it is absolutely forbidden. Customers are not allowed to test drive the underwear.

MINDER: (*Shouts.*) We don't want underwear! We want tops and bottoms!

MARTHA: Yes, sir.

MINDER: For a friend!

MARTHA: Ladies' tops and bottoms for a friend . . .

MINDER: Yes.

MARTHA: This friend here?

MINDER: No! For a friend in prison!

MARTHA: I see. You want ladies' tops and bottoms for a friend in prison.

MINDER: Yes.

MARTHA: (*Pause.*) What size is he?

(*Blackout.*)

Episode Four

(MARTHA *stage right*, MINDER *stage left*. PARTIAL LIGHTING *only stage left. The* LIGHTS *grow hotter stage right around* MARTHA *as she speaks.*)

MARTHA: Are you there?

MINDER: Yes.

MARTHA: The clothing arrived.

MINDER: Oh, yes?

MARTHA: Blue is my favourite colour.

MINDER: Blue is the colour of hope.

MARTHA: Yes. Well— It's that time of year again. September.

MINDER: September. Yes.

MARTHA: This is the month of pardons—of amnesty—
forgiveness—freedom.

MINDER: Yes.

MARTHA: In September of every year, they come through that
gate—and they choose twelve people—and they set them
free.

MINDER: Yes.

MARTHA: I have been here, now, nine Septembers.

MINDER: Eight. This one is not yet over.

MARTHA: Yes. It is not yet over. But it is still number nine.
(*Beat.*) What are you doing today? I wonder.

MINDER: Sitting in the shade.

MARTHA: Oh, Minder! You sound so weary of it all. I'm sitting in
the sun. I love the sun. It is spring here, now, you see. Spring—
and the month of pardons.

MINDER: We're thinking of you, Martha—all of us—and praying.

MARTHA: (*Pause.*) When they come through the gate, you never know. I mean—they come for you, and sometimes, it is not an amnesty. Sometimes it is not a pardon. And it is never forgiveness. Never. (*Beat.*) Thank you for writing—all these years. Just in case. (*Beat.*) Some people . . . sometimes, they come through the gate and they choose you—and you disappear. People disappear. It is not always a good thing—to be chosen.

MINDER: We are with you, Martha.

MARTHA: On the other hand—a person can be set free. Pardoned. Hah! Pardoned! How dare they "pardon" me. I did nothing wrong. Only what I believed was right. And I will believe it was right to the day I die, Minder. Yes. To the day I die. (*Beat.*) Are you afraid of death, Minder?

MINDER: Yes.

MARTHA: So am I. And here I sit—waiting for the gate to open. (*Beat.*) If it opens to an amnesty, I will see my children.

MINDER: Yes.

MARTHA: Well—Minder—here they come. Goodbye.

MINDER: I won't say goodbye. I can't. (*He turns upstage, becoming another person.*) MAR-THA!

MARTHA: Yes. That is me. (*She turns upstage, and slowly walks into the wings.*)

(Pause.)

MINDER: (*Turning front.*) Ladies and gentlemen—after almost ten years, Martha was released from prison—and reunited with her children. And here she is.

(*Enter* MARTHA KUMSA, *no longer imprisoned in Addis Ababa, but living in Toronto with her children.*)

She was welcomed with a loud and prolonged standing ovation which caused her young son in the audience to ask: *why is everyone standing up? Are they angry at my mother?*

Stone Orchard
1987
Article

Indefinite Detention, Incommunicado, In Solitary Confinement

Saturday, March 7th: For the very first time this year, the door stood open all day and we opened all the windows. We have been so desperate for spring—and here it is.

This spring, I celebrate the twentieth anniversary of being a published novelist. In the spring of 1967, I went to New York City and someone handed me *The Last Of the Crazy People* bound between hard covers. What an extraordinary sensation that was. Being published at all had not seemed possible. . . .

On the phone today, as if to bring me back to the inescapable, Christina Hartling from *Quill and Quire* wanted to check the Little Sisters data. Books that cannot get across the border into Canada. It all seems so unreal. Twenty years ago, a Canadian publisher turned down *Crazy People*, saying: "this book tells about a young boy who kills his family, Mr Findley; and I'm here to tell you, I can't publish a book like that. The public would say I was nuts. Children don't kill their families in Canada."

Oh.

And now these books that can't get across the border. Impounded. Books by Oscar Wilde and Jean Genet and Quentin Crisp. I can hear somebody saying it, now: *"these books are downright advocates of homosexuality—and I'm here to tell you, people don't engage in that activity in Canada!"*

What a year it's been.

Friday, January 2nd: I'm sick of being president of the English-Canadian arm of PEN International. I'm sick of heartfelt writing. I'm sick of making heartfelt speeches. I'm sick of telephoning people and saying: "we need your help again." I'm sick of telegrams, sick of letters, sick of midnight interviews and sick unto death of thinking the following will never end:

. . . *Zwelakhe Sisulu has again been arrested in South Africa* . . .

Again.

The news of this arrest arrived by post this morning. Zwelakhe Sisulu is a respected journalist, a Nieman Fellow, editor of *The New Nation* and a director of Article 19, a new human rights organization designed to monitor and protest instances of censorship. From 1980 to 1983, he was restricted under a banning order, and from July 1981 to February 1982 he was detained without trial. In the summer of 1986, he disappeared. Through the efforts of his wife, who spread the word of his disappearance by means of the press outside South Africa, Sisulu was finally located in a prison and released. And now—this letter:

Zwelakhe Sisulu has again been arrested . . .

I have sent the appropriate telegrams and have written four letters in his behalf. Sending the telegrams, I also have to send some

others to Tehran in behalf of a British journalist who has disappeared some place in Iran and who, we fear, has been arrested.
This man's name is Roger Cooper. On the telephone, having
contacted CP/CN Telecommunications, I get an operator who
obviously thinks he has a minor madman—maybe just a crank—
on his hands. When I say that one of the telegrams is to go to the
Iranian president, Ali Khamenei, he says: "ahem . . . could you
hang on for just a moment?"

"Certainly."

(I'm sick of this.)

It is obvious the operator is checking me out: "there's a guy here
claims he's a writer. Timothy Findley. Anyone heard of him? He
also claims there's a writers' organization called International PEN.
Has anyone heard of that?"

(Sick of this, too.)

Thank heaven, someone down the line of operators has either
heard of PEN or of me and the operator comes back on the line
with a slightly modified tone of respect. "Okay," he says. "Shoot."

(I would like to.)

I read the burden of my message with absurd formality. It is, I
admit, a most peculiar feeling to be addressing yourself to the
president of Iran.

By the time I get to the Sisulu telegrams, all being sent to
Pretoria, there is, at last, a chance to burst out laughing. One of
the messages is addressed as follows:

> To: Major General S.H. Schutte,
> Head of Security Police,
> Police Headquarters, etc.

Major General "Shoot," eh? Head of Security Police? I thought,
for a moment, I had stumbled inadvertently into the pages of a
comic novel by Evelyn Waugh.

(I would like that, too.)

But no such luck. The message regarding Zwelakhe Sisulu gave short shrift to that—and our laughter died.

I am sick of this.

Later, I telephoned to Susan Crean, who chairs the local Writers in Prison Committee and to Margaret Atwood, last year's president of Canada's English Centre of PEN who, this year, is one of its vice-presidents. They, too, sent telegrams and Crean sent letters.

I wondered if the telegraph operator left the line to check on them, the way he had on me. I found myself thinking: it is a kind of madness we're all engaged in: sending telegrams to plead for someone's life.

Atwood said something that disturbed me. She said: "you know that, in Iran, they aren't going to pay attention to anything Susan says, or that I say." And I said: "why?" And she said: "we're women."

The power to persuade is mitigated, somehow, everywhere you turn.

I'm sick of it.

Saturday, January 24th: Someone phones from the *Vancouver Sun*. This is to check on how PEN means to respond to the current problem there of Customs Officials impounding shipments of books that are destined for the Little Sisters bookstore, Vancouver's best-known outlet for gay literature. Some of the impounded titles are by Oscar Wilde and André Gide, Jean Genet and Allen Ginsberg. I listen to all of this, already thinking: I am sick of this. There is a code of which I had not been aware before. It seems that, among the apparently thousands of reasons a book or a magazine can be impounded is if, within its pages, there is depiction of anal sex. This prompts me to remark that, if that is the case, then practically every American novel written in the last twenty years will have to be impounded because practically every American novel written within the last twenty years contains the phrase: stick it up your (THIS IS A FAMILY NEWSPAPER)!

I tell the reporter that the English Centre of PEN Canada has already decided it is prepared to donate appropriate monies to the British Columbia Civil Liberties Association, who will, it is hoped, be bringing a court action concerning Little Sisters and the impounded books sometime in May. I also tell him the English Centre will donate the equivalent in monies to the Glad Day Bookshop in Toronto, which is suffering from the same harassment. The latest book to be impounded at the US/Ontario border is *The Naked Civil Servant*, by Quentin Crisp. The thought of this is so pathetic a person can only laugh. There is no one I would rather take survival lessons from than Quentin Crisp.

Friday, February 6th: There is a long and exhausting meeting of the PEN Executive. Exhausting, but also exhilarating. Good things have happened. Some good things. We have had a communiqué concerning one of our prisoners—a journalist whose name is Martha Kumsa. Martha Kumsa has been imprisoned in Ethiopia for some time and, while we have known that Martha was in prison, we did not know how to make contact. Now, a card has arrived. A Christmas card. The only words are the printed text of the card: Merry Christmas and a Happy New Year. But it is signed, in her own hand: *Martha*—and she, herself, has drawn a Christmas tree. More important, there is an address. We can write to her.

Michael Scammell has come to the meeting. Scammell is an English writer currently teaching in New York State and he has been, for the last ten years, the international chairman of PEN's Writers in Prison programme. Mary Lou Finlay, the journalist, is also there in behalf of Zwelakhe Sisulu. Finlay is a Nieman Fellow and she has come to explore the possibility that the Nieman Foundation and PEN might work together for Sisulu. We decide this is a good idea. June Callwood also mentions that a prominent Canadian lawyer is travelling to South Africa and perhaps we could send a letter to Sisulu with him. This, too, receives a positive response. Things have begun to look up.

Monday, March 2nd: We have had another success. Our prisoner in Lithuania, the writer and human-rights activist Antanas Terlakas, has been released from prison. The fact is, he has been released for some time, but the news of it was somehow censored. However, that hardly matters. The thing is, he's free, and this is plainly wonderful.

But there is still no word of Martha, although we have written since we received her card. And there is still no real news about Sisulu, although the Canadian lawyer came within an ace of being allowed to visit him. And this morning, there was another of those letters in the mail: this one from the Iranian Embassy in Ottawa. Roger Cooper is going to be tried on charges of spying and espionage. *There seems,* this letter concludes, *to be no ground for concern.*

Somehow, I am not persuaded this is true.

Tuesday, March 10th: It's spring now, or nearly. And I want all this to end: the prisoners hidden away from the world, the doors unopened, the closed hearts, afraid of words—the shuttered windows and the shuttered minds. *Don't let the air in—don't let in the light!* Imagine. The earth turns upward into the sun—and everything that's capable of life is on the verge of freedom. Everything, that is, but those in prison and the words that put them there.

And I'm sick of it.

Aren't you?

Stone Orchard
1989
Verse satire

The following poem was written for inclusion in *Barbed Lyres: Canadian Venomous Verse—A Collection of Satirical Poems.* The poem was considered potentially libelous, and was dropped from the book's contents. Unfortunately, Tiff was not aware of this until the book was published. Had he known, he would have included a disclaimer to the effect that the last two lines in no way implied anything about the minister's sexuality, but only warned about a hypothetical view of his sexuality that might be engendered should he "protest too much" about homosexuality in literature. wfw.

Otto-Eroticism
A cautionary poem for Mr. Jelinek

He can be awfully Otto-cratic
With reactions Otto-matic.
Always sees as pornographic
Homo literary traffic.

If a cover shows a man
In a posing strap and tan,
Law enforcement persons can it;
At the border, Otto-ban it.

Maybe Otto should beware the
Inquisition arbitrary.
In the new gay dicktionary,
Otto-da-fe is a fairy.

Stone Orchard
1993
Speech excerpt

Canadian Heaven

It intrigues me that people can still ask: what does it mean to be Canadian? It's a question, I've been told, that was asked of a British parish priest, decades ago, after he'd returned from a visit to Canada. What were Canadians like? He received so many questions, he finally decided to answer them from the pulpit. And so, one Sunday, this is what he said:

"You want to know what Canadians are like? I will tell you. Imagine, if you would, the entire population of the world walking down a single road, together. At one point, this great multitude comes to a crossroads, where each branch is plainly labelled with a signpost. Most of the people choose the road whose sign proclaims: "THIS WAY TO HEAVEN." However, a relatively small number of people wheel off in a second direction. These are the Canadians—and they have chosen the road whose sign reads: "THIS WAY TO LECTURES ABOUT HEAVEN!"

Stone Orchard
1992
Article

The Valour and the Horror

The resentment over the premiere broadcast of *The Valour and the Horror* has something disturbingly in common with the resentment over the events depicted in the television series itself—the tragic overkill apparent in the World War II bombing of German cities by Canadian and other Allied forces. It is the resentment of those who realize for the first time that in war, there can be no glory. Not only can there be no glory, there can be no dignity and little honour. What there will be is terror, bravery, revulsion and agony. And death. In other words, precisely what the title of Brian and Terrence McKenna's brilliant television series tells us: there will be valour and there will be horror.

What is most surprising about the reactionary opposition of those who want to silence what the McKenna brothers have achieved is that so many expressing opposition are battlefield veterans themselves and, consequently, men who should be most aware that glory is a lie. They appear, however, to be telling us otherwise.

It is now a commonplace that in war, the first casualty is truth. As an example of this—and one outside the McKenna series— bring to mind the well-known Canadian war correspondent who, on his return to England after the disaster at Dieppe in August of 1942, reported that he had entered the town of Dieppe that morning in the company of Canadian troops and while there, was witness to a completely successful operation. This was a lie. The truth is, he sat offshore on a command ship and knew before the raid began exactly just what he would broadcast. Only a handful of Canadians made it into the town; many more died on the beach or were taken prisoner there.

Such lies may be well meant, but in denying the scope of the horror, they also deny the scope of the valour.

In light of the events of World War II, it is astonishing that anyone could imagine the behaviour of the Allied High Command was impeccably civilized. Does no one remember the ending of what began at Hamburg and Dresden—to say nothing of Berlin, where I personally witnessed the results of what can only be called Allied barbarism. This onslaught on civilians ended with the dropping of one atom bomb on Hiroshima—and of a second atom bomb on Nagasaki. Not one; two. Not once; twice. Who, with an ounce of sanity, could claim that two bombs were necessary? On the other hand, would either bomb have fallen if the massive raids on Hamburg, Dresden and Berlin had not taken place?

This is not to say that the Allied High Command was by any means alone in perpetrating horrors. These words tell us otherwise: *Hong Kong—Leningrad—holocaust.* War, being war, calls up the worst in all of us. And perhaps the best. Horror and valour. Valour and horror.

As a writer, it is my job to seek and to confront the truth. As filmmakers, Brian and Terrence McKenna have shown the same approach. In researching the incidents presented in *The Valour and the Horror*, they interviewed hundreds of soldiers. While it was being filmed, the series was given the full support of the Chief of the Defence Staff. It is an entirely responsible, fully documented and laudable piece of journalism—a landmark for which the majority of Canadians are grateful. If it were not controversial, it would be worthless; it would be mere propaganda. Propaganda, however, is what its opponents would have it be. Not to put too fine a point on it, they would prefer that it had lied. They object to its truths.

This is fine—or it would be—if Brian and Terrence McKenna's critics had stated their opposition to the series in the normal fashion—in the traditional ways that negative criticism is voiced—as letters to the editor—as critical responses in the press—as refutations and arguments carried out in public forums. What is dreadful about what actually happened is that the series' opponents have chosen to censor and to silence the McKennas. And they have done this by striking a Senate Committee to do their work for them, urging that the government ban the programmes from further telecasts.

Further, they have reached inside the Canadian Broadcasting Corporation—where the government has no business reaching—and they have staged a coup in there, effectively damning *The Valour and the Horror* through the medium of the CBC ombudsman.

What has become of the government's long tradition of an

"arm's length" policy in broadcasting. What has become of freedom of expression?

Go back to the beginning, we are being told. Start again. Tell us there was no war, but only noise and furor. Tell us that dust and rubble are only scenic effects. Tell us that no one died—that people merely disappeared. Above all, tell us we meant well. We meant well.

We meant well. We meant well. . . .

Language

Cotignac

1994

Fable

The Unicorn and the Grapevine

. . . the Bodhisattva, life-traveller on the way to becoming Buddha, was once an antelope . . . speaking in human language that had been perfected in the course of a hundred incarnations. The colouring of this antelope was as bright as pure gold, and with the soft gemlike lustre of his horns and hoofs, he was of surpassing beauty. Knowing how slight humanity's compunction was, he preferred to stay in the depths of the forest, avoiding human contact.

Thus it is written concerning one of the many incarnations of Buddha; and thus can we call to mind another creature of great beauty who once lived in the wilds, far from humankind. This was a magical creature of wisdom and of gentle powers—including the power of human speech: the Unicorn.

Many have lamented the passing of this wondrous and unique beast. One new-day writer, in telling the story of the universal Flood, relates how the Unicorn—that flower-fed marvel of the forest—perished on board the Great Ark, a victim of human brutality. As has been said before, and as can still be said, to our dismay:

cruelty is nothing more than a failure of the imagination. It was the extinction of the Unicorn, our new-day writer explains, that caused all the magic to fade from the world.

Sadly, I must confess: that new-day writer is your present storyteller. But wonders never cease, and I can tell you now that your storyteller no longer holds to new-day ways. You will see the truth of this when I reveal to you what has since been discovered regarding the fate of the Unicorn, and the magic it carried onto the earth.

This splendid beast, whose powers so exceeded its delicate dimensions, first came into being within that same Supreme Imagination that created us all, and that created, too, the magnificent world in which we all live. When time was ripe for its birth, the Unicorn stepped out of the Supreme Imagination into the sun-dappled seclusion of the forest, and thus, into the experience—and the greedy grasp—of humankind.

In time, as other storytellers have noted, the Unicorn eluded our grasp and abandoned its forest home. But not through death. Not through extinction. The Supreme Imagination does not embrace and will not tolerate extinction. Instead of disappearance, it decrees transformation: not obliteration, but the evolution of one being into another. (If you search the word *another*, you will find the word *one*, itself transformed.) This way, the Unicorn retreated into the safety of the human imagination—where anyone can catch a glimpse of its beauty, whether in paintings or in paragraphs. Wherever the human imagination thrives, the Unicorn lives. When human imagination fails, as has been said—it dies.

It is not just the Unicorn born of the Supreme Imagination that lives in this inner realm. It is every unicorn that ever stepped upon the earth. Let me tell you of one of them.

There was once a unicorn whose name was "Half-wit," because his head was adorned with but a single horn. He suffered dreadfully from ridicule. Other hoofed creatures proudly displayed a pair of horns—horns being the outward sign of wit and wisdom.

One day, angry and hurt, Half-wit resolved to take action against his disfigurement. He chose a place in the forest where a rocky outcropping thrust a hard, sharp edge of obsidian out towards the trees. Measuring carefully with his eye, the unicorn lowered his head and charged at the rock, hoping it would split his horn in two, and thus provide him with an acceptable appearance. Unhappily, he misjudged his aim, and the tip of his horn, deflected by the bright obsidian, buried itself solidly in an adjacent cleft. And there it stuck, despite his frantic efforts to free himself from the rock's unyielding grasp.

The other animals gathered to laugh at the unicorn's plight. "Half-wit! Half-wit!" they cried. "He will soon have no wits at all!" He suffered their cruel humour in silence until—looking down—he saw what was happening near his blue-veined hooves. There, the shoot of a budding grapevine had begun to grow up the rock towards the unicorn's head. It was the kind of grapevine along which news is able to pass. The voice of this particular vine reached out towards the ears of the animal assemblage:

"Tell me, you who scorn another's adversity, what is the most magnificent thing you have ever seen?"

"The sun!" cried a voice.

"And why," said the grapevine, "do you call the sun magnificent?"

"Because," the voice said, "although it leaves us at the end of every day, it never fails to return to light both the business and the pleasure of our lives."

"I see," mused the grapevine, sprouting three new leaves and two new tendrils even as it spoke. "And what, may I ask, is wonderful?"

"The moon!" another voice called out. And then, in response to the grapevine's query: "because it looks down at us with a changing face that signals how time is passing . . ."

"Indeed," said the grapevine, waving its leaves and flourishing its purple fruit. "And what, pray tell, is inspiring?"

A third voice was heard: "the stars are inspiring . . ." and, without waiting for the question, "because their patterns in the sky draw pictures that tell us the stories of our beginnings . . ."

The grapevine grew in silence for a moment, and then sent its words once more towards the circle of animals. "Does everything magnificent, wonderful and inspiring reside in the sky?" it asked—itself straining upwards. "Do you mean you look around you and find nothing here to marvel at on earth?"

As the animals shuffled their hooves and shifted their eyes, the grapevine continued: "look, then, at what is growing in this very rock that holds the unicorn so tightly in its grasp. Do you not see? Here is the gold magnificence of the sunflower, reaching up and out towards the blazing orb from which it takes its name; and the white of the wondrous moonflower, opening its petals only at night, beneath the light of its namesake—and the inspirational blue of the starflowers, hanging in their own intriguing patterns from their stems."

The grapevine twisted back towards the unicorn, rustling its words in the direction of the rock's prisoner. "Feed, I charge you, on these earthly wonders, unicorn—and let them free you from your present predicament."

The unicorn turned his head as far as he could, and, reaching out with lips and tongue, tasted of the triad—sunflower, moonflower and starflower. All at once, his eyes widened, and, to the amazement of all who watched, he withdrew his horn from the rock—as one might draw a silver sword from its sheath. At last, he was able to stand erect once more.

Many of the animals—even those who once had laughed at the unicorn—stamped their hooves in approval. Others leapt to the branches around them and sang out their happiness in a song that echoed through the whole wide forest. After all, there is nothing that lives that does not celebrate freedom.

"Tell me, grapevine," the unicorn said at last, when the stamping and the singing had ceased, "what can I do to repay you for setting me free?"

"You can teach all unicorns to live on a diet of flowers," said the grapevine, "from now until the end of time. Thus will the eyes of the Unicorn remain wide open to all that is magnificent, wonderful and inspiring here on earth. And from the flowers themselves will come a truly magical power—the power to conquer space and time."

"To conquer space and time!" The unicorn pranced with excitement, while the other animals muttered their envy. "But still, I ask," said the unicorn, "what must I do to merit such wondrous power?"

"Why," said the grapevine, in a quiet voice, "you must spread the word of all the wonders you encounter in your days on earth. You must tell every being that breathes—all the animals and all the people—about the marvels of the place you share."

The unicorn stopped prancing, and thought about this. "*All* the animals?" he asked. "And *all* the people?" He frowned at the grapevine. "But how can I possibly go everywhere? And how will I ever have time to speak to everyone?"

The grapevine had become quite weary with its growing and its freeing of the unicorn and now its words could hardly be heard. "Did I not tell you that unicorns would conquer space and time?"

"Yes," said the unicorn, "but *how?*"

No more words came from the grapevine. It had curled around the rock, and now it was entirely still and silent.

The spectacle of its growth and the wonder of its wisdom seemed to have concluded and the animals began to drift away. For his part, the unicorn, held prisoner for so long, realized how thirsty he was, and he went in search of water. He knew he must be careful where he drank, since many of the pools in various parts of the forest were poisonous. He would have to test the scent and try the texture and taste the edges of every pool before he could drink.

When at last he found a pond he knew to be safe, and having

drunk, he decided to leave a mark that would speak the message for others: *here you may drink your fill.*

And so he scraped with his sharp white hooves at the pond's rocky border, and having left his message, moved on.

This was how he fulfilled his part of the bargain made with the grapevine. Wherever the unicorn went, he left his distinctive marks that advertised the wonders of what he found—the pure, sweet springs of water, the tenderest shoots of bamboo, the thickest patches of berries. And once we had learned to read his messages, just as the grapevine had predicted, his words conquered space and time because they could be read no matter how many miles or days the unicorn had travelled since creating them. How, then, can anyone say that magic has faded from the world. How can you say it, with evidence to the contrary right before your eyes. Are my words not speaking to you now, though miles and years now lie between us? And if there is still such potent magic as that—who knows?—there may still be a Unicorn in some wild forest yet to be imagined. A forest of sunflowers, perhaps. Or a field of moonflowers and starflowers gazing up towards their namesakes. But of course, his existence is entirely up to you— since, after all, it is your imagination—if you have one—that must invent him.

Stone Orchard
1993
Entries in the Dictionary of Neologisms

New Words

flus-trate: n [fluster + frustrate]: to produce a state of nervous tension through confrontation with something that does not function; usually denoted by the biting of lips and the making of

fists. *This birdhouse kit has left me so flustrated I could spit nails!*
Can also be used as the basis for a noun: *After the cursor had
jammed for the nineteenth time, Allison was reduced to a state of
utter flustration.*

mulroned: [Mulroney + marooned] pron. *mull-rooned.* A word of
Canadian origin, referring to the state of nations that have first
been crippled and then abandoned by their leaders. The occasion
of its coinage was the dismemberment in the 1990s of the Canadian union of provinces, at the instigation and under the guidance
of then Prime Minister Brian Mulroney (pron. *Mull-roo-nee*).
*Once the dirty deed was done and the broken nation had been mul-
roned in the frozen north, Brian retired from politics and became the
permanent house guest of George and Barbara Bush.*

Stratford
2003
Translation Traps

International writers' festivals offer wonderful opportunities to
study what happens when writers of many different nations and
languages gather under one roof.

I remember one year at Harbourfront's festival in Toronto,
when writers from Spain and Mexico were present. To my amazement, neither could easily understand the other's Spanish. Too
much distance and too many centuries had intervened, to the
point that some of their conversations had to be carried out in
some other tongue they held in common, such as English or
French.

One of the Mexican poets was a gorgeous redhead. Her teeth
and eyes flashed as passionately as her words—and, as with many
of the festival's international guests, she was invited to read in her

own language, pausing at the end of every stanza for an English version to be read. Leading Canadian writers were invited to voice the translations.

The beautiful poet, therefore, was paired with the Alberta writer George Ryga—wonderful, but outwardly phlegmatic.

Here is an impression of what we heard.

The redhead launched into a poetic aria whose intensities and staccato qualities were outdone only by its length. Finally, at the end of her initial outburst, George Ryga offered a deadpan, monotoned translation: *the house . . . of love . . . is . . . empty.* A polyglot friend assured us that the poetry was outstanding—and we believed him. In fact, the experience left us wondering if English is not sometimes a little too economical.

Other international gatherings held more demonstrations of the hazards that can beset any venture into another language. Having suffered repeatedly as a result of my own linguistic inadequacies, I offer the following examples of translation traps in full sympathy with those who fell into them.

I was a delegate to the 1986 Congress of International PEN—an organization active on several fronts, including trying to gain the release of writers imprisoned for what they had written. The Congress, that year, was held in Switzerland, in the beautiful lakeside city of Lugano.

As well as delegates, there were observers—people from many countries who were free to report their observations to their fellow citizens, but who were not supposed to take part in the discussions.

There was more than one session in which volley of opinions gained steadily in volume, intensity and invective. I don't remember the subject, but I do recall the moment when one of the British observers could no longer preserve her silence in the face of what had just been said. She shot to her feet and began to express her outrage. Immediately, another of the observers, an Asian, stood up to proclaim her out of order, but his own passion got the better of his usually impeccable English. "Mary ... Mary!" he shouted. "You are ... you are ... *illegitimate!*"

Pandemonium. Until order was finally regained.

The following year would see the Congress held in Korea, and so the delegation from that nation was large in Lugano. The leading delegate, in fact, was invited to give the keynote address—a talk on the subject that had been selected as that Congress's theme.

Whoever translated the theme into English did not do a terribly good job. *Border Literature.* This did not refer to what might have been written in the region where England meets Scotland. It was meant to express the idea that writing should know no boundaries—that it should be allowed to move freely all around the world.

When the delegate from Korea was introduced as keynote speaker, Bill and I were relieved to discover that he would deliver his address in English. Relieved for several reasons, a wish for accuracy being one of them. Everyone had been outfitted with earphones through which could be heard an appropriate simultaneous translation of the proceedings. Appropriate, that is, to the listener's native tongue—but not necessarily to what was actually being said.

The English translation we were hearing was apparently being voiced by somewhat prim British spinsters. I remember one instance in which an exchange between the German and Italian delegations grew absolutely vicious. Even with my almost nonexistent capacity to understand either language, I could tell that the argument was laced with the profane and the obscene. And what were we hearing through our headsets at that moment? Gentle, feminine tones that said: "I very much fear I feel some disagreement with what my honourable friend is saying. . . ."

And so, as I said, we were relieved that we would hear the keynote address in our own language.

If I tell you that before long, our attention wandered, it is no reflection on any of the speaker's abilities. His thoughts were heartfelt and his words well chosen and well spoken. It was simply that once the point had been made about the need for writing to move freely across boundaries, there was not a great deal else to be said about it.

He suddenly regained our attention by pounding on his podium. In nearing the end of his speech, he was more and more excited—more passionate. As he launched into his final statement, his Korean accent re-established itself. To us, that statement was absolutely electrifying.

"Ladies and gentlemen! Little Richard mus' not be held captive! Little Richard mus' be *freed!!!*"

Bill and I looked at each other. *Little Richard?* Who on earth was holding *him* captive? And . . . *why?*

Slowly, it dawned. *Liter . . . ature.*

We were both extremely grateful that the applause and cheers the talk had deservedly won served to cover our laughter. Most of it, anyway.

In all fairness, I must now confess to some of the language pitfalls into which we have fallen over the years—most of them since we began spending time in France.

I first made a fool of myself in our Provençal village of Cotignac when I went into the village to have a haircut. Bill, who was a little more fluent, usually accompanied me on errands, but this time, I decided to brave it alone. After a nervous cigarette outside the premises of *la coiffeuse*—and a quick, silent rehearsal, I entered.

"Bonjour, Madame. Voulez-vous écouter mes chevaux?"

Would you listen to my horses?

Madame was very kind. She twinkled at me and replied: *"bien sûr, Monsieur. Où sont vos chevaux?"*

And then she gently corrected me. *"Voulez-vous couper mes cheveux . . ."*

Well, I was close, at least.

★   ★   ★

What might be called creative translating does not always work. On one of our many visits to the Normandy town of Dieppe, Bill wanted a change from his usual glass of wine. He rarely drank spirits, but in hot weather, would occasionally indulge in a Margarita or a Bloody Caesar. Since the first was Mexican and the second distinctively Canadian, he thought the safest thing to do was to order an American drink. He chose a Bloody Mary. But what, he wondered, was it called in France?

When the waitress appeared, he took a chance and asked for *une Marie Saignante.*

We still don't know just how profane this must have been. All we know is that the girl gave a faint scream, ran from the room and did not reappear. Someone else took over our table, and we each ordered a glass of wine.

Years later, we discovered what a Bloody Mary is called in France. You guessed it: *une Bloody Mary.*

Certainly, *une* of the most dangerous territories in any new language is swearing. It is so easy to be profane or obscene without intention. That is why Bill and I were happy to receive a book from a translator friend, its purpose being to teach one how to swear in French.

I have to admit that the book was so long and the study of French swearing so exhaustive that we did not gain a great deal from it.

On the other hand, we have since discovered that paying careful attention to French subtitles on English films can be most instructive. We now at least recognize some of the words, even if we seldom have occasion to use them.

Back in our early days in France, however, our innocence nearly brought us to grief.

The first time was in 1995, when we bought a small property in Provence to use as a writing retreat. It meant getting some of our belongings there—and the first to arrive were the books we needed. Several cases of them. Very heavy cases.

Our property is a series of small terraces that cascade down a valleyside. The road is at the top, with a narrow, slightly twisting driveway leading down to the house level. When the truck arrived, Bill went up to suggest that the driver back his truck down the driveway, since we had discovered for ourselves that it is much easier to back *down* a slope than it is to back *up*.

The French word meaning "to walk or drive backwards" is *reculer*. Unfortunately, there is a similar-sounding verb whose meaning was euphemistically and charmingly expressed by Neil Simon in his play *The Odd Couple*, when he had Felix Unger simply sign his initials at the bottom of an angry note to his roommate: *F.U.*

The look on our truck driver's face quickly told Bill he had used the wrong word—and gave him the power to reach for the right one. All was well, and the cases were unloaded at the bottom of the driveway.

The second moment of danger was in Paris in 1996—a year later, when I was made Chevalier de l'Ordre des Arts et des Lettres. There was a gloriously big reception with more flashbulbs going off than I had ever seen. Applause. Cheers. Interviews. It was heaven.

Then, the Head of le Centre National du Livre took a few of us out to a special luncheon—accompanied by his charming wife. They were a delightful couple, and had obviously been warned that Timothy Findley, at that point, did not speak a great deal of French. Consequently, the entire meal was conducted in English.

That certainly made matters easier for Bill and me—but by the end of the meal, we knew we simply had to say something to our host in his own language. Over coffee, Bill briefly deserted the general conversation while he silently tried to put a few appropriate words together in his head. Then, as others had begun to move around the table, speaking to people they had not been able to chat with during the meal, Bill slipped over to one of the Canadian journalists present—just to make sure his grammar was correct. He whispered the words to our compatriot, who burst into astounded laughter. The journalist then whispered back to Bill.

When we got home, Bill explained to me why he had offered our thanks to the host in English.

He had been about to say to the Head of le Centre National du Livre, *Monsieur, Mr. Findley and I wish to thank you for your superb generosity and hospitality—and would you mind if we fucked your beautiful wife!*

Bill added, with just a touch of petulance: *in my university days, I swear* baiser *meant "to kiss"* . . .

Other Writers

Stone Orchard
1993
Article

Wild Animals I Have Known

I first encountered *Wild Animals I Have Known* when I was a boy growing up in Toronto. It was read to me by my father, for whom it had also been one of childhood's literary centrepieces. Part of its magic comes from the fact that the author, Ernest Thompson Seton, began his professional life as an artist and this book, like most of his others, is enhanced by a profusion of charming and informative drawings. As a complement to all the full-sized illustrations, almost every page of *Wild Animals I Have Known* has some detail of animal life set out in pen-and-ink sketches in the margins. For these alone, the book is guaranteed to enchant any child.

Adding to my early fascination with these narratives was the fact that each time my father read one of them to my brother and me, he would take us down into the Don Valley and show us where the story had taken place. Saturday afternoons in spring and fall were often spent seeking out a likely location for Raggylug the Rabbit's confrontation with the snake—or the spot near the river where Redruff the Partridge had saved one of his chicks from a marauding squirrel.

All the deep ravines that feed into the valley of the Don River are still pretty much as they were back then, wooded with oak and maple trees and lush with undergrowth. But the valley itself, which then could only be traversed by horse trails and a train track that followed the course of the river, has since been scarred by a great roaring highway that cuts against the natural flow of the land. It is sad to go there now—if you knew the place in its verdant years. But the ravines remain a blessing and a haven for beasts whose lives are the echoes of those told within the romantic tradition, and who appear in *Wild Animals I Have Known*—the rabbits, crows and foxes of another time.

In writing about these stories, I have to temper the phrase *romantic tradition* with a caution. Romantic they are—certainly romantic enough to qualify as authentic adventure stories with dashing heroes, alarming escapades and narrow escapes. But Seton himself gives warning in his preface that *the life of a wild animal always has a tragic end*. And indeed, only one of these beasts escapes with his life as his story concludes. This, I think, is what ultimately gives *Wild Animals I Have Known* its staying power—namely, its unbending honesty about the facts of life and death. There is not a single sentimental thought put forward in the book, no deliberate pulling at the heartstrings, nothing manufactured, nothing falsified. Seton's purpose was to reveal the passionate pursuit of survival that lies at the heart of every animal life—a pursuit for which, it seems, much of humankind has lost its passion.

In setting these indelible lives before us, Seton also instills in his readers an unavoidable response. Anyone who can read this book and set it down without gaining a sense of compassion for the animals with whom we share this planet is clearly doomed to lack a sense of compassion for fellow human beings. And surely it is never too soon to encourage that sense of compassion in any child who can read.

Perhaps this seems an overly serious response to a book that is, after all, intended for children—not only for their edification, but more, perhaps, for their entertainment. *Wild Animals I Have Known* is filled with amusing incidents and anecdotes and the idiosyncrasies of its characters are often as humorous in their consequences as the idiosyncrasies of an eccentric neighbour or wily school chum. Half the fun of trouble in a story is knowing that trouble is sure to come, especially to those who court it either through stupidity or pride.

There is much to be learned here, too, from the ways in which animals, whether by instinct or by experience, thwart the enemies who hound them and survive the worst of the circumstances in which they live. There are also enchanting encounters in all these stories with the sheer charm of Ernest Thompson Seton's imagination. As when, for instance, he sets out the seasons of the moon as perceived by Redruff the Partridge: the drumming moon—the berry moon—the moulting moon—the snow moon—et cetera. Or when he draws a map, showing how Raggylug outwits the hound who is chasing him by circling round him so many times, in so many directions that the poor dog is dizzy and fails even to see the rabbit when, at last, Rag "freezes" practically under the dog's nose. The reader, of whatever age, will also be able to learn the various tunes of crow-music, set out on five-line staves and even given key signatures by the author.

When my father died, my brother and I inherited his books—but his copy of *Wild Animals I Have Known* was so dog-eared and ragged from eighty years of family reading that it was almost unusable. Its back was torn and some of its pages were missing. I recently had a gift of the British edition of 1902—and I prize it dearly.

I cannot recommend this book highly enough. It is a classic, yes—but there are better reasons than that to have it in your library and to make it available to children—and to adults. We live in a time when nature is increasingly being placed in hazard—not only by what we do out of ignorance, but what we fail to do because we have ceased to pay attention. This book's best gift, from the moment of contact, is the dedication to life that is implicit in its title. The word *known* says it all—because to be known is to survive, at least for as long as it takes to be seen.

Stone Orchard
1985
Speech

Riding Off in all Directions
A Few Wild Words in Search of Stephen Leacock

You may wonder why, as the author of books with titles such as *The Wars* and *Famous Last Words, Not Wanted on the Voyage* and *The Last of the Crazy People,* I am writing in celebration of Stephen Leacock. The name of Leacock, after all, is synonymous with laughter, while my name, if I have one, is synonymous with madness, mayhem and Armageddon. If the connection between Professor Leacock and myself seems somewhat forced, to say the least, perhaps I can explain.

I have been living for the past twenty-one years on a farm just forty miles south of Orillia, where Leacock lived. But that is not the connection. On the other hand, there is some connection in the fact that the farm where I live is barely seventeen miles to the east of Sibbald Point, where Stephen Leacock is buried. All one needs to know is that the burial site at Sibbald Point and the homestead site at Orillia face each other on opposite sides of Lake Simcoe.

Now, it just so happens that, back in the days when Leacock was up there alive near Orillia, my so-called Grandfather Findley (the so-called will be explained when I come to the end of this connection) had his summer residence down near Sibbald Point. If they had possessed the right kind of telescopes, they could have seen each other fishing. But that is not the connection.

The next thing one needs to know, in order to make the connection between myself and Stephen Leacock, is about the graveyard at Sibbald Point—the graveyard where Leacock is buried but where my so-called Grandfather Findley is not buried; not buried because he refused to be buried there. Perhaps with good reason, from his point of view—again, as you will see when I come to the end of this.

The connection continues. In the graveyard at Sibbald Point, where my so-called Grandfather Findley refused to be buried, lie not only the remains of Stephen Butler Leacock, but also the remains of little Maisie Roach, otherwise known as Mazo de la Roche.

Now, what follows is of immense importance. What is wrong with Canadian literary sleuths that they have failed to discover, and therefore have failed to reveal, the story of the love affair between Mazo de la Roche and Stephen Leacock?

Do they think it is by pure and simple chance these two are buried within kissing-distance of one another? Well, let me tell you, it is not by chance.

For anyone who cares to think about it, the *grande affaire* between Stephen Leacock and Mazo de la Roche is as plain as the nose on Cyrano's face. The trouble is, and has been for far too long, that nobody has cared to think about it. And, therefore, our great Canadian literary sleuths have missed the multitude of clues that are virtually massed before them, for all to see, in the works of both Leacock and de la Roche.

Consider: Jalna, where Mazo's Whiteoaks family lives, and Mariposa, where Stephen's best-known characters live, are both on the shores of a lake.

Consider: the year 1912. It was in that year that old Granny Whiteoaks had all her teeth removed. And it was also in that year that Stephen Leacock's pen gave birth to all the citizens of Mariposa. I ask you: *is this not Cadmus sowing the dragon's teeth in order to create a whole new race of men?*

Well, one could go on and on and on. The references are legion . . .

How many readers are aware that *Jalna* is the word for butterfly in an obscure Hindi dialect?

How many readers are aware that *Mariposa* is the word for butterfly in Spanish?

How many readers are aware that the title of my second novel is *The Butterfly Plague*?

How many readers are aware that early in my acting career, I played the role of Peter Pupkin on television, in a weekly series adapted from Stephen Leacock's *Sunshine Sketches of a Little Town*—his tales of Mariposa.

How many readers are aware that, later, in the early years of my writing career, I adapted Mazo de la Roche's *Jalna* epic for television?

One last question:

How many readers are now aware of why it was that my so-called Grandfather Findley refused to be buried in the graveyard at Sibbald Point along with Mazo de la Roche and Stephen Butler Leacock?

This is what I have always suspected. Because the man I knew as Grandfather Findley refused to be buried along with Stephen Leacock and Mazo de la Roche, it is my firm belief that he had some connection with their hitherto unknown liaison. I cannot prove what that connection may have been, but given all the literary clues, I can only conclude that I am not descended from Thomas Findley, but from that unsuspected and illicit union of literary giants.

Here before you is none other than the grandson of Stephen Leacock!

Stone Orchard
1993
Speech

W.O.

You never get to spend much time with W.O. Mitchell—a meal's worth, perhaps, or the time it takes to have an anecdotal evening, watching him trying not to look at his watch. It's not that he doesn't like people—not that he doesn't enjoy another person's company, singly or in groups. It's just that he gets nervous if he thinks the conversation is getting too serious, and that someone is going to ask him to explain his books or talk about the meaning of life. You can't expect him to give pithy answers—tie things up with bows or speak the last word. What you can ask Mitchell to do is tell you a story. This way, you can wheedle almost anything you want to know from him. Just don't let him know you're asking.

I guess it's true: there is not a better storyteller alive than William Ormond Mitchell. It is a pure, unadulterated delight to watch him wind up and go with an anecdote—rising from his place at table, eyeing the distance to see if his punchline is out there waiting for him—hearing him begin with his trademark hesitancy: *I shouldn't tell you this—but here it is* . . . All of this is magical foreplay. Not a bad analogy. By the time the punchline is achieved, the laughter is orgasmic.

He has fed so many images into my head. The anecdotal past of my whole generation has much of Mitchell in it, the sort of anecdotage that goes with having a family, antecedents, ancestors. The voices, for instance, of John Drainie's Jake and Billie Mae Richards' Kid, real and everlasting as neighbours—someone you can visit in your mind as vividly as if they had lived up the road. The images, too, that are conjured of the prairie—which seems, at times—even in all its three-dimensional reality—to be a place invented by W.O., because he gave it shape and distance and all its smells and sounds. "This is your prairie," the young Brian says in *Who Has Seen the Wind*, as he watches his future self and the ghosts of all children stepping out across the wondrous landscape laid out before them under Mitchell's hand. That prairie, first encountered over forty years ago, is still my prairie, now.

We speak of Bill as "W.O."—which gives his name the kind of grandeur that suits him. Grandeur, that is, with a wink and a brushing away of snuff from the lapels. There ain't no guff about W.O. There ain't no guff—but there's a lot of splendour.

Let me tell you what I mean. Make a picture of an empty restaurant. Somewhere in the depths of Toronto, even deeper in the depths of winter—deepest of all in the depths of morning. Somewhere in the neighbourhood of dawning, cold and bleak and blowing. Out in the kitchen the cooks and one or two waiters have assembled and the cashier is picking up her first cup of coffee. She has already seated two bleary customers in a mercifully shadowed corner—me and my companion, Bill Whitehead. We have worked the whole night through, editing tapes for television. Now we will have our breakfast and go home.

Simultaneously, the coffee-revived cashier and a new customer enter the room from opposite doors. Remember that aside from us in our darkened corner, the whole restaurant, with all its multitude of empty tables, is spread out before this new customer. Of course, the customer is instantly recognizable as W.O., in spite of an all-night session with friends that more than likely involved a good deal of drinking. His famous white hair is dishevelled. His famous lapels with their famous stains from his famous snuff are turned up, perhaps against the cold. His eyes are . . . well, his eyes are red. He doesn't look, to be frank, terrific. And I guess he doesn't feel terrific, either. Anyone else would seek the dark, as we had, and soothe his hangover in the quiet there. But no. This is Mitchell—W.O. And I was speaking of *splendour*.

He chooses a large round table right smack dab in the middle of the room. "I'll sit down here," he says. Which he does.

Food is ordered. W.O. sits desolate. He sighs. *The Globe and Mail* is spread out beside him, but his eyes cannot endure the thought of print.

Bill and I, sympathetic, ignore him. The last thing he wants, we surmise, is company. But we are wrong about this. We have forgotten his innate politeness, his genuine adoration of conversation, his need for the motor of speech. He sees us. He rises. He crosses the room. He asks that his breakfast be delivered to our table and he joins us.

Seated, without greeting, he toys with the snuff box, places some on the wrist, sniffs, dusts—and speaks.

Did I ever tell you about the morning I was caught on the road by a blizzard and the nearest town was twenty miles off and . . .

This is what I mean by *splendour*: unforgettable—unforgotten.

One last thing to say—about the woman he married. Like Bill, she goes by her initials: *F.C.S. Merna. F.C.S.?* you say. *I never heard her called F.C.S. Merna. What's it stand for . . . ?*

Well—I'll tell you.

Whenever Bill loses his glasses, the snuff box, his fishing rod, his pen, his shoes—his *mind*—he calls out: *for Christ's sake, Merna! Where's my . . .* whatever. And there you have them: William Ormond and For Christ's Sake Merna.

It would be unjust, as we raise our glasses now, it would be unthinkable not to toast them side by side. So—here's to W.O. and F.C.S. Merna: hail—but never farewell. Not ever.

Cotignac
2002
Article

Mordecai Richler

I will never forget my surprise when I first discovered how shy he was and—what is the word?—courteous. At heart, he was a gentle, thoughtful man—as most courageous people are.

It took a long time for me to realize *the curmudgeon* was a polished performance—and let's face it, he did it better than anyone else in his time. And where would we be as artists, politicians and everyday Canadians if he hadn't given vent to his well-considered attacks on poseurs, parasites and politics? Lost, that's where—somewhere behind our own self-made, self-centred and self-protective screens.

His honesty was breathtaking. After he had published the hardcover version of *Oh, Canada, Oh, Quebec*—which he called *A Requiem for a Divided Country*—I wrote to him, praising his gritty depiction of the way things really were. The subsequent attacks on him were a mixture of vicious denial, personal vitriol—some of it anti-Semitic—and accusations of everything from racially motivated hatred of French Canadians to treason.

Well.

He survived. As well he should.

When he replied to my letter some weeks later, it was from under this blanket of personal abuse, but with the heart from which his integrity had never been dislodged. He wrote that he was grateful for what I had written—but, in so many words, he also wrote: *you have no idea how lonely your letter was.*

Scotch—cigars and brandy. Guys—bars and armchair sports. An unmatchable love and respect for his wife, Florence, and their children, both mutual and happily adopted. All this, and a writer of unsurpassable honesty, critical brilliance and creative joy, summed up in two unforgettable words: Mordecai Richler. A friend and colleague is missing—and missed—but his books abound and his presence clings.

Atlantic House, Maine
July 1969
Journal

Within the Canadian writing community, Tiff's closest friend was the poet Phyllis Webb. When we first encountered her in 1964, she was programme organizer for a CBC radio series called *University of the Air*, while we were writing and voicing material for a new series called *The Learning Stage*, for which Tiff covered the arts and I, the sciences. Within three years, the two series merged, with Phyllis as programme organizer and Janet Somerville as producer. At first the series was given a title we found both cumbersome and unfortunate: *The Best Ideas You'll Hear Tonight.* Soon, it became simply *Ideas*— and is still going strong.

During our two or three years of working with Phyllis on *Ideas*, a strong and lasting friendship was formed—particularly between her and Tiff. He loved both the poet and the person. It was unwelcome news, then, when we learned that she was moving to British Columbia—first to Victoria and later to Salt Spring Island.

Over the years, Salt Spring became a frequent destination on our trips west, but that first separation was initially sad. WFW.

To the Lady Phyllis:

You are no less hidden now
Than on your other island in my mind,

Which is not to say you are more hidden—
Neither less nor more.
But this physical remove is not like you.
I have always been able to catch you
    in the blue watch of the night,
Sitting, cornered in your room
(The one I built for you in my own palace of inadequacy,
Or the one you rent from time to time in mortal cities.)
But now, it seems, you've moved out.

They call it "west"—where you've gone,
But "west" of what?
"West of the horizon in forgotten eyes."
I never averted mine without due warning
And this is all the poem I can get
To let you know
The same goes for you.
I saw you signal once: "I'm leaving"
And you left.

You are no less hidden now
Than on your other island in my mind.
But there, at least, impressions of your mask
Pressed profiles in the sand.
And I could come ashore, then,
And know that while you were due to leave it—
You left it, once or twice (how careless of you!)
Behind you and I keep them in my sand museum—
A place for stranded touches,
Those orphaned, particularly by the high tide
                    of fear and reticence.

Findley as Writer

Stone Orchard
1969
Journal

I do not want to seem to be anything.

I want to be.

But it hurts, so often, to be what you are instead of what you would like to be—if you were able. Why is it—and how can it be—that you hurt yourself—your own sensibilities by saying and doing and being things—feeling things that are so contrary to your own ideals? Where, then, does the IDEAL come from? From what source?

If I should die right now—this instant—I should feel so unfriendly—so unkind—so shallow—a selfish . . . some kind of hateful and monstrous person. And yet, that really is an unreal view. Because I'm not that definable yet. And I think that's what I'm saying: I should die undefined—which would be awful.

There's nothing else to make of life except to perfectly define yourself—to perfectly define your own existence. To be so utterly what you are that you can be perfectly perceived by others, which is an aid to them and everything to you. And which is happiness—I guess.

And yet—of course—implicitly, there is the calling to be

perfectly what you are—not perfectly what you want to be. For that's quite different. Absolutely—in fact—different altogether.

Isn't it.

Stone Orchard
1989
Journal

The only standard of success you can really abide by is your own sense of it: have you accomplished what you set out to accomplish? And you never do. Not completely. If you did, you'd probably quit right there. But of course, there's the reality. I recognize all the trappings of success that have accrued around my work and my name—but I suspect the reason for whatever success I've had has something to do with something that happened years ago.

It was when I was having a terrible time with the work. Nobody seemed interested in what I wrote—and I was on the verge of giving up. And Bill sat me down in our living-room, and asked me to imagine that other people were sitting in all the other chairs. He put a stone in my hand, and told me that's all I had. Then he went around the room and asked "everyone" for a carrot. And some "people" gave him a carrot. I couldn't. Then he asked for a piece of wood, and some gave him that. Again. I couldn't. Finally, he asked for a stone—and nobody had a stone but me! I had the stone. That was connection. When they ask for a stone and you have a stone, then something happens, and for me, that something was a book called *The Wars*. That was my stone. That was what was in my hand when it was what people wanted. I think I'd had good work prior to that, but no one wanted it. When that happens, tough. I don't mean that to be cruel. Only that nothing can be done about it. If you try to write a "carrot" when you don't have a "carrot" inside you, then you're going to write what that hateful kind of person writes. All you can try then is to satisfy your ambition by putting something out there that isn't you. It won't be a true carrot, however successful it seems to be. End of story.

Vancouver Island, B.C.
November 1977
Letter

Tiff's first two novels—*The Last of the Crazy People* and *The Butterfly Plague*—were rejected by Canadian publishers until they had appeared in the US. Neither novel attracted much critical attention in either country, which, for, Tiff, resulted in an eight-year fallow period as he struggled with a despondency that seeped inevitably into his writing. The manuscripts he offered to Canadian publishers during that time were both depressed and depressing—including his first attempt to write his own version of *Heart of Darkness*, which he finally managed to complete twenty years later under the title *Headhunter*.

Finally, in late 1976, he began work on a short novel set in a period that had deeply affected both Tiff's country and his family—World War I, in which his uncle had fought and been badly wounded. The novel was published in 1977: *The Wars*.

That was the first Findley novel for which we did a promotional tour—and the trip began badly. Toronto's *Globe and Mail* assigned the book to a writer of comic novels set in World War I, Donald Jack. Not surprisingly, his review of *The Wars* was, to say the least, dismissive.

No other reviews appeared until our tour reached Edmonton, where we were told that Margaret Atwood had written about the book in *The Financial Post*. I immediately found a copy of the paper—and can still see Tiff reading it in the hotel lobby, caught in a single shaft of sunlight from a high window. WFW.

Dear Peggy,

Alec Guinness said I was the clumsiest actor he'd ever seen. I trip over safety-pins and barge into teacups. (Grace eludes the anxious?) It may be I am writing this for you on a sheet of yellow paper with a pen that makes blobs all by itself—in the hope that yellow blobby paper will hide the fact I cannot think how to say what wants to be said without bumping into all the chairs and tables between the thought and its articulation. Graeme says— "say nothing in response to praise." Therefore, I say nothing. Here, instead, is a sheet of yellow paper with blobs on it that want to be words. I hope you will accept it in lieu of whatever other expression I might have mustered to articulate the whoops— shouts—smiles and dances that were performed ad lib on the terrace of an Edmonton hotel this morning after Willy returned with your piece in the *Post*.

Love,
Tiff

Stone Orchard
April 15, 1978
Journal

Cold—dark—stormy. Four kittens were born to Mother—very difficult births. When she went into labour, she gave a great cry and I thought either she will die—or be afraid and kill the litter. However she was, it turned out, a terrific battler and as each kitten emerged, she was very eager for it and did all the standard things with great style. The kittens were born in a rocking chair in my workroom. . . . After the third kitten . . . there was a hiatus. The pause was so long I went to take my bath. I was very deeply depressed—as I had been for weeks. Work was not going well— my general health was very run down—lack of sleep—profoundly nervous, etc. I was quite far gone into a "low of lows"—I lay in the bath, trying to relax, but unable. . . . Then, the telephone rang. (About 11:00 a.m.) I heard WFW answer, heard him say: "yes. He is. Just a moment, please . . ." and he came to the door. "I'm sorry," he said, "looking at me in the bath—"but, even soaking wet, I think you should answer this call." He looked strange—as he held out my blue robe. Not smiling—but nervous—expectant—very tense—almost shaking. I thought: *someone has died.* And went to the phone in the hall, flooding water all over the tiles. I did not even have a towel—just my long blue robe. I picked up the phone and sat on the hall stand. "Hello?" "Hallo! Mister Findley?" "Yes." "Good morning!" (He was French.) "I am André Renaud. I am phoning from Ottawa to congratulate you . . ." "Thank you." (I didn't know why I should be congratulated except that it might have to do with having been chosen to receive a Canada Council grant I'd applied for.) So I said: "it's very good of you to phone. Uhm . . . ?" And he laughed and said: "you wonder why I am congratulating you?" "Yes." "I have the honour to tell you that your novel *The Wars* has been awarded the Governor General's Award for fiction in English . . ."

I was stunned. Totally. I said: "my God . . ." three times. The man was charming. He laughed and so did I. "You do not believe it," he said. "No." "It is true . . ." He told me he makes these phone calls once a year and *loves* it. He likes the pleasure and surprise it always generates. I thanked him—I could hardly speak. I said: *"Merci milles fois!"* and he said: *"bon, merci."* And he rang off. He had told me a letter would follow. I had been sitting very far forward on the seat so as not to get it wet—and now I fell forward onto my knees. It was weird. WFW was standing in the living-room. Mother's fourth kitten had been born during the phone call. A male—pure grey.

I kept babbling: "I don't believe this! I don't believe it!" WFW roared with laughter. He said that as soon as he heard who it was, he knew what it was about. I said: "I'm not allowed to tell the press—only family and very close friends." So I phoned Mother and Nancy [Colbert, the agent] who were both delighted. Then I phoned Margaret [Laurence] and said to her: "I cannot contain the news—I have a cat who has just given birth to a kitten we are going to call G.G. . . ." And Margaret roared with laughter. "I've known since March 1st, kid!" she told me. *It had been a unanimous decision*—no other book was considered. This made me very proud.

About an hour later, Ken Adachi [literary critic at *The Toronto Star*] telephoned. He said: "I'm just phoning to say hello . . . I hear rumours . . ." I took a deep breath. He had been so good—to the book and to me. So I laughed and I said: "you mean about the birth of our kittens." He laughed. "Well?" So I said what I had said to Margaret—that it was true and that the last born will be called G.G." Then I said: "there are rules. Please don't break them on my account . . ." (He was very good and contained the news until the last minute before others could break it—and it gave him a scoop by one day. I did not feel this was wrong—and there were no repercussions.)

In a year, I have been published successfully—well reviewed—toured the country—been Chairman of the Writers' Union—dealt with the remainders issue—gone so many times to Ottawa I have lost count—and won the Governor General's Award.

My God, indeed.

Winnipeg
1985
Notes for a Seminar

A Writer's Craft in Fiction

(These notes were put together as part of a seminar on creative writing which I taught in October 1985 at the University of

Winnipeg. They lack, above all, the inventive and exhilarating responses of the students in Professor Al Reimer's class.—T.F.)

The first question every potential writer must answer is: *why write at all?*

The truth is, too many writers write for the wrong reasons. Among the most salient of these wrong-headed reasons are self-aggrandizement, self-justification and vengeance. None of these should make up or take up the energies of fiction and, indeed, there would have to be extremely strong reasons to give them a rightful place as the motives for any form of writing. But so far as fiction is concerned, it must always be borne in mind that the self—which is to say the writer—has no place at all on the page. In fiction, the writer must remain at all times out of view, beyond the awareness of the reader, completely hidden. This means, equally, that whatever motives the writer has for doing what he's doing must also be hidden. Better by far that there be no motive; and—above all—that there be no personal motive.

Perhaps the apparently wrong-headed reasons for writing fiction given above should be examined—but only briefly. They are all such poor excuses for sitting down to write, they don't really warrant much attention. At the same time, they cannot be ignored, because they embody most of what is generally misunderstood concerning what the writing of fiction is about. Fiction is not about self.

The first misguided reason is: self-aggrandizement. In short, if the reason you want to write is to make a name for yourself or to amass a fortune, look elsewhere. Certainly people have made names for themselves as writers and even, from time to time, pulled down a fortune doing it. But the people who have done this were—ninety-five per cent of the time—writers to begin with: the Maughams, the Hemingways, the Mailers, the Capotes of this world. On the other hand, even the briefest glance at this list—

beefed up with any other names you care to include—a Hailey, perhaps, or a Cartland—will show there is a price to be paid and a sacrifice to be made if writing is what you want and fame and fortune is what you get. Something killed Hemingway: it wasn't his talent. Something destroyed Capote: neither was that his talent. In Norman Mailer's case, the man has survived—but—(this will be a matter of opinion)—has the writer survived?

The actress Ruth Gordon once remarked, with a good deal of insight: *it's fine and dandy to have a talent—yes. But what an artist needs, besides the talent, is a talent for having talent!* It is this secondary talent that writers such as Maugham and Hailey and Cartland nurtured: the talent to recognize your limits and to make the most of what you do best. Before all else, the Maughams, the Haileys and the Cartlands were and are supreme craftsmen: wonderful storytellers and, above all, hard workers. Writing—never forget it!—is work—and if you don't regard it as work, then you aren't a writer—you're a dilettante. The thing to remember about the writers I've mentioned so far is that all of them were writers first and foremost. The writing—the writer—was primary. The entrepreneur was secondary.

So far as self-justification is concerned—*I'll show those so-and-sos!* and *They can't say that about me . . . !*—such motives for writing are about as childish as motives can be. Self-justification leads to all that is worst in the uses of language—ostentation, rhetoric and propaganda. Forget it. We have enough of that on television talk-shows and, alas, too much already in print—much of it written, oddly enough, by derailed politicians. The fictions of Haldeman and Erlichman, Gordon Liddy and Charles Colson are a case in point. Which brings us to the last worst reason to write, which is vengeance.

Vengeance will out—and that's the problem. Once it is clear that a given book has been written to settle a score or to get even with someone—nothing will save it. Every scene and every gesture will be forced and false and every word and sentence will reek of prejudice. Luckily, no immediate or mighty example of vengeance fiction leaps to mind—and this may tell the tale. As a motive for creating fiction, vengeance can be equated to lead: it sinks quickly out of sight. But for want of any other example, think of *Mommie, Dearest.* Clearly, the survivor here is Joan Crawford. As for what's-her-name, who wrote the thing—she, in the well-remembered words of George S. Kauffman, is *forgotten but not gone* . . .

The only real and the only good reason for putting words on paper—for saying: *this is what I will do* and for believing that writing is what you should do with your life—is necessity. Need. The fact is, I should reword that and state as flatly as I can that the only reason a person should become a writer is the absolute necessity—the absolute need to make the making of fiction the passion of your working life.

I don't believe a person ever does learn how to write on a once-and-for-all basis. I think what really happens is that you learn how to write, both painfully and joyfully, each piece of work as it brings itself forward as a candidate for your attention. But there are a few standard problems that have to be faced with every piece of writing and some of these follow.

STORYLINE: *A storyline is like a clothesline—without it, all you have is a hamperful of damp sheets* . . . I don't remember who said that, but it bears repeating. To begin with, a storyline is a convenience for both the writer and the reader. The story needn't be complex or convoluted—indeed, the less complex and convoluted, the better. Plots can be complex and convoluted: not storylines. The simpler the story, the more room you give yourself, as a writer, to manoeuvre.

Still, there are too many writers who think they can get away with writing books that have no storyline at all.

Well, these people say, *when Beckett writes, he doesn't tell a story.* . . . This is always said with immense but misplaced confidence and it shows a lack of understanding of what it is that Beckett—and some others, Chekhov among them—are really doing with their "story-less fictions." Beckett, after all, requires of each of his immobilized, imprisoned or entombed characters that they have a story in their past—a failure to make connections, a losing track of someone they loved or a longing for something or someone they need but cannot name. And it is these active stories that make the inactivity of his characters lives the wondrous, readable nightmares that they are.

One more example: Gertrude Stein. Much of her work, so people say, was writing for writing's sake. But I think not. Yes, indeed, she was in love with language—words and sentences—but through the words and through the sentences she managed, nonetheless, to tell at least some fragment of a tale and always to conjure sufficient glimpses of a person or a place to make it possible—and, I think, imperative—for us to make a story.

Above all, it should be remembered that both Samuel Beckett and Gertrude Stein began their writing careers by practising and learning their craft in much the same way that painters do, by learning and mastering the problems of line and form.

And they did this by writing stories—such as *Murphy,* in Beckett's case and, in Stein's case: "Melanctha." I am not, myself, an easy disciple of Beckett's prose—though I love his plays. But if anyone wants to read a good example of what an innovative writer can do with a story, read "Melanctha." It is, quite simply, a masterpiece and it settles once and for all that, when Stein set out to redefine the uses of her language, she began from absolute comprehension and absolute mastery of how that language worked in its classic forms.

★   ★   ★

The question arises over and over and over: *but what's the difference between a storyline and a plot?* My favourite definition of plot is the possibly apocryphal story of how the word *plot* evolved. For this, we must go to the theatre—and specifically to Shakespeare's theatre. Back in the 16th century, theatres weren't—backstage—what they are today. No cue lights, no lighting board, no elaborate system of call-boys and Tannoys. All they had in the wings, where the actors waited to go on, was a wooden board upon which was chalked the general outline of the play, scene by scene. Consequently, when the actors asked—as actors tend to ask quite often—*where the hell are we?* they only needed to look at this board to find out. *ACT I: Scene I: Ghost on battlements* or *Act I: Scene II: King, Queen, Hamlet* or *The Court* . . . etc. And this wooden board, which gave, to all intents and purposes, the outline of the play was called the *platte*. And thus, the *plot*. In other words, the means by which the storyline unfolds. A ghost, a battlement, a king, a queen and a man called Hamlet residing in a court provide the plot for a tale—a storyline concerning murder.

The story of Hamlet is easy enough to grasp, after all. His father dies; his mother marries his uncle; his father's ghost appears, tells Hamlet he was murdered and asks him that all-important question: *and what are you going to do about it?* Well, let's not get into that! The main thing is, the story is in the action—a murder. The plot is in the people—in Hamlet, Claudius, Gertrude, Polonius, Ophelia—and how they do or do not cope with the story they've been given. And thereby hangs a tale in which the simplest of stories has been made to mesmerize not only actors, but scholars, readers and audiences for centuries because of its extraordinary plot.

This brings us neatly to the subject of character.

The first thing I want to say about character is personal—though I'm certain other writers would have their own examples of this. I cannot say how many times I have been asked this question: *In* The Wars, *tell me who Robert Ross really was* . . . And my answer is always the same: *Robert Ross was—and is—himself.* But people, many people, don't want to hear this. They want to believe that he really did live, which means, conversely, they do not want to believe that I made him up. That he did not, in fact, live.

But the thing is, he did live and he does live inside that book. When I say that Robert Ross is himself, I mean he is as much himself as you are yourself or I am myself. He is just as whole and complete as the rest of us. The only difference between Robert Ross and you and me is that we live here—and he lives inside a book. He is a fiction. But for all that—I repeat—he is whole. That is what fiction means: *life, if you like, being lived in another dimension.*

All characters are—and must be—inside the writer. At least, they must spend a good deal of time inside the writer before they make their way onto the page. After all, it is the writer—and only the writer—who can provide the human dimensions of a character so that everything that character does is both believable and recognizable to the reader. I read, too often, characters who do things I can't believe in: who do things only because the writer has told them to. But when I don't believe, as the reader, it can surely only mean that the writer, too, has not believed. It seems to be inevitable that, when a character's behaviour is not believable, it is unbelievable because the writer has failed to draw the character up through himself.

By *drawing the character up through himself,* I mean that all the good and all the bad, all the sweet and all the sour, all the appealing and all the abhorrent qualities in every character must be found by the writer—inside himself. There is no escaping this. You cannot make up human behaviour and expect your readers to believe it simply because you tell them it is so. If what your characters do does not rise directly from your own absolute conviction—then you have no right to put it on the page. And, plainly, the only way to gain this conviction is to run the given behaviour—whatever it is—through your own emotional channels and your own process of reasoning. Run it through your innards—draw it through your nervous system. Be an actor. Haul each and every character and each and every thing that character does and thinks and says up in front of every mirror you've ever looked in. This is your job. Not to make us believe the unbelievable—but to make us believe that what we innately understand, but cannot articulate, is true. Fiction is validation: truth made clear.

Finally, fiction is not an extension of reality. It is, instead, a distillation of reality.

All of us are trying to find our way through the chaos of real life. Most of us cannot get through the mess and the mass of what surrounds us. Forward movement, in real life, is constantly blocked by this mess and mass. Some people call this *not being able to see the trees for the forest.* But a few people can find the trees and these few can deal with or eliminate the mess and the mass—and these are those who write fiction, who make up stories, novels and plays by creating order out of chaos.

What we do as the readers of fiction is find our way through an ordered process towards the solutions that we seek in our real lives. Note: I did not say *answers.* I said *solutions.* Solutions are doors—as books are doors.

And the answers lie beyond those doors, beyond the books we read—in ourselves and in the way we can learn, through reading fiction, how to deal with chaos.

Fiction articulates—at its best—the questions we cannot articulate for ourselves—and it does this by showing us people who are like us, making choices. Aside from that—by telling us stories, it keeps our imaginations alive and functioning, so that we can begin to imagine our own answers. And that, after all, is what really matters.

Stone Orchard
1999
Speech

A Writer's Nightmares

My worst moment as an author? Which one should I choose????

The first happened just after I'd published my second novel. It's called *The Butterfly Plague*, and although it's still in print, thanks to Penguin Canada, it's the least known of my books. Its first Canadian publisher had picked it up from the States and didn't even know I lived in Ontario. They forwarded all my fan letters to New York. All two of them. And I kept going into bookstores and failing to find *The Butterfly Plague* on their shelves. Finally, I asked a bookseller: why not? The lady I spoke to scurried back to her office and emerged with an open catalogue. She was smiling sympathetically. "Well, you see, Mr. Findley, your book is all about . . . Hollywood." She pronounced it much as she might have mouthed *Sodom and Gomorrah.* And then she continued: ". . . and men who wear women's clothing and . . ." here there was a long pause before she whispered: ". . . unnatural *sex.*" I blinked. "So you see," she said, "that's not really the sort of thing *our* readers would choose." "Ah," I said, "and what are your readers reading this season?" She closed her catalogue and beamed. "We've had *great* success with *Portnoy's Complaint* and *Myra Breckinridge!*" I said nothing. Masturbation—and transsexuals in Hollywood. Yes.

Then there was this one: imagine that you've spent four years writing an extremely difficult, complex novel—a novel whose centrepiece is based on an historical event—and you discover, the month before submitting the novel to a publisher, that a popular writer of thrillers has just published a book whose entire plot is a retelling of the same historical event.

This was what happened while I was finishing a novel called

CANADA'S WEEKLY NEWSMAGAZINE

Maclean's

OCTOBER 5, 1981 $1.00

Fiction's brightest season

This photo of (*clockwise from top left*) Robertson Davies, Margaret Atwood, Timothy Findley and W. O. Mitchell was taken for the cover of *Maclean's* (October 5, 1981).

Timothy Findley in 1984 outside a place he called Arkwrite, where he wrote his novel *Not Wanted on the Voyage*.

Tiff inside Arkwrite with his collection of toys, 1984.

This photo of Tiff and Bill was taken at Stone Orchard circa 1990, inside the gazebo where Tiff often wrote.

Tiff at Stone Orchard with Whisper the cat, 1992.

Timothy Findley relaxes with some of his many cats at Stone Orchard.

Findley at the Toronto Arts Awards in 1994, where he was recognized for his lifelong contribution to writing and publishing.

The author at his writing desk, in his Stratford home, 1999.

DATE: 12th MARCH 1993

FOR: IRIS

PAGES (including this one): 1

FROM:

PEBBLE PRODUCTIONS INC. (Timothy Findley/W. Whitehead)

Box 419

Cannington, Ontario

LOE 1E0

(705) 432-2719)
) PLEASE KEEP CONFIDENTIAL
FAX: (705) 432-2756)

DEAR IRIS —
BOOK ARRIVED
SAFE AND SOUND THIS
A.M. WEIGHT: 800 GMS.
SEX: AMBIVALENT. STATE
OF HEALTH: EXCELLENT.
PARENT OF CHILD: EXUBERANT.
THANKS FOR MID-WIFERY. LOVE — TIFF.

Timothy Findley's fax to his editor, Iris Tupholme, upon the arrival of his novel *Headhunter*, 1993.

Tiff in his atelier—which he and Bill had converted from a garage—where the author most often wrote while in France.

Timothy Findley at his home in the south of France, 1997.

Tiff and Bill in the rotunda of their Stratford home, 2000.

Famous Last Words. One of its major scenes tells how, early in World War II, British commandos landed in neutral Portugal and literally kidnapped the Duke and Duchess of Windsor and got them to the Bahamas—just as a group of German sympathizers were plotting to force the royal pair into fascist Spain.

Bill Whitehead and I were staying at an old seaside hotel in Maine, feverishly trying to meet the publisher's deadline, when I saw something in the *New York Times* that almost stopped my heart. The big thriller of the season was a book called *To Catch a King*—and it told how, early in World War II, British commandos landed in neutral Portugal and . . . etc., etc., etc.

Panic!

Bill drove into Portland, bought a copy and quickly read it. I don't think I blinked even once while I watched him. Finally, he closed the book and said: "no problem. It gives a completely different take on the story. Get back to work. . . ."

As I picked up my pen I thought: "well—let's hope we never have to do *that* again. . . ."

Hah!

About fifteen years later, I was working on the final draft of *The Piano Man's Daughter.* The title character's father is killed in a bizarre accident, and her mother then marries the president of a piano factory in turn-of-the-century Ontario. One morning, on the way to my desk, I turned on the radio to listen to *Morningside,* and to my delight found Peter Gzowski interviewing Alice Munro about her latest collection of stories, *Friend of My Youth.* The delight didn't last long. The next question I heard was about a story in which a woman marries the president of a piano factory in turn-of-the-century Ontario—a factory in whose sawmill a man is accidentally beheaded.

Well, with years of experience and some measure of success behind me, did I panic? You bet I did. . . .

Bill dashed out and bought a copy of Alice's book, and read the story while I managed to choke down a couple of glasses of wine—

without blinking. At last he reassured me that although the two situations were similar—the two plots were completely different.

That time, when I picked up my pen again, it was not to continue with the book, but to write to Alice. It occurred to me that this was an opportunity for a little fun. You see, in my book, the woman who marries the piano-factory president grew up as a farm girl, and views the industrial revolution with some alarm. In fact, on her way to make her first visit to the factory, she remembers the headlines she has read in the papers: GIRL'S ARMS TORN OFF BY GIN-WHEEL . . . MAN CRUSHED BY STEEL PRESS.

And so I wrote to Alice Munro and explained why I would like to add one more headline to that scene: WORKER DECAPITATED IN PIANO FACTORY. Would she mind? Alice wrote back: *mind?? I'd love it. Just think what will happen when all those future Ph.D. candidates get their hands on our books!*

Stratford
August 3, 1999
Journal

Neither of us thought we would leave our farm, Stone Orchard, until forced to by ill health or death. We had spent almost thirty-five years there, lavishly expanding the house, lawns and gardens and enlarging the pond to give it an island and a population of colourful Japanese koi.

Once we had achieved a writing retreat in France, however, it became almost impossible to maintain Stone Orchard. In a sense, we had created a high-maintenance monster. And so, with tremendous regret, we put it up for sale.

What we needed was a Canadian base without plants or pets—something we could simply lock up and leave whenever we needed uninterrupted working time abroad. And we found it in the form of a condominium in Stratford, Ontario—a town both of us knew well and loved, having each been actors in the Stratford Festival Company.

Some of our oldest friends lived and worked there—including Bill Hutt and Martha Henry.

Like most of its kind, the condo was slow to reach completion, so we rented a lovely little house for 1998, our first summer there. Tiff began work on a new novel, *Spadework*, in which members of a Stratford family must overcome the consequences of a simple accident—the severing of their telephone lines by the thrust of a gardener's spade. Our rented house, with a fictionalized location, became that family's house, as Tiff tried to fit his writing hours around bouts of public appearances and teaching. wfw.

All last week at Humber College with ten students, five of whom were quite promising, the rest not. Two had written extremely accomplished pieces and are with promise—but not quite there. Two others need to get through two or three new drafts but had submitted basically good work. So difficult to be truthful about the failed pieces—but one must be, otherwise there's no point. Diplomacy, of course, but honesty—and they dealt with it very well . . .

. . . now we only await my bedroom chairs, which are being reupholstered, and the remaining cabinetry, including living-room TV installation—library ladder (me)—screens for WFW's windows and kitchen cart. Then, the final paint touch-ups and we're done. It's looking wonderful . . .

Now—must concentrate on *Spadework* and have only *the rest of August* to make early notes and also deal with Martha's [Henry] notes re: *Elizabeth Rex*. Have been "watching the town"—learning its streets—its people—its overall atmosphere . . . I haven't the wife's name yet, though I think she is a cutter at the Festival. The husband is an actor whose name is Griffin. They have a seven-year-old son (?) whose nanny is Mercedes or Mercy. I think the gardener's name is Quinn, but I don't know the names yet of the Bell man and his wife—or of their two-week-old child who is perilously ill. The use of real people—the Hutts, Henrys, Bedfords,

Monettes is going to be problematical—but must be faced . . .

Element of guest director—totally fictional—someone who has directed Griff in this year's play (*Much Ado*? Claudio?) and wants to bed Griff—and, if Griff will agree to this, he will be given . . . something truly stellar in the next season. Griff will say yes—in the same moment more or less, as the wife succumbs to the Bell man . . . oral sex is the link, here.

All of this happens in the summer of '98—the year of Bill [Clinton] and Monica [Lewinsky] and endured in the atmosphere of all the ghastly jokes and jibes . . . and yet, the reality is different than what the public perceives. *They're* all out there doing it, because it's the only ""safe" sex left—or so we're told . . . and they're all laughing at something they do but call "despicable."

Stratford
August 6, 1999
Journal

Yesterday, I found the wrought-iron bench in the park dedicated to Susan, Ruth and Jack Wright, who perished by fire in Brent's [Carver] house. Very moving. I wept. There was a live rose attached to the bench and a note which read: *Happy Birthday Grandpa Jack.* . . .

Today, I must set something down about the Bell man . . . His progenitor . . . came to reconnect the phone line at Mary Haney's house after Matt [Mackey] had severed it with his spade.

His physical presence was virtually overwhelming. Not beautiful . . . nothing "classic" in his form or features—just rampant, raging sex. His jeans bulged—and, of course, he wore a utility belt—always sexy—why? Perhaps it's just the multiplicity of hard, rigid "tools" hanging around the hips . . . I very rarely get an erection just by seeing a man—but in his case, I did—and could not stand up! It was extraordinary. He hadn't been gone five minutes before the whole of *Spadework* fell into my lap—you should pardon the expression!

Stratford

1999

Timothy Findley Interviews Timothy Findley

Who am I?

I will give the answer I would not give to any interviewer other than myself: I am a living, white, male homosexual who writes in Canada.

Why would I not give that answer to someone else?

There's a lot of negative talk in this politically correct, deconstructive age about dead white males dominating Western literature. Certainly, dead white males are being dumped on. For myself, I prefer not to dump on Shakespeare and Socrates—any more than I'm prepared to dump on Jane Austen or Emily Brontë. Or Langston Hughes. Or James Baldwin. The past is the past. It is where we all come from. All of us. To deny that is to deny who we are. I'm not prepared to do that. Here and now—I'm alive. Evolving. Becoming whole. Part of my evolution—part of the wholeness I hope to achieve depends on where my culture comes from—its failures and its triumphs. If I lied about these failures and triumphs, I would cease to evolve. I would become an egocentric, self-defined, self-satisfied prick, blind to reality and deaf to humanity. If you redefine your past, you condemn your future. Being white—being male— being alive—I have an obligation to accept the failures of my white male predecessors. And their triumphs. These I can work with. With lies, I cannot. Thank you, but I do not believe in intellectual suicide.

How does gender affect my writing?
Oddly enough, when I write a female character I don't sit around thinking about sexual differences. Let me explain. This goes back to the image of William Hutt, portraying Lady Bracknell in *The Importance of Being Earnest.* He did this with immense success. It was a stunning performance—in many ways, a performance of genius. I had a long conversation with Bill about this—because at that time I was writing something in which a man had to assume the role of a woman. And I wanted to know how, as a performer, William Hutt had accomplished this. Because you never, for one instant, had any sense that you were watching a drag act. You never said: "that's Bill Hutt playing a woman."

What you did say was: "there is Lady Bracknell." And therein lies the secret. Not to write to a sexual recipe when you're writing in another gender's voice. What you write to is the character—and you write from within the character. Whatever kind of character I write—I don't think outside of the voice. I never think: now I'm trying to see a woman—or a ninety-year-old—or a cat, or whatever. I garner everything I know about the character by being inside the character. So when there are things that pertain to the body in which they take place—to its sex and its age, for instance, those things emerge quite naturally because I am telling from the inside, looking out—not from the outside, looking in. This was Hutt's process.

I'll never forget one incredibly indignant letter I had from a woman after I'd published a book called *The Telling of Lies,* which—it so happens—is narrated by a woman. This letter just blew me away! *Mr. Findley, you have described a moment when this woman is so alarmed, the hairs on the backs of her arms are raised. Are you not aware that women do not have hair on the backs of their arms???* Golly. For one moment, I thought I must have been seeing things. But many women do have hairs on their arms. So I wrote back, suggesting my correspondent take another look—at herself, or at her friends. This is typical of the militant voices in this kind of issue: *you're going to get it wrong if you try to imagine what it's like to be like me. I'm the only one who knows what it's like to be me.* This way, all art, all creativity, all social change would cease.

It's the problem of concentrating only on the differences between people—and forgetting the similarities. If you focus only on differences, you might as well be talking about an alien race. Creatures from another planet—or another species. Grass, for instance. Although I think I have a fair idea what grass must feel like when it's cut. . . .

Talk about being white, as a writer.
Black or white, if you try to get into some other skin, your job is to get it right. The differences—and the similarities. All you have to do, if you're white, is get off the plane in a predominantly black country, and you immediately understand what it is to be other, and how that affects how you move, look, see, present yourself, speak—everything. The stuff you accept as being inherent—your physical integrity. This is a good place to begin imagining otherness. You have to think about your willingness, and your ability, to stand there entirely as yourself. That, it seems to me, is what we are all having to learn to do these days—to be entirely ourselves. Unapologetically. But thoughtfully.

Does being a Canadian affect my writing?
Place affects any writer writing anywhere because you see the world from where you are. If it happens to be the country of your birth—which is to say, the country from which your whole root system is rising—then, of course, place has a doubly important role to play in how you see as a writer. Canada, and more specifically, southern Ontario, provides me with my vantage point. This is where I gain my view not only of other Canadians, but of other cultures, other terrain. I also see the past from here. And the future—if I'm looking. Place affects a writer's voice because place is where a writer breathes.

As a homosexual, why haven't I written a homosexual novel?
Well, I have. That aspect of me—my homosexuality—has a presence in everything I've written.

But why haven't I written a novel that deals exclusively with homosexuality?
I haven't yet encountered a homosexual character who's going to gather a whole novel around him. Or her. On the other hand, I have recently written a play whose central character is a homosexual. *The Stillborn Lover.* And the action centres around how that character's homosexuality affects his life as a Canadian diplomat. But the play isn't only about homosexuality. It's also about loyalty. It's also about memory and loss of memory, because the diplomat's wife has Alzheimer's. I can't tell any story that concentrates on a single aspect of character. Some can do this—I cannot. If it's the story of a homosexual, and if it's a good story, it's impossible to have that homosexual interacting only with other homosexuals. He has to interact with the whole range of people who touch and affect his life. You could say that I've never written a heterosexual novel, either, because I've never written a novel that concentrates exclusively on a sexual relationship of any kind. I have no interest, as a writer, in creating a book whose plot is driven by sex—any more than I want to create a book whose plot is driven by automatic pilot.

I can't imagine writing exclusively for homosexuals, either. To talk to ourselves may be amusing and informative—but what good does it do? I don't want to read in a ghetto. I don't want to live in one. There's only one way in which such writing might be helpful—and that's with the young, who may be having a hard time dealing with their homosexuality. We live, I'm afraid, in a world that's increasingly homophobic—and I think it's our job, as the elders of the homosexual community, to do everything we can to get the young through the door and into the fullness of their own lives. We must teach them the value of being whole. And their right to be whole.

So who I am affects my writing, but doesn't confine it?
Yes. With one exception. My writing doesn't depend exclusively on my being white or male or Canadian or homosexual. But it does depend exclusively on my being alive. The only confining element for a writer . . . is death. As long as I'm alive . . . mentally and physically . . . I'll be able to write. And—I might add—I don't mind being a white male homosexual Canadian, either. Just so long as being a white male homosexual Canadian doesn't get me shot. This death thing—I'm not sure I care for that. *The grave's a fine and private place, but none, I think, do there embrace.* They don't write novels, either.

*Theatre Tours
and Final Curtain*

Can You See Me Yet?

Ottawa
1976
Play

The first of Tiff's plays to be produced on stage and subsequently
published was called *Can You See Me Yet?* It was set in an asylum for
the insane, and ten of its eleven characters played double roles. The
eleventh character, Cassandra—played stunningly by Frances
Hyland—was a new patient, a former missionary who saw the other
asylum inmates and their nurse as members of her own family, whose
photographs were in an album she carried with her. In the play, it is
never determined whether the pictures actually were of her family, or
simply portraits she had gathered during her missionary wanderings.

The play was first performed at the National Arts Centre in
Ottawa, and was directed by a former colleague from our Red Barn
Theatre days, Marigold Charlesworth. She and Tiff had great fun
working out the simplest transitions from an "asylum scene" to a
"family scene"—using the addition of a hat, a sweater, a jacket, or a
cane to transform a patient into a father, a mother, a son or an uncle.

The following speech was delivered by Clare Coulter, who doubled
as Cassandra's aunt, but at this moment was playing a patient who
saw her rag doll as one of her many children. WFW.

The garden of the Asylum for the Insane at Britton, Ontario, late summer 1938.

ENID: I wish they wouldn't show us things like that. People killing dogs and everything. Like that movie last night. I mean, I do like Deanna Durbin—all that singing is very nice, but the other things: those newsreels. why do they do it? I don't want to see a cave in China falling in on fifteen hundred people— all of them crawling out on their hands and knees through the rubble. Trapped, they were; using it as an air-raid shelter, and then it collapses on top of them. Seven hundred dead. I mean, why do I want to see that? Thank heaven I didn't take the children. Not that I almost didn't, what with it being Deanna Durbin, but still I say, what's the point? The towns being shelled, the whole of Shanghai falling to the ground, the bombs, the hordes of refugees, and Spain, plagues, diseases, fevers. What's the use of it all? I mean, how can it help to *see* an earthquake? How can that help me? I want help, not famine, drought, *disaster*. These people don't know what they're doing. And they used to make such lovely movies. Don't you remember? Clara Bow and Rudolph Valentino. Oh! The number of wandering hands I had to slap off my knees when *they* came on! Now it's all floods and Fascists— whatever a Fascist is—all those people who go around with their hands in the air . . . as if they wanted to leave the room. And their chins stuck out. It's pointless. What is a person supposed to understand from it all? And that girl's lovely voice . . . oh, it was marvellous. Fourteen years old, from Winnipeg . . .

Findley as Actor

Stone Orchard
1988
Article

Phantoms of the City

Since this is Toronto's Year of the Phantom, it might be of interest to relate a few of the episodes surrounding the story of yet another phantom who has haunted Toronto's theatres for over fifty years. This particular phantom does not compose music, however, and is not devoted to opera. His passion is for the movies and he has been in our midst since an evening in 1937 when he fell in love with Shirley Temple at the old Imperial Theatre on Yonge Street—the very same building that currently houses his operatic namesake. In order to set the two apart, I shall call the Toronto original The Fantom of the Films.

Who was this creature and how did his extraordinary passion manifest itself? Take that initial encounter with Shirley Temple in 1937, for instance. The Fantom was then aged seven and had been taken by his parents to see Miss T. in her latest hit, *Wee Willie Winkie*, one of those stories loosely based on the writings of Rudyard Kipling and set—as always—somewhere near the Khyber Pass.

The Fantom, who had entered the theatre clothed in the body of a boy and wearing a polo shirt, shorts and running shoes, did not emerge from the theatre that way—and here is why.

Somewhere about three-quarters of the way through Wee Willie Winkie's adventures, Miss Temple was obliged to hide beneath her bed—with her dog, I think—for fear the savage horde would do her in. But Miss T. could not afford to indulge in quivering terror for long. She had to save the garrison! Which is exactly what she proceeded to do, dressed, it should be said, in Victor McLaglen's bullet-riddled pith helmet and a kilt and army jacket especially designed for the child by Edith Head. Consequently, the boy who had made his way into the darkened theatre dressed in shorts and shirt emerged to descend the grand staircase, wearing his father's pale (but unriddled) brown fedora pulled down over his ears and with his mother's cardigan tied back-to-front around his waist—which gave him a dandy kilt to kick his knees against as he marched to the nasal whine of the bagpipes roaring in his mind. Thus was the Fantom born. For weeks he refused his own name, insisting that he be addressed as *W.W. Winkie, thank you.* . . . He even took to sleeping under his bed with his trusty dog, Danny, at his side. It was a trying time for his parents.

But the Fantom's parents, who more or less began to adjust to the mad obsessions of their child, whatever his name might be, were not the only ones who had to cope with the Fantom. There were also friends and relatives, teachers and strangers, not one of whom was spared the Fantom's presence. When he gave his name, it might be Mickey Rooney, it might be Freddie Bartholomew—it might, on the other hand, if the Fantom was in his singing mode, be Deanna Durbin. Today, Jane Withers—tomorrow, the world! Note that, as the Fantom aged, the wraiths from the screen to whom he played body-host were being adapted to his years. In 1942, when he was twelve, the Fantom played host to Roddy McDowell, who had just appeared at roughly that age in *How Green Was My Valley*.

The Fantom's first major crisis came when, in 1944, he

attempted to welcome Elizabeth Taylor into his repertoire. Not only Elizabeth Taylor, but the girl she was currently playing body-host to herself, the androgynous Velvet Brown. It was Velvet Brown who won the Grand National Steeplechase and who had to flatten her budding breasts with painful tapes, in order to play the role of a man, since girls were not allowed to ride as jockeys. And not only did Velvet have to flatten her chest, she had to flatten her teeth; she wore a tedious brace, which both embarrassed and pained her.

Since the Fantom was a teenage boy in the midst of his own rather dazzling puberty, he had no breasts to flatten and he had no braces on his teeth to embarrass him above the waist, shall we say. His personal embarrassments were flourishing in other regions of his being and body, and he did not quite know how to stage the hosting of a girl—Miss Taylor/Velvet Brown—who was herself attempting to play the role of a full-grown man. Imagine, if such things amuse you, the Fantom, aged fourteen, alone and naked in the bathroom, binding his breastless chest with yards and yards of surgical gauze, just to see what it felt like. Imagine his mother insisting, as mothers will, that he *open the door at once*—the worst that can happen to a teenage boy no matter what room he happens to be in. And what must his mother have thought when her son explained: *everyone's doing it, Ma. There's a contest amongst the guys at school to see who can get the flattest chest.* . . . Unh-hunh. As for the braces on his teeth, the Fantom had discovered new and disturbing uses for bobby pins and wads of rolled-up toilet paper. Choking put an end to all that, just as not being able to breathe put an end to the yards and yards of surgical gauze. Elizabeth Taylor/Velvet Brown was forced into the open without accoutrement or props and she became the Fantom's initial triumph of body-hosting by insinuation alone. If you believe—you are.

Perhaps you are thinking that this is the way female impersonators are born. Not true. It is the way that actors are born—and writers: men and women who cannot *be*, except by insinuation.

Which is to say: *I am not I—but I am. And if I can make you recognize who I am by insinuation alone, then I have succeeded, whether as actor or as writer—or as both.*

And so, when on some future excursion to your favourite repertory film showcase, you should chance to meet Simone Signoret standing in the lobby after a screening of *Madame Rosa*—or if you should be accosted by a wild-eyed Robert Newton lurching toward the nearest bar when you have just been watching *Odd Man Out*— or if Spencer Tracy should happen to be over by the water fountain, muttering "Cherce!" as you emerge from *Pat and Mike* and—yes—even if Shirley Temple is marching to imagined bagpipes down the grand staircase after *Wee Willie Winkie*, you will think for the briefest moment it is I—but then you will know it is not that fellow, Findley, at all. It is the Fantom—still.

Stone Orchard
1989

I started acting because I loved the theatre, and I left school. I was about sixteen or seventeen and had been ill. Consequently, I missed Grade ten, but I had a tutor. I was flat on my back in bed most of the time, but I could sit up in bed or put on robes and slippers and eighteen pairs of socks and go and sit with scarves on at the dining-room table. This poor man was supposed to teach me *all* the subjects and try to keep me up to date—but I wouldn't let him. All I wanted was history and reading and art. When I finally regained my health, I was going to have to go into Grade ten at an age when everybody else had gone on. It was dreadful. I think I did about a month, if that, and immediately it was perfectly clear I had no business to be in that school—Jarvis Collegiate—or in any other school. And my parents were wondering what the hell was going to become of their beloved son.

They went to see the vice-principal and he, I think, must have been some kind of genius, because he said, "Mister and Mrs Findley, I urge you to let your boy out of this school into the world he wants to enter—the world of the imagination. He's going to be all right. He will find his way. He's intelligent enough to survive in that world. He doesn't really need to do this." So they let me out. I had enlightened parents and an enlightened vice-principal. Wow! And I got a job when I was seventeen. And it was wonderful.

While I had a job by day, I started in the amateur theatre and gradually got to the place where I could leave other kinds of employment and be in the theatre. I had radio work, a long time in a repertory company, and when television began in Canada, I started working in television, and consequently went to the first year of Stratford, went on to Great Britain, etc. And I did that until 1962, at which time I left acting because in the mid-1950s I had started to write and was encouraged in my writing by the actress Ruth Gordon and by the great American writer Thornton Wilder. It was while I was in a Wilder play starring Ruth—*The Matchmaker*, which, years later was made into a musical called *Hello Dolly!*—that Wilder became my mentor, and it was soon apparent that I could not have done both—acting and writing. I had a good career as an actor, and I could have gone on acting and made that my career and been, I think, successful—mostly because I'm a character actor, and you're likely to keep working as such. But I don't have the kind of intellectual energy that will allow me to spread my effort in two directions. And I wanted writing more, and so in 1962 quit the theatre, cold turkey, with my partner, Bill Whitehead, who had been in the theatre as well, and we both went into the world of writing—Bill as a documentary writer for television and radio, and me as a writer of fiction.

I was incredibly lucky to have Thornton Wilder as my mentor. He was a very great man as well as a very great writer. I had idolized his writing before I encountered him in person. I came to idolize him in the best sense—recognizing that this was a very great person, with great capacity to give and to articulate and to force exploration. I think of Thornton Wilder very much as being the sort of person I imagine Socrates must have been—a provoker, with a great sense of fun and a great sense of intellectual daring and intellectual frolic. And also deeply serious.

From time to time, I regret having given up acting—only because there are all kinds of roles I would have loved to have played that I had not achieved the stature to play, or the age. At the time I left the theatre, I was only thirty-two years old. But now, I would be suitable for many marvellous roles—some of the older men in Chekhov, and in Shakespeare. I would have loved to play in the works of Harold Pinter, and could have.

So, every time I have to give a reading, I recognize very quickly that the nerve-wracking aspect of acting is not something I miss at all. And I'm very grateful I don't have to face it every night.

Acting, though, did help me as a writer, because it allowed me to be able to read in public situations, and to play the role of a writer reading so I didn't have to face that without the necessary techniques.

The whole experience of being in the theatre was like a wonderful apprenticeship for writing. It taught me about language, about the shape of scenes, about dialogue, about character. I approach the writing of a character in exactly the same way I used to approach the playing of one. I look into my own centre to find the core of the character—to find why and how that character is saying and doing whatever it is.

The other thing I regret losing—but am now beginning to get back through writing for the theatre—is the wonder of rehearsals. The greatest aspect of theatre for me has always been to watch a piece of work grow and become itself during the rehearsal period.

One thing I have learned—both as an actor and as a writer—is that you can't be *taught* to be either. You can only be taught how to be better at your craft. In other words, I think all artists are born. It is not always evident that the artist is there until the circumstance reveals it. A door opens. For me, it was getting sick and ultimately leaving school and getting into amateur theatre. That's how the door opened for me, but once I was there, I realized: *this is what I am.* I think one is born with the capacity—simply because it is a capacity. You cannot teach someone who is not a writer how to write. The same for an actor or a dancer. Only a dancer can benefit from what can be had in dancing class. The voice, for the writer, must be there. There must be a lack of blockage. The writer has to know, instinctively, how to get the words out onto paper. You have to have a capacity for freedom. And that is not a capacity with which everyone is born. It's simply part of who you are, if you have it. The rest, once you recognize this is what you are, is all very hard work. No one, not even the greatest of *born writers*, can manage without craft. They don't simply sit down and write. That does happens, I think, on very rare occasions in music. Mozart, who could hear another person's symphonic work and go away and write it all down, correctly. That is the capacity we call genius, and it's very rare, however many dumb and rather stupid people seem to think that genius is all over the place. It ain't. There are few true geniuses. There are very great writers—Dante, Shakespeare, etc. But that's about as far as genius goes.

Stone Orchard
1996
Anecdote

The Leap

It was exciting news. In 1953, I was among those chosen to be part of the acting company in the opening season of Canada's Stratford Shakespearean Festival. I was only twenty-two, and would be working with some of the most talented people in Canadian and British theatre—including the director Tyrone Guthrie. One of my roles was Catesby, the King's henchman, in *Richard III*. This meant that I had to make an explosive entrance into the scene in which Alec Guinness, alone on the battlefield, was to cry: *my kingdom for a horse!* Guthrie wanted this entrance to be physically *alarming*, having already devised some entrances for other actors that were pretty spectacular. Pacing around the stage, he looked up at the balcony and—while my heart sank—asked if I could burst through the drapes that covered its entrance, jump up onto the balustrade—and leap down onto the stage. That's right. A ten-foot leap through the dark, and *not* land on Alec Guinness, whose single spotlight was the *only* light there was. What else could I say but: *sure.* I tried it, and—to my dismay—it worked. This meant I had to do it in every performance. Somehow, both Guinness and I survived. It was only in later years, looking back, that I realized how well that single move summed up what had happened that summer. Canadian theatre took a leap into the unknown—and, to judge from what's been achieved since, it landed on its feet.

London
October 22, 1953
Journal

> In 1953, following the first season of the Stratford Festival of Canada, Tiff and Richard Easton, the first recipients of what was to become the Tyrone Guthrie Award, were sent to England, sponsored by Tyrone Guthrie and Alec Guinness. Tiff was enrolled in London's Central School of Speech and Drama and installed in the Guinness household with Alec, his wife, Merula [Merry], and young son, Matthew. WFW.

I should say a word about the party last Sunday, which was rather wonderful. . . . Nerve-wracking to say the least, but I did settle down inside finally and did have a wonderful time. Sir John G.

[Gielgud] told some wonderful stories about his recent holiday in the South of France and Italy . . . voice beyond belief and really staggering presence. Very shy—very lonely man . . . Totally honest and open.

Dickie Burton, a very charming young man. Wonderful humour and wit. Obvious intelligence. It makes me more and more sure that his Hamlet is wrong merely from inexperience and immaturity as an artist, and that in time to come he will be very good . . . Kay Walsh invited Dick and me to lunch at Ealing, which we must do. Irene (Worth) looked a bit tired—but obviously must be working hard as the new show opens on Monday next in Liverpool. Went to see [Donald] Wolfit in *Volpone* last night. My God!!!!! Fantastic. The worst production of anything imaginable. The company too bad for belief . . . How could anyone, and with such obvious purpose, too, surround himself with such dreary people? . . . Beyond a doubt he must either be mad—or totally in the wrong profession. Amen!

London
December 25, 1953
Journal

Had a wonderful but very lonely day. Got up around 9:00 and Matthew brought up tea to us, which was jolly nice. Went down to breakfast and then we all opened presents, which was a wonderful sight. Everyone had the loveliest things. Alec gave me a leather cigarette case and the most wonderful pyjamas I've ever had—silk . . . Matthew, a record of Dame Edith [Evans] reading poetry, and Merry, the most wonderful recording of *The Rape of Lucrezia* by Benjamin Britten. Also a lovely tie and some hankies, ostensibly from the animals.

London
December 26, 1953
Journal

I feel today an overwhelming sense of gratefulness for what Alec [Guinness] has done for me. While somehow it has been tangible in a way—plays and galleries and museums and meeting people and school, the major thing is intangible as anything can be. I am here. I have been living with a great man. I have taken part in his life and he has taken part in mine. He has given me confidence, education and values, but above all I think he has awakened in me an awareness of what I am and what I am about and what the world is about and why there is a work of art and why we create and where I fit into the scheme of the world. And above all, he has taught me that I must live my own life and find within my own heart the sense and meaning of my life. . . . Now I have confidence in the fact that things can happen, even though I don't have confidence in myself.

More and more is able to happen when I am willing to let it.

London
January 14, 1954
Journal

Last night the news came through!!! Alec [Guinness] had tea with Mr. Beaumont. Dick [Easton] and I are both to have a year's contract with Tennants, which is unbelievable news. We are to expect to work very very hard, which sounds monumentally exciting as it will be tremendous to be worked hard. What glory to be back on the stage. On February 1 rehearsals start for *The Prisoner*. There is a rumour that if nothing else turns up there are parts for us both in a London production of a Thornton Wilder play [*The Matchmaker*] which Guthrie is doing. How exciting to know I will be working for a year. Of course there may be nothing decent to go into and maybe I will turn out of it badly—but I have high hopes. I don't want to let myself down with a fabulous chance like this.

Will be drawing approx. £2.10 a week, which isn't much but is certainly enough to live on. Imagine me in London digs! Cooking on a burner and putting pennies into geysers for hot water. It sounds like old times in Canada, except that the prospects are so much higher and the city so much more intriguing to live in.

Other wonderful news is that the tour of *The Prisoner* will be five weeks. Edinburgh and then two weeks in Dublin, then Manchester and Cambridge. Is it really all true? Still, still and ever more, I can't believe it's me.

London
January 18, 1954
Journal

But oh, how sad I am. I walked in London today and I miss so many people. If only I had a friend. A close, close friend who understood me and loved me. What I would do for that—and to always have that friend—forever.

There is a tangle of everything inside me, biting at my insides to let itself out. I wish that the evolution of greatness wasn't so terrifying and painful. The long hallway of doors that I must shut seems endless, and beyond each one of them seems something more desirable than the one before. But none of these things am I allowed. Inside me the finger points the way and a tiny head shakes itself at the physical yearnings and the shady fantasies of imagination . . . I have nowhere to turn but into my own arms and into the mind of God, through the genius of other men.

London
January 31, 1954
Journal

Today it all began. The new life. And it is as exciting a life as ever I could hope for. The stamping of cold feet, the rubbing of cold hands, the impatience to get on the stage, the envy at another actor's grace, the sudden quiet when someone really feels something correctly and everyone waits for him to finish. The glances from actor to actor: "well, I wonder how good you are . . ." The despair when the director makes you feel like an utter fool, the worse despair when you make yourself feel a fool and the catastrophic upheaval within when you *are* a fool . . .

Alec gave me a wonderful gift tonight. His make-up box. He has bought a new one and gave me the old one. My first "relic" *du théâtre*. I will say to my grandchildren: "and this make-up box was given to me by Alec Guinness in 1954 when I was doing my first play on the London stage. It was called *The Prisoner* and Mister Guinness (perhaps by then Sir Alec) was playing." "Did you really know Alec Guinness, Grandfather?" "Know him. Why of course I did. I was his protegé. He was my teacher." "Did he teach you how to act?" "No. But he taught me what acting is. And much more than that, he taught me a great deal about myself and about other people." "What do you mean?" "Well, he taught me to look for the Truth. That was the first thing he taught me." "Didn't you know what Truth was?" "No, I guess I didn't. (Perhaps I shall say then "and I still don't"—but I hope not.) But I was aware of it, and he began to show me how important it was and how to cut falseness out of my life and of course, out of my acting. You see, he believed that you could not be a "true" actor unless you were a 'true' person." "Was he a good man, Grandfather?" "Not a goody-goody man. He was a strong man. Sometimes I was very unhappy about some of the things he said to me. . . . He was a good man, yes. But a very strict—a hard man." "Why was he

hard?" Because he had trained himself to throw away the unnecessary things in his life and he wanted me to throw away these
things, too. And that wasn't easy. But of course, it was worth it."

Stone Orchard
1989
Article

Katharine Hepburn and Robert Helpmann

In 1954 I was performing in a play called *The Prisoner* at the Globe
Theatre in London's West End. My part required a very great
number of props, all of which had to be counted over before each
performance.

On matinee days, the actors rarely left the theatre between performances because, in England at that time, the curtain came
down about 5:30 and went back up at 7:00.

The curtain falls, of course, when a play is over—but as soon as
the audience has left the theatre, the curtain is raised and a battery
of cleaning women comes in to vacuum the aisles and pick up discarded programmes. Visiting celebrities very often take advantage
of this moment to come up out of the house and reach the stars'
dressing rooms simply by crossing the stage instead of going outside and having to face the mob of autograph seekers hanging
around the stage door. . . .

So there I was, late on a Wednesday afternoon, standing in the
wings counting over my props after the first performance, when I
heard somebody coming out of the house and over the footlights,
preparing to cross the stage. Of course, I leaned forward to see who
it was—and there were Katharine Hepburn and Robert Helpmann.

In those days, Hepburn affected a scarlet opera cloak. Helpmann,
for his part, always affected high-heeled shoes—because of his
shortness. The image, then, is of two of the greatest stars of all

time—suddenly marching into the presence of a traumatized young actor (me)—thinking they could escape unrecognized.

Well—they couldn't.

The scarlet opera cloak swirled into view—with Hepburn's neck and head above it. Clickety-click, clickety-click—the high-heeled shoes tipped the image of Robert Helpmann perilously forward in my direction.

I stepped from behind the property table. I don't know what I had in mind. Perhaps I was thinking I might just say "hello." But instead, I felt myself floating towards the floor . . .

Not in a faint. No such luck.

I had curtsied.

And I mean the full court curtsy of another age, the kind once offered only to the kings of France.

Miss Hepburn paused and stared and blinked.

Mister Helpmann was more succinct. Regarding my lowered self, he said: *Oh no, dear boy—no need! No need!*

And they both swept on.

Cotignac
1996
Article

Digs

While I wasn't *born in a trunk*, I lived in one for fifteen years. This was when I was an actor, 1947–1962. There were moments back then when I felt like a ventriloquist's dummy, packed away between engagements, speaking only the words allotted to me by the playwright.

There's a lot of invisibility and a lot of silence in an actor's life, from the moment he leaves the stage to the moment he goes back on. God, it was a lonely time. But wonderful. I wouldn't have missed it for the world. It gave me access to the fund of necessary solitudes a writer requires in order to function—solitudes peopled with all those interior companions who inhabit your work, but not your life.

The trunk I lived in had been my father's during World War II. Neatly stencilled on the lid—black on Air Force blue—was FLO A.G. FINDLEY—C2425. I was younger then, of course, and stronger—and used to carry the trunk on my back. I can still feel the metal bump of it against my bum, and the burns from the leather handle. A flat trunk, with one removable tray. I had no suitcase, only a shopping bag, from time to time—often filled with laundry, plus the irresistible paperbacks, mostly Penguins, bought in market stalls. This was in England: Liverpool, Manchester, Newcastle, Leeds. Also Brighton. Also Oxford. Also Cambridge. Bournemouth and Norwich. Always to Scotland—Glasgow, Aberdeen and Edinburgh. Sometimes to Dublin, whose streets were in my genes; where I could find my way unerringly back home, drunk and riotous through the dark.

Home.

For an actor, home is mostly *digs.* The word, I think, is Australian—short for *diggings.* No one in the theatre ever talks of *lodgings, bed and board* or *quarters.* These are all civilian references. And a non-civilian breed of women has been in charge of theatrical digs since well before the turn of the century. In all my time in the theatre, I never once had a landlord.

In Dublin, I arrived with my trunk on a rain-wet afternoon, impossibly romantic in the misted views of row-houses, each one more dilapidated than the next, all of them redolent of stories waiting to be told. I rang the bell and waited, standing on the Georgian doorstep, watching myself being watched from a dozen windows, all lace-curtained, each with a single inquisitive face beside the single hand that had pulled the curtain aside. *Who is it this time? Male or female—young or old?*

The door in front of me opened.

"Yes?"

"It's me," I said. "Timothy Findley. With *The Prisoner* company."

The Prisoner was the play being toured, with Alec Guinness and Wilfrid Lawson. I had a small but wonderful role, playing the inquisitor's all but silent secretary in Bridget Boland's account of Cardinal Mindszenty's ordeal at the hands of Hungarian communists. A Catholic play, just right for Dublin.

"Ah, yes. The lad," said a woman barely seen in the shadows. "Enter and be welcome."

As my eyes adjusted to the light, I saw that she was middle-aged—a beauty still who, in her youth, must have set the world on fire. She wore a ratty mink coat and an ankle-length silk nightie. Her feet were bare. "Go later to your room," she said. "Now, come with me."

In the kitchen, the table had been set for one. "Sit," she said. "That's you." Her name was Mrs Higgins. "And I don't mind just plain Missus, if it suits you." A bottle of Jameson's was produced. Cigarettes were lighted. Mrs Higgins, clutching at her mink, sat opposite, each of us with a glass, and before she went to the stove to prepare my supper, she told a tabloid version of *The Troubles*— all of its greatest moments in vivid detail, all of its people conjured, all of its martyrs named. Her father, Donnell, who had fallen then, was resurrected between us there in the twilight. Tears and intensity. Laughter with a twist of rue. All of Ireland was in her voice— or so it seemed to me. I was enchanted.

After I had eaten, I unpacked my *home*—postcards and photographs set on the bureau, flashlight and crucifix on the bedside table, books beside the chair. The crucifix was the last surviving remnant of my grandmother's Irish Catholicism, and still it sits beside my bed, protecting me—I like to think—from all the crashing aeroplanes and sinking ships in my dreams, if not my life.

Few of my digs were as splendid as those overseen by Mrs Higgins, whose splendour was all in her presence, not in material opulence. The sheets were worn, the food was spare—but a person could survive by means of Mrs Higgins alone, who had the gift of survival in her being and the gift of life in her words. Other landladies thrived, or so it seemed, on the expectation you could live on a diet of words such as *no* and *never*.

I depended for survival on the continuity lifted from my trunk. No matter where I was, if I could see my parents and my brother in their cheap brass frames, my postcard Cézannes, Monets and Modiglianis sitting on the bureau and my orange Penguin Waughs and Fitzgeralds, I was safely at home.

One of my Modiglianis was a female nude.

Oh, you can't have that there, Mister Findley! Anyone might see it! This was Manchester.

In Birmingham, the landlady bought a half-dozen eggs for my daily breakfast, each one just a bit more *off* than the one before. When I pointed out they were rotten, she apologized profusely. *Isn't that strange*, she would say. *And I bought them only yesterday.* Next morning's egg went down the toilet. On the Saturday, fearing I might not be able to bear what lay beneath the shell, I carried the egg inside a handkerchief and dropped it down the nearest sewer.

MISTER FINDLEY! This was in London. *MISTER FINDLEY—I KNOW WHAT YOU'RE DOING IN THERE! AND I WARN YOU, STOP AT ONCE!*

Think what you will, my sin was nothing more than running a bath beyond the prescribed three minutes. Given the fact that all hot water was delivered from a gas contraption called a *geyser*, three minutes' worth was barely one inch deep. *Madam*—I forget her name—would stand outside the bathroom door with a watch, and listen.

Others were intolerant of light. Their houses were equipped with automatic switches, inevitably timed to leave you in the dark just halfway up the stairs. Some had rules about personal acquaintances. NO ONE OF THE OPPOSITE SEX TO BE ENTERTAINED PAST TEN. Clearly, these women had never heard of homosexuality. *Have all the men you like, Mister*

Findley, but if I ever find a woman . . . Mrs Brown of Leeds expressed this with great authority: *I know you actors!* she said. *Don't you think I don't! The minute my back is turned, you're into one another like knives!* An interesting analogy.

A life in rooms is a life under siege. Every eye is upon you. And when you leave to go to work, the sense that every eye is upon your belongings is palpable. Steeped in honourable traditions: *we never snoop, we never peek*—theatrical landladies nonetheless know everything there is to know about their guests. *Went to Lawton's, did you? Quite agree—they have the best underwear in town* . . . Still, as the years go by, you become their own. They play into your lives the way that trees play into gardens. All the right protective shade is offered—all the right fruit is produced.

You travel often in the company of other productions—plays and operas, ballets and orchestras—every single performer carrying *home* in a bag. *You again!* the landlady will say. *And here's your favourite marmalade! You again! And no doubt all your socks need mending* . . . This is what greeted you, setting down your suitcase or your trunk. *You again! And I have that chicken stew you like on the stove!*

It's a profession: making a home of one part actor, one part landlady. Something about it makes you think of animals. *Nesting.* Bill Whitehead, my companion, says: "you could nest anywhere, Tiff." And yes, I could. I've had the practice.

London
March 8, 1955
Journal

I must add a word here to my "memorable performance" information. Siobahn McKenna's St. Joan, which I saw on Tuesday last, is without compare. I certainly never want to see another St. Joan—that is certain. Too good . . . to be able to pin down with descriptions. For me the tears didn't come (and I think, rightly so—absolutely rightly) until she said, in the epilogue: "oh, no, it is the Saints must pray"—and fell on her knees in prayer—and I was like a man standing in a wilderness who is struck by a flash of lightning when there have been no clouds in the sky—no rain and no thunder—and nothing to see for miles on end—and suddenly something hits you—and it doubled me up—a stomach blow—and then you could only hear her voice and see her kneeling in the shimmer of your own tears cast over the lights around her. Oh, it was—it was unbelievable and unforgettable. "What is it, Lord?" That is what you really said inside to yourself. "What does it mean?"—because if we knew, we should know, I think, almost everything.

London
April 24, 1955
Journal

Had a fabulous conversation with Ruth G. [Gordon] on Saturday. Just something about young artists having nothing to portray except desperation. And so on—about young people today and what they were aware of. I want to write her something—but I must think it out carefully before even beginning—such a subject is highly flammable and dangerous—especially for me.

London
May 2, 1955
Journal

Ruth [Gordon] and Garson [Kanin] are both absolutely unbelievable people. They have given me a typewriter and ten pounds to do typing lessons. And a beautiful grey suit. And Miss Ruth said the most astounding things tonight. I can't even remember, she said so much—mostly about me being talented. And I don't understand. I wrote her a story. Now, all this. But she said some pretty potent things I don't want to forget—and which I never will. About not wasting your talent. About full expression—and I kept being a fool and saying how kind they were—but she said something about that. She said: "it is not kindness. It is seeing that you do the right thing."

And she is now the third person to intimate that my career (not my career, my real *place*) is as a writer, not an actor. She was wonderful! "Oh, you can act when you want to—but you're really a writer."

What? What is it? What have I got? And why don't I know about it so I can do something about it?

I want to.

I won't fail.

I *can't* fail.

Not me and not her.

And not whatever it is.

Edinburgh
September 11, 1955
Journal

The Old Vic production of *Julius Caesar* yesterday was the epitome of everything bad in the theatre. Do you remember that Danish lad who, because of his accent, constantly referred to this group as the "Old Wick"? Now I see there a perfect description. How many bright fires used to burn—and how limp and damp it is now. The Old Wick, indeed. Drooping.

Stone Orchard
1991
Article

An Unforgettable Journey to Russia

The journey I am about to describe took place at a time when I was still an actor and working in the UK. This was in November of 1955. I was twenty-five years old.

Peter Brook's all-star production of *Hamlet*, with Paul Scofield playing the title role, had been invited to the Soviet Union, where we would be the first English-speaking company of actors to play in Moscow since the Revolution of 1917. I had been cast as Osric, the kind of small, flashy part young actors kill for—though, luckily, in this case no corpses had accumulated.

Having rehearsed in London, we opened and played in Brighton and Oxford before the historic journey took place. Everyone, including Scofield—normally Mister Cool himself—was riddled with nerves. We were all about to be part of a momentous theatrical event and the prospect overwhelmed us. For one thing, this was before the age of commercial jets and the distance to Moscow, in terms of hours alone, was vast. It called for one-and-a-half days of air travel, with stops in Berlin and Lithuania.

Another factor creating tension was the Cold War climate in which we had to make the trip. In the West, we were locked into an American-dominated foreign policy, syndicated by that coldest warrior of all, John Foster Dulles. As for the Soviet Union, the ghost of Joseph Stalin, dead for two years, hung like a pall over the Presidium. And making matters worse, the 1951 defections of British diplomats Guy Burgess and Donald Maclean were still a major source of embarrassment between the UK and Russia. It was not, by any means, the easiest time to be made the representatives of cultural detente. It was, however, a most exhilarating time.

The initial part of the journey, from London to Berlin, was

made aboard a BOAC airliner of enormous size—the pre-jet version of a 747. We left mid-afternoon, arriving over Germany a good deal later than had been expected. The delay was caused by an encounter over the lowlands with a storm that seemed determined to blow us back to England. There was also a display of thunder and lightning worthy of Stephen Spielberg and, at one moment, the airliner fell eighty feet through an air pocket. The jolt at the bottom of this fall was almost lethal and I can still recall the sound of the bang it caused, and the sound of rattling bolts and screws as the aeroplane began, we were certain, to come undone around us. At this point, being a novice flyer, I turned around to look at my fellow passengers, most of whom were experienced air travellers, to see how they were reacting.

I should not have done this. . . .

Everyone on the plane was pale with fear—and it didn't help when, with something of a shock, I noticed for the first time the grim, silent features of the man who was seated four rows behind me on the other side of the aisle.

His presence, I cannot really tell you why, was somehow unnerving. Perhaps this was only because my catching sight of him had come as a surprise. But why was he with us? What was he doing on board our aeroplane?

It was Graham Greene.

No one had told us Graham Greene would be joining our excursion. After all, we were on a chartered flight, which meant he had to be one of us. He had, in that moment, the grey appearance of a stowaway and, when he saw me looking at him, his expression begged me not to draw attention to his presence. He was so intent upon not being recognized that I had to look away. Settling back into my fear of flying, I was able to take a little solace from the fact that Graham Greene had obviously been as frightened by our fall through the air as I had been. His knuckles, just like mine, were bone white and rigid. I also derived some comfort from the long-shot hope that maybe God took special care of special people.

Surely He would not destroy that all-star cast of *Hamlet* and their newly revealed companion, the starry author of *Brighton Rock* and *The Power and the Glory*. Could God afford the headlines?

I suspect that, more than likely, most of us were making up those headlines for the next three-quarters of an hour as our wounded aeroplane slowly made its escape from the storm: SCOFIELD, WYNYARD, CLUNES, URE, BROOK ALL VICTIMS OF FIERY CRASH! My version added: BODY OF FAMOUS AUTHOR ADDS MYSTERY TO AIR DISASTER!

When, at last, the image of West Berlin presented itself below us, the Kurfürstendamm ablaze with lights, a cheer went up that might have come from a shipwrecked crew when land has been sighted.

Emerging from the plane at Templehof, several of us touched the ground with trembling, grateful fingers, swearing we would never fly again. But, of course, we still had the flight to Moscow before us, no one guessing what a nightmare that would prove to be.

We stayed for most of the night on the Wansee shore in one of those grand hotels where marble is mixed with neon to produce a kind of kitsch peculiar to Berlin. No one slept. Everyone drank a great deal and waited nervously for 4:00 a.m. This was the hour when the cavalcade of official limousines would arrive to take us away under cover of darkness deep into the East German countryside.

Somewhere out there was the military airport from which we would make our departure for Moscow.

I remember all the tastes and smells of that night—of Turkish coffee, brandy and of German cigarettes and the warm aroma of Knize Ten cologne which have remained for me the signals of oncoming intrigue. The company sat en masse at a congregation of little tables spread beneath potted palms in the large café adjoining the hotel lobby. This, in spite of the fact that all of us had been assigned the comfort of beds and bathrooms. Nobody wanted to sleep for fear of missing a second of the great adventure.

I looked for Graham Greene and spotted him sitting with two male strangers beyond the palms, locked in a conversation that might, for all I knew, have been about the weather. On the other hand, because he was Graham Greene, I supposed the subject of their talk must be espionage. There had long been speculation, because of the tales in some of his books, that Greene was in the employ, one way or another, of the British Secret Service. Or perhaps he was tracking down another murderous Harry Lime. Certainly, he couldn't possibly have tagged along just to see the sights. Graham Greene a tourist . . . ? Never.

I was also intrigued by the fact that, although he had never once approached nor been approached by any one of the acting company's leading lights—I had nonetheless caught a glimpse of him in an upper corridor of our hotel engaged in a deeply serious conversation with one of the company's walk-on players. This was a woman whose presence in the company, while entirely welcome, had been somewhat mysterious because of her utter lack of acting talent. Still, since the theatre overflows with such people, no one had given it a second thought. This charming woman was with us—and that was that. Or rather, that was that until I saw her with Graham Greene in the corridor of that Berlin hotel. And, when she finally came downstairs to join us in our cafe, passing Graham Greene without a flicker of recognition, I was quickly made aware that, if this lady couldn't act on stage, she could act the socks off every one of us in real life. What else could she be but a government spy? An agent whose job, once Moscow had been achieved, would turn out to be some sort of secret mission. After all, she was the only member of our company, besides Peter Brook himself, whose Russian was impeccable.

At 4:00 a.m. on the dot, the limousines arrived and we were divided into groups of six and eight and required to sit in the cars with blinds drawn tight. Each of the vehicles was driven by a military driver and, after we had been locked in place in the back, a dark-suited gent got in up front and said, in Russian: "move!" It was all very strange. But it was also funny, because our hosts were doing precisely what all the Cold War movies had told us they would do. The only thing they didn't do was call us Comrade.

We seemed to be in the cars for a very long time, even as long as an hour and a half, before the official silence was broken. I have often wondered since, if we were driven any real distance at all. Or was it an exercise in disorientation and were we only driven around in circles? At any rate, there came a moment when, still in transit, the dark-suited figure turned around and said, in English: "you must raise curtains now." And when we did so, what was revealed was a flattened rural landscape, lighted by sunrise, showing much distressing evidence of the war—the skeletons of blasted houses and the absence of trees. Also, in spite of the early hour, there were endless lines of men and women setting out on foot along the roads on their way to work.

This landscape with its depressed population made it all too obvious how spoiled we had been in the West with our relatively quick recovery from the war. Everything there was as dark and as bleak as I remembered it being at home in the late 1940s—a bleakness from which we had emerged, in the 1950s, into a Rinso-white and over-polished version of prosperity now called the Eisenhower era. But there in Eastern Europe, ten years after the war had ended, the people seemed unable to escape from its hardships. Inside the cars, we all fell silent.

The airport, once we got there, was set behind a double row of high wire fences. Soldiers—all of them shockingly young and armed with equally shocking submachine guns—strode up and down and watched our arrival with a mix of boylike curiosity and adult wariness. It appeared, in every way, still to be a war zone and we, though nothing overtly malicious happened, were treated for the moment more like prisoners than as guests.

Do not be looking, someone said, as we were escorted into an aeroplane hangar. Do not be looking and do not be speaking. Thank you.

But looking and speaking were the only two things that any of us wanted to do. Where the hell were we? And where the hell were the washrooms? Where the hell were the aeroplanes that were going to fly us to Moscow?

The sight of all of us standing there must have been odd for the soldiers and officers in charge of us. We were not exactly "ordinary" looking. Actors—in those days, at any rate—always looked like actors: standing straighter, with more self-awareness; wearing their clothes with a sense of theatrical style; presenting themselves as if they were really there and not pretending they wanted to hide. Added to this was the fact that Diana Wynyard and Mary Ure had been dressed for the tour by the front rank of British designers—their clothes being advertisements for English chic. Not that chic was an issue in Russia, back in the days before Raisa Gorbechev, but the press of the Western world was covering our excursion and the British government had decided it was a perfect opportunity for showing off the best of British haute couture. The only problem was, not many people hang around military installations wearing Hardy Amies cocktail suits and Norman Hartnell clutch coats. Or, for that matter, stiletto heels . . .

Speaking of actors and haute couture—we had in the company one of the theatre's true eccentrics, the late and entirely delightful Ernest Thesiger. Mister Thesiger's eccentricities began with what nature had given him—a long, rather horselike face with a long, tilted nose. He was also tall, thin and angular and his hands, which had been badly damaged in World War I, were also long and thin and angular. In order to regain his use of them after they had been crushed during a bombardment on the Western Front, he had learned to do needlepoint and had become so proficient in this art that he was taken up by Queen Mary as her sewing companion. In fact, the widow of George V and Ernest Thesiger bore a strong resemblance to one another—each of them squinny-eyed—each of them dedicated to Edwardian dress and each of them employing the same hairdresser, who turned them out in identical mauve-rinsed, marcelled waves with curl-framed foreheads.

The thought of them together, bent above their sewing frames, scandal-hopping through *Debrett's Peerage*, conjures the image of a high-class act in turn-of-the-century music halls: MA'AM AND ERNIE—THE TATTING TATTLERS!

Ernest's other notable eccentricity also stemmed from the fact of his damaged hands. Convinced they were unbearable to look at—they weren't—he had begun wearing rings on every finger and, sometimes, even on his thumbs. These rings were often very large, and most of them were antiques. Some had once belonged to historical figures such as Napoleon and Marie Antoinette. His prize possession was a poison ring that had actually been used by Lucretia Borgia. I can still hear him saying: "used, my dear—if you get my drift!"

It was Ernest Thesiger who, when he had been asked to describe his impression of the Western Front, first uttered the famous lines: "oh, the noise, my dear! And the people!" And it was Ernest who sported our company's only fur coat on our journey to Moscow. He had longed all his life to wear a fur coat and now he had the perfect excuse. Turning up his luxurious collar against the wind that invaded our hangar, Ernest surveyed the NKVD agents who were acting as our shepherds and said to me: "you know what we should do the minute we get to Moscow, dear boy? We should march straight off to the Kremlin walls and write, in the biggest letters we can make: BURGESS LOVES MACLEAN!"

"But we don't have any chalk," I said.

"Not to worry," said Ernest. "I've brought a whole box."

And he had.

When, at last, they paraded us out of the hangar and onto the tarmac, all we could see by way of aircraft were two or three DC-10s, a cargo plane the Americans had used in the war. Large numbers of these had been sold to the Russians for the same purpose. Now, they had the appearance of old tin traps: long past their youth and long past salvaging. Thank heaven we don't have to fly in those! we all thought. But then, with a dreadful determination, our shepherds turned on the tarmac and started to lead us directly towards the DC-10s and, all hearts sinking, we realized these derelict crates were to be our transport to Moscow.

Our scenery and stage crew had preceded us. Now, the actors and the costumes were boarded and the engines were started. Everything shook and the propellers screamed. Inside the planes, we were seated in rows down either side of the fuselage—one row on the left, two rows on the right—death rows, we were certain. Taxiing down the snowy, ancient runway we were given such a ride that I realized for the first time what it was like to see the world through the eyes of Carmen Miranda: one-and-two-and-three . . . lurch! One-and-two-and-three . . . Bang!

Et cetera, et cetera, until we took off.

It was a flying nightmare.

Somewhere in the Baltic States (I think it was in Vilna) we stopped to have lunch. In the meantime, we had flown over Poland which, in winter at any rate, had much the same appearance as parts of northern Ontario where it broaches the Manitoba prairie. There were a lot of small lakes below us—many trees and occasional farming communities. It was all very beautiful and somewhat reassuring. At least, if we fell, I would feel at home—which, of course, could not be said for anyone else.

Lunch was wonderful. We ate at huge round tables spread with pure white cloths and all around us there were other tables where various military personnel were eating—all of us being served by women dressed entirely in layers of thick white clothing. The soldiers and the airmen came from every region of the Soviet Union—exotic Mongols and flat-faced Slavs, black-haired Armenians, blond Ukrainians and red-faced Muscovites, and all their varied languages gave the room the feel of Babel. Once, when the sun came out, all of us paused and, after a moment's silence, said:

"aaaah!" The effect of this was such a pleasant surprise that every-one laughed. Even Graham Greene was laughing, tucked in a private corner sitting alone at a small, white-clothed table. I wondered what would become of him now that we were about to depart on the final leg of our journey. I wondered if, at last, he would break his silence and speak with us—or would he maintain his distance and disappear, once we'd arrived?

As the afternoon wore on and the early winter darkness swept all sight of the earth away below us, we were offered Russian tea by our stewardess. This tea, which is both unique and delicious, is drunk with lemon zest and broken lumps of sugar from tall, thin glasses in silver holders. But, as the stewardess brought it around, it became quite clear that her supply of glasses and silver holders was somewhat more than slightly limited. In fact, she had only four of each and, consequently, only four passengers could be served at a time. No explanation was ever offered for this, but I cannot believe that, in all of Russia, they could not have found enough glasses to serve more than four of us at once. The reason, I am more inclined to suspect, had to do with the fact that we had entered—about the time the tea was first offered—a blizzard whose proportions were vaster and more violent than any blizzard I have experienced here in Canada. And that is saying a very great deal. Ernest told me that, in broken English, the stewardess had admitted to him: "now there is some possibleness we shall not be able to be landing . . ."

"Oh?" I said—white.

What, I wondered, would we do instead?

Increasingly, as the flight wore on, it became apparent that we really were in trouble. It became very cold in the plane. Everyone put on an overcoat. Blankets were offered. The pilot was attempting to climb above the storm—but he was failing to achieve his goal. The snow, it seemed, went all the way to heaven.

Nobody spoke, which is the way of people in jeopardy, it seems. Neighbours retreated into private thoughts. We turned very slightly away from one another. The DC-10 began to shake and shudder. I thought how young we all were—even Ernest in his seventies. It is always too soon to die, I guess.

Moscow was at last achieved. At least, the sense of it was achieved, straining somewhere out there trying to be heard on our radio. The stewardess came out of the cockpit at one point and beamed at everyone and just said: "yes!"—and then turned around and disappeared again. But the city was there. We could feel it.

Sometime later, the plane began its descent and all at once—the same as over Berlin—the lights of the city began to wink at us one by one through the blowing snow. First, you would see them, then they would be wiped away, and then they would return, closer— more of them, multiplying like insects. Finally, searchlights appeared, finger-beams probing the blizzard. Everyone sighed.

But we were not down, yet.

Round and round and round the airport we flew in circles and as each circle was completed, the pilot banked the plane a little more until, as the circles were beginning to make us all dizzy, the plane was literally flying on its side and those of us on the up-side were holding on for dear life.

And all the while, the searchlights seemed to be holding us up in a cat's cradle of crossed beams.

The stewardess made another appearance and told us, practically standing on her head to do so: "there is no need to worry, please. Our pilot was in war planes and is best we have!"

I'll bet!

Then, the moment came when we had been cleared to land and the plane levelled off. Now, the whole storm rushed past our tiny windows and all we could see was its white and incandescent light. When the wheels touched the earth, we still could not see what was there below us.

Once the plane was stilled and sitting in its designated place, everyone applauded. The stewardess smiled and waved as if she had done it all alone. In fact, I think we all felt as if we had done it alone: kept the whole world alive. It was a wonderful moment.

Then the door was opened and the sound of the storm swept in with a burst of snow—and everyone laughed. We all lined up to make our departure. And it was only then that we became aware we were not alone.

Racing over the great, wide field of the aerodrome, a hundred people and more came running through the beams of light and the streaming snow—and they were all like small round balls of fur being blown towards us, jubilant in thick black coats and round black hats, and all of them, every one of them, carrying armfuls of flowers. And as each of us stepped from the plane, a dozen hands reached out and thrust red roses, carnations, snapdragons, tulips, lillies into our chests and we were virtually embraced by all these flowers and then we were swept away through the snow and the lights and the people towards the warmth of lounges, bars and cafés that awaited us.

Only then did we realize who these people were. They were all the actors of all the theatres in Moscow. I doubt that anyone could ask for a better ending to a journey than that. Someone very wise had known that the language of kind—of actors and of theatre people everywhere—is universal.

As for Graham Greene, he chose that moment to slip away as I had thought he might. He did not return with us, and I don't know how his journey ended. But if, as I suspected, he had come for some liaison, for whatever reason, with Burgess and Maclean, then we held one thing in common. I, too, met Guy Burgess during that month in Moscow. But that is, very much, another story—not to be told until I'm old. The real adventure was in getting there.

Toronto
August 23, 1956
Journal

I have been reinvited to play in *The Matchmaker*. I am to play Rudolf again and I go on Tuesday next. We play in New York until January '57 and then we tour until June. All I so far have heard about the tour is that it includes an extensive stay in Chicago and Los Angeles. I hope we also hit San Francisco and New Orleans, which are the other two American cities one really wants to visit. Anyway, I am overjoyed at the thought of five months in N.Y.C.—and I am going to do my damnedest to come out of this next year firmly established on my way to the ultimate. N.Y.C. and L.A. can be especially rewarding if I concentrate and make an effort to meet people and make good contacts. Anyway, it's all a terrific challenge—and I'm very grateful for its timeliness. It simply couldn't have happened at a more fabulous time.

On train to New York
August 28/29, 1956
Journal

Typical of myself to travel in the midst of complete chaos. First off, the train goes via Buffalo—while my visa waits untended in Niagara Falls!!! So I am sitting here in my little roomette waiting to find out if I shall be permitted to cross the border or not. The Customs man has wired to Buffalo, which will, in time, wire Niagara Falls to check slips. I cannot quite face having to spend all night in some ghastly station—also I cannot afford it, as I have now exactly four dollars and some odd cents to my name. Problem two, money. Problem three—I had been booked into the wrong roomette on the train. How terribly typical. However, without such incidents, what is a journey?

So. They did "yank" me off the train. I got through Fort Erie, where one poor Italian was taken off—it meant he would miss his ship which sails today. Immigration officials do the nastiest things in the kindest way. I got off at Black Rock. There, I carried "Spencer" [umbrella], and it rained. I felt singularly filmic, which made an entertaining moment of a time when I should have been raging mad. I wasn't, really. I found it quite interesting. I got off and I paid for a phone call to Niagara Falls, where they checked and verified my petition for entry. Then I went and had a ham sandwich in a small bar where the man was quite angry because I ordered food at 1:00 in the morning. Two truck drivers—a waitress and some sort of woman in a clinging black dress. I think she was feeling failure, too.

Anyway—they put me on another train (this one) which came through at 1:30 or so—and my bad night at Black Rock was over. Not until, however, I had seen and watched all the lights of Canada and great flashes of lightning across the river. It looked as though Canada was on fire. Then I watched a train being shunted and it rained and rained and here I am. Short sleep—but I feel wonderful. I have had breakfast and feel quite up to arriving. The Hudson River is on my right as I sit here and I must give up trying to write as the motion is very upsetting—and just sit and watch as we go by. The view is consistently fabulous—even just now as a garbage dump goes by. There was an old unpainted ship hulk, too—a sailing ship of the old times. And presently a seagull—which is so appropriate that I will close with it.

The Deep Blue Sea

Everyone in Canadian theatre—everyone of a certain age, that is—has a Milly Hall story. Amelia Hall, that incredible actress/manager who, with Sam Payne, started Ottawa's Canadian Repertory Theatre. *I get no kick from Sam Payne; Amelia Hall doesn't thrill me at all . . .* We all used to sing it—because we loved her. And Sam.

One summer, Milly was in summer stock at North Hatley, in Quebec—playing the leading role of Hester in *The Deep Blue Sea*. Hester ultimately kills herself by turning on the gas jets in her fireplace, so Milly decided she would subtly lead the audience towards this tragic event by playing several of her scenes leaning back, with her elbows on the mantel. All through rehearsals, there she was, elbowed along the top of the box that was standing in for the fireplace. Then came the cue-to-cue, the rehearsal when the actors first encounter the set. And there was Hester's fireplace and there was its mantel—its top a good five feet from the floor. Milly was something like five-foot-two—if that. But she stuck to her guns—or, at least, to her mantel—even though there were moments when she gave a slight impression of a bat hanging from

its perch. And the marvellous thing is—being Milly—she somehow made it work!

Rhinoceros

There is only one thing worse than missing a performance. In
1961, I was playing in Ionesco's *Rhinoceros* at Toronto's Civic
Theatre on Queen Street—and those were my drinking days. One
Saturday morning, I awoke in an alcoholic haze, bleared at the
clock—and went into total panic. It was twenty to two, and we had
a matinee at two! I called a cab, set a record for getting dressed,
and dashed unsteadily down the stairs, out the door and into the
waiting taxi. I asked the driver to get me to the theatre *faster than a
speeding bullet.* He complied. We tore through the streets and
pulled up at the stage door just as the old City Hall clock began
striking the hour. Only, it didn't stop at two. It struck nine times.
And that was when I realized that, although I'd been able to see
the hands on my bedside clock, I hadn't been able to tell them
apart. It hadn't been twenty to two at all—but ten after eight. In
the morning. Home I went, had a stiff drink—and decided the
only thing worse than missing a performance is *thinking* you've
missed one.

The Rivals

It was the spring of 1962. I was working at the Central Library
Theatre in a season of repertory. We had come to the opening
night of the third and final play in the repertoire: Sheridan's *The
Rivals.* Already playing Genet's *The Balcony* and N.F. Simpson's
One Way Pendulum, we were all exhausted. Rehearsals of *The
Rivals* had not gone well. I was playing Captain Jack Absolute, and
Cosette Lee was Mrs Malaprop—that heavenly woman who mud-
dles her words. *He was the very pineapple of perfection!* In Act One I
was waiting in the wings, desperately trying to remember my own

first line, when Cosy Lee staggered off into my arms—almost in tears. *They're not laughing!* she wailed. *Mrs Malaprop—and I didn't get a single laugh!* Later, so I was told, Tommy Hooker, the stage manager, took Cosy aside and quietly informed her that, more than likely due to nervousness, she had been meticulously correcting all the malapropisms in her first scene. . . . After that, all was well and the play was critically very well received.

For Love or Money

Every actor eventually dries, but not every actor forgets the line that gives the play its title. At the Red Barn Theatre, Jackson's Point, Ontario—in the summer of 1962—Judy Sinclair and I were in a romantic comedy called *For Love or Money*. In one scene, our characters argued about the future of their relationship. I was to declare: *there are lots of girls who'd go to bed with me at the drop of a hat!* And Judy was to snap back: *well, I wouldn't go to bed with you for love or money!* As always in stock, lines are shaky—and we both fell victim to opening night jitters. When the moment came, all I managed was: *there are lots of girls who'd go to bed with me . . . er . . . uhm . . . lots of them!* This so threw Judy that all she could come up with was: *well, I wouldn't go to bed with you . . . for . . . for* anything! Which so threw *me* that a few lines later, I found myself sneeringly observing—in a total non sequitur: *well, some people are just standing around* waiting *for a hat to drop.* . . . Stage management heard its cue—and a hat fell from the flies all the way to the stage. Judy and I looked at it in horror as the curtains closed and the audience launched into somewhat puzzled applause. *A hat????*

Stone Orchard
1996
Memorial

Robertson Davies

My first encounter with Robertson Davies was in two ways theatrical. In retrospect, it seems like a single moment. To begin with, I was an actor in one of his plays. And then I read *Tempest-Tost,* his wonderfully funny, sometimes sad and often wicked evocation of a small university town's amateur production of Shakespeare's *The Tempest.*

The town in question was based, somewhat more than transparently, on Kingston, Ontario—the home of Queen's University and, it so happened, of the International Players, the repertory company which produced the Davies play in which I appeared.

It was a nightmare. I was twenty-one years old and had to play a man in his forties. To play the greatly old is something of a treat for a young actor. To play the middle-aged is hell on wheels!

The middle-aged—take a look around you, sometime—take a look around you right *now,* for that matter—and you will discover what the young actor also discovers. The middle-aged are all pretending to be twenty!

Now, I ask you: *what is a twenty-one-year-old actor to do?*

I opted for deep disguise. Clothes that did not fit. A hat that did somersaults every time I leaned sideways—and a beard that had a life of its own. A life, I discovered, that was not on my person. The beard, it seemed, had some ambition to play out its existence, like the hat, on the floor of the stage.

Oh, well. You have to suffer public embarrassment sometime—and you might as well get it over with. I did, however, think that *massive* public embarrassment was a little harsh.

The play was called *At My Heart's Core.* I wish it was more often performed, though I would suggest abjuring the use of beards. A portrait of Robertson Davies in the lobby would suffice.

Yes—it is true. Davies's plays are difficult—principally because he uses them as debates. And debates are another kind of theatre—not so much drama or comedy as dialogues in the Platonic manner. Nonetheless, there is a place on the stage for debates—for heated argument and reasoned response. Especially if the words and the ideas are generated by a master. Think of George Bernard Shaw. And think again of Robertson Davies.

He loved the theatre. He thrived in its presence—he adored its panoply—he reflected on its uses—he used its reflections. There is much of theatre, much of what is both theatrical in mood and theatrical in mode, in all his novels.

His love of theatre, his great respect for it, and his profound knowledge of its history and its people were reflected in his person.

I once did an interview with Robertson Davies on the subject of 19th- and early 20th-century theatre in Canada—and one of the most telling images he evoked was of the great English actor-manager John Martin-Harvey.

Martin-Harvey's career bridged the turn of the century, and he often took his company on tour across the US and Canada. Consequently, as a small boy, Robertson Davies saw Martin-Harvey perform. But perhaps more importantly, he saw him walk down the street.

It was winter. There was snow. A figure of majestic proportions strode towards the young boy, who was on his way somewhere in the company of his father.

Everything stopped.

There were scarves flying back in the wind. There was a Trilby hat pulled down above the eyes. Even full-face, there was the power of a gorgeous profile. A cape was appended to the shoulders of a greatcoat. And there was a walking-stick . . .

"Who . . . who . . . who was that!" said the boy.

"*That*," said Rupert Davies, "was Sir John Martin-Harvey—the actor."

Indeed.

Now conjure, if you will, the tea room of the Four Seasons Hotel in Toronto on a late winter's day last year. Bill Whitehead and I are seated directly in line with the entrance. The entrance is angular—it involves steps—and also provides a break from darkness into light. Very theatrical.

All at once, the entire room falls into silence.

Is the angel of death passing through?

No.

It is Robertson Davies.

He wears black. His beard is white—the beard of beards. His hair, beneath a tilted Scot's beret, is also white.

I cannot tell if the coat is an Inverness, with cape attached or a full-blown cape. Certainly, it is capacious—fulsome and useful for making an entrance.

Did he make an entrance?

Of course he did.

Bill and I sat watching. Should we speak?

Of course not.

Any actor knows that.

Robertson Davies went to his table, sat there alone, ordered and drank his tea—and *everyone* knew it. *Everyone.* If any small child had been present and had asked: "who . . . who . . . who is that?"—the whole room could have answered.

Only when making his exit did Professor Davies stop at our table. We rose. People did that. It was automatic in these situations—and we had our conversation standing.

Then he was gone.

I never saw him again. Not in the flesh—only on television—only in the papers.

Now, listen. What had I seen that day?

A great actor?

Yes.

Yes. Because it was a role he played.

The role of Robertson Davies.

Was he a ham?

Not by a long shot.

It was a gigantic presence—yes. But a gigantic presence comes to nothing if there is not a giant inside.

I suspect only Brenda Davies knows what it really cost him to *play* the giant as well as to be one. A lot, I would think. He was a shy man. A quiet man. Oh, yes, he *was*.

I saw him only once without his gigantic presence intact. This was at Massey College in Toronto, when he was Master. Some of us had gathered to discuss something or other—and he came down to the Library wearing a loose sweater, the hair upstanding where his hand had brushed it aside, the beard presentable, but not combed. He'd been working before he came to join us.

We talked for an hour—no more. He barely raised his voice. He was succinct one moment, distracted the next. Then he went away and we all left. On that occasion only—ever—I called him Rob.

Cotignac
1998
Memorial

For Donald and For You

I send these words across the Atlantic, and although I cannot be there to speak them aloud, Bill and I are with you in spirit to celebrate the life of an old and dear friend.

I have known Donald George [Davis] since the late 1940s. Good heavens! *Fifty* years. It seems impossible that any of us has seen so much life—but the joy of it is that our generation boasted so many wonders—and still does. How lucky we are to have lived when we have and to have spent our lives in one another's company. If I were booking passage on a voyage, I could not imagine a better passenger list.

It was in our time that Canadian theatre came of age. It was in our time—and of our crop—that a generation of actors, directors and playwrights stood up, hand in hand, and without apology said: WE ARE HERE. And into this magical time the Davis brothers and their sister Barbara injected a shot of sustaining adrenalin. Through their foresight and generosity, our theatre in English-speaking Canada received a whole new world of golden opportunity—and, above all, of survival.

Donald and I had our fling when we were younger—*very* brief, and mostly just for fun. He was a great companion, sweetly caring and never possessive. In the days of our youth there was a lot of good, healthy rioting. We drank too much, we set our lungs on fire with endless cigarettes, we played our music too loud, we danced and roared through too many nights and saw too many dawns— but, oh! I would not have missed it for all the world. Talk about *chimes at midnight!*

It was wonderful, too, to watch Donald making his way up the professional ladder, becoming such an extraordinary actor and managing all the ages of man with such flare. In what I called his *Wellesian* days, he flourished as never before. The great voice lowered and boomed, the body blossomed, sometimes out of control—but he used both superbly.

I am so proud—and thank heaven Donald knew it—that he performed in my own work, both on radio and in the theatre. When I was told he had been cast in *The Stillborn Lover,* I literally cheered. His portrayal of Michael Riordon, his last role on the stage, was insightful, powerful and properly sinister.

Bill and I join you in saluting Donald George Davis—a good companion, a generous benefactor, a gallant sufferer, a joyous reveller, a wicked and delightful prankster, a grand performer and a loyal friend. It was our privilege to know him. It remains our privilege to remember him.

Stone Orchard
1998
Tribute

Herbert Whittaker

Some years ago, I wrote a drama for an old friend, Frances Hyland. It was set in an asylum and it was called *Can You See Me Yet?* Emerging from one of its performances, I bumped into Herbert Whittaker in the theatre lobby. It was at the National Arts Centre in Ottawa—and there he was, in the famous overcoat and the famous scarf, turning the famous hat in his fingers. "You know what I think, Tiff?" he said. "I think you should try a comedy . . ."

One or two years later, emerging into the lobby from a performance of the play I had written for William Hutt—a rollicking entertainment about John A. Macdonald—I bumped yet again into Herbert Whittaker—overcoat, scarf and hat. "Well, Tiff . . ." he said—and he sighed. "I guess I was wrong."

Me: giving a speech at the Heliconian Club. Herbie rises from his chair while I am still in mid-flight.

"Where are you going?" I ask him, setting down my pages.

"I'm going to see a play," he says. He picks up the overcoat, the scarf, the hat.

"Well—I hope you enjoy it," I say.

"I'm sure I will," he says—and he begins to walk away.

"Goodbye, Herbie!" I shout after him.

The audience laughs.

He doesn't answer.

There is an icy blast of winter air.

The door closes.

A week later, we are at a party.

"Did you enjoy the play?" I ask him.

"No," he says. "I left after the first act."

"Did you?" I say to him. "Well!"

"Yes," he says. Then he smiles. "But they didn't say goodbye."

This is some time ago—early in the 1960s. Herbie is designing a production of *King Lear*. William Hutt is playing the title role. They are rehearsing in Toronto.

Bill Whitehead and I are living in Richmond Hill and I come down into the city to dine with Hutt and to hear his lines.

All through dinner, he is tense and uncommunicative. He hardly says a word. This is not, by a long shot, typical.

After the meal we ascend in the hotel elevator some storeys to Hutt's room. He has hardly spoken of the play at all—except to tell me that Herbie has given it an Arctic setting. It will be known, in the future, as The Eskimo Lear.

Bill hands me the book.

We begin the scene in which Lear is being refused all comfort by his daughter Regan. Bill gets all the way through to *O, reason not the need!* And then he stops dead in his tracks.

He sits with his head in his hands and heaves a sigh.

Then he says: "you realize, of course, that Herbie wants me to wear horns . . ."

Another sigh. Then: "AND BRANDISH A HARPOON!!!"

Howl! Howl! Howl!

One last encounter.

Herbie is directing Thornton Wilder's *A Life in the Sun* at the University Alumnae Theatre. Herbie has loved the play since he saw it in Edinburgh some twenty years before. The sense of occasion is doubled by the presence of Thornton Wilder's sister, Isabel, who has published a new edition of the play following her brother's death. Knowing that Thornton Wilder had been my mentor and that Miss Isabel is an old and valued friend—and that I had been in that Edinburgh production years ago—Herbie goes to special pains to see that I am there to greet Miss Isabel and to speak with her from the stage when the performance is over. It is an enchanting evening and it will be the last time I am likely to see Isabel Wilder before her death—and we have a fine reunion. About two years later, she takes to her bed and, though she is blind now and incapacitated, her companion takes dictation and sends along her letters. One of the last of these was very short, indeed. All it said was: *I'm so old!* Yes. But so alive. Like Herbie.

Here we are—all together—after much time in one another's company. All of us, here in this theatre, celebrating Herbert Whittaker's time with us and our time with him. God bless you, Herbie, and thank you.

And now, I take pleasure in introducing another old friend. Ladies and gentlemen—William Hutt—seventy, this summer—and horny as ever!

And that, Herbie, is all your fault!

Stratford
2000
Article

William Hutt

Looking back over the fifty years since we met, I see a tall figure, graceful but angular in movement and distinctive, too, for its stillness. There was then, and there remains, a feeling of containment that gives a sense of power and energy. I think of toughness, honesty, courage, insight and imagination—all the characteristics that make a great actor, and not incidently, that also make a great friend. I remember—with love, laughter, gratitude and wonder—five decades and more of William Hutt.

In 1953, I shared with him the excitement of performing in the inaugural season of the Stratford Festival of Canada, which has become the most stimulating and prestigious seasonal theatre venue not only in this country, but in the whole of North America. Since then, I have joined the hundreds of thousands who have been mesmerized by William Hutt's unique creativity and daring. He has thrilled audiences in London's West End, on Broadway, on international tours, and, for half a century, in Stratford, Ontario, where from the very beginning he insisted on speaking Shakespeare's lines in unadulterated *Canadian*. The words were, and remain, clear and pure—without unnecessary flourishes or vocal trickery. There is nothing grand in William Hutt. Greatness, yes—but without ostentation. None.

His final Lear in 1997 brought the power of Shakespeare's text to new heights. His performance was on a par with the interpretations provided in our time by John Gielgud and Paul Scofield. As with these giants, his reading was utterly unique—matchless. The same was true of his Prospero, performed in 1999 at the age of seventy-nine. It was an unforgettable farewell to the great roles. But what a legacy of other memories he has left us.

It was in the 1965 Stratford season that he appeared in *Henry IV, Part Two*—and achieved the amazing feat of playing three roles in the same scene. The setting was the barnyard of Justice Shallow's farm, complete with live animals—sheep, geese and dogs. Shallow is one of Shakespeare's greatest comic creations, and his entrance is heralded by the text. We therefore prepared ourselves to see Hutt's version of him with some excitement. What we heard, offstage, was the sound of a chicken laying an egg. Clearly, this was not an everyday chicken nor an everyday egg. This was history's noblest chicken—a majestic queen of the fowl with a diva's vocal range, and she had just laid the most beautiful egg since the beginning of time. At the end of her delirious cackling aria, there was one of the most unforgettable entrances ever made on the Stratford stage—perhaps on any stage. The wonder-egg, itself, materialized before our eyes. Of course, its means of transport was Shallow's extended hand, but the hand, somehow, seemed invisible. Hutt had also played the uproarious chicken and now he played the egg. The audience literally cheered. Oddly enough, I wept. I wept the way one weeps at the most joyous of Mozart's music. I wept at the brilliance of the moment, and the artistry of its creator.

In that same season, it was not an egg that made an entrance onto the Stratford stage—it was pure charm. Utter, absolute charm, in the form of Chekhov's lost and childlike Gaev in *The Cherry Orchard*. Playing Gaev, Hutt seemed to float a few inches above the floorboards, wafting through a dream in search of the perfect snooker shot. It was a poignantly beautiful, accomplished and sustained vision of a man whose society was doomed by the social upheavals taking place in Russia at the turn of the century. What was so poignant was the magnitude of the dream that had been lived by a whole privileged class—until change brought the dream crashing to the ground. William Hutt's Gaev showed us exactly what it was like to have your feet forced down to earth, to be planted firmly and tragically—in reality.

Ten years later, the play was *The Importance of Being Earnest*—with a tall, imposing Lady Bracknell who bore a startling resemblance to Britain's late Queen Mary, grandmother of the present monarch. Not unlike Lady Bracknell, Queen Mary, in her time, was a formidable figure of regal hauteur. It was William Hutt who played the dowager dragon. One of the younger members of the audience was heard to remark: "if I didn't know it was a woman, I'd think it was a man." After the performance, I asked Hutt how he had managed to achieve the woman—and his reply was illuminating. "I didn't concern myself with gender," he told me. "I simply played the character. And because the character is female, I naturally found the woman."

The 1994 Stratford season brought *Long Day's Journey into*

Night—and the miracle of Hutt's magnificent portrayal of James Tyrone, the parsimonious father who had once been a great actor. Never had it been made plainer why his sons both loved and hated their father. All the depths and all the shallows were there, perfectly distilled and perfectly presented. And best of all, for the sake of those who could not see this incredible production, it became the basis of a feature film. *Long Day's Journey* was but one occasion when Hutt was matchlessly paired with our greatest actress, Martha Henry. Together over time, they have created tragic and comic married couples and wonderful sparring partners—not only in the classic plays of Chekhov, Molière and Shakespeare, but in modern plays, some of which have been written especially for them, including my own *The Stillborn Lover*.

When we first met, Hutt was thirty, I was twenty. It was 1950, and he was already one of the leading actors of the country—having returned from the battlefields of World War II with the Military Medal. He had enlisted in 1941 to become a member of the 7th Light Field Ambulance, and was decorated for his bravery in the Italian campaign in 1944 when, under mortar bombardment, he volunteered to push through the minefields in order to find a suitable location for a temporary field hospital.

Our meeting occurred while I was an acting student in Toronto. The school had received a call asking for a juvenile actor to play in Sidney Howard's *The Silver Cord*—a drama about a possessive mother and her two sons. I auditioned and was cast as the younger son, the one most disastrously tied to his mother. The director was William Hutt. Under his guidance—incisive, witty and sure—the play was a hit. And my career as an actor was given a marvellous beginning.

Ultimately, I was to blossom as a writer and, as a result, it was my good fortune to write more than one role inspired by Hutt's talents. These he has played on television, the stage and in film. Whatever good fortune I have had has been augmented by his presence.

In the 1970s my partner, Bill Whitehead, and I wrote a television series about the building of the Canadian Pacific Railway—adapted from two excellent books by Canada's most popular historian, Pierre Berton. Hutt played our first prime minister, John A. Macdonald. His John A. was wickedly funny, powerful and almost unbearably moving. Shortly afterwards, Hutt took Macdonald onto the stage in a play I wrote especially for him: *John A.—Himself.* As it turned out, Macdonald and Hutt were well matched. By then, the actor had become Artistic Director of the Grand Theatre in London, Ontario—and thus by necessity, had become part politician. On the other hand, John A. Macdonald is depicted in one of the political cartoons of his time as the consummate actor, playing his starring role in *Her Majesty's Theatre at Ottawa.* Here, the match took on magic.

Given the player-politician character of both men, I structured the play as an evening of Victorian theatre, presented as if Macdonald were, indeed, a great actor-manager on the eve of his farewell performance. The first act dealt with his public life, and was presented as Victorian music hall. Parliament was a troupe of acrobats whose human pyramid kept collapsing. The press was represented by a ventriloquist who could make his Macdonald doll say anything the press required in order to shoot him down. There were patter songs in the style of Gilbert and Sullivan and a production number about the building of our national railroad, featuring its architect as a magician. But even better was to come.

In the second act, a Victorian melodrama, Macdonald's life began to fall apart. Public uproar over his political conniving in the building and completion of the railroad; private despair over his crippled daughter and his faltering marriage. Both sets of pressures took him straight to the bottle. The hair on the back of my neck still rises as I remember the first rehearsal of a scene in which Lady Agnes Macdonald denounces his behaviour. She was played by Jennifer Phipps with the all-out fervour of a great Victorian tragedienne. Macdonald stood listening as she pulled out all the stops. When Jenny was done, Hutt paused and then reached into his pocket for a handful of coins, which he tossed onto the stage at her feet—the ultimate ironic accolade for a great performance in 19th-century theatre. It was electrifying, and remains one of my prime memories of Hutt, the inventive actor—the writer's best friend.

Bill Hutt has the ability and the willingness to know his friends as well as he knows the characters he plays. He has the integrity, the courage and the honesty to tell them when and how they are heading in the wrong direction. He also has the generosity to support them whenever they are right. This I know, because I am one of his most fortunate friends.

There have been times in my life when, as with John A. Macdonald, despair has driven me to the bottle. One of the most disastrous of these times occurred in the 1970s, after my first two published novels were all but ignored by critics and public alike, and when everything else I had submitted to publishers had been savagely rejected. *You're nothing! You don't know how to do this! You can't, because you haven't an ounce of talent!*

Well, Bill Hutt would have none of that, in my behalf.

None.

I had gone far down into drink and despair. Gone so far down that I could not write. Circumstance had left me alone in the farmhouse I shared with Bill Whitehead—and I did not want to be alone. So, I called up some friends and invited them to dinner. Some came from Toronto, an hour and a half away. Bill Hutt drove all the way from Stratford—almost three hours, by car. And what they all found on arrival, of course, was neither dinner nor a convivial host—but a man who could hardly stand or talk.

But that man can remember that night—and will never forget it. As Margaret Atwood and Graeme Gibson stood amazed in the doorway behind me, William Hutt turned in the courtyard beside the open front door of his car and yelled at me . . .

Yelled at me . . .

"You bastard—if you give up now, with all your goddamned talent—I hope you roast in hell."

He got in, slammed the door and drove off—in a cloud of summer dust. He knew, you see, the value of punctuation!

Did I recover? You bet I did. Because I came in time to understand the true meaning of love. Love is . . . *push*. Towards *survival*. As parents say to dying children: *"LIVE!"*

Be.

Well . . . I have *been* ever since that moment in the courtyard. Thanks in large measure to the goading and the support of friends such as William Hutt.

Are there words to express my gratitude? Probably not. What can I say to William Hutt besides *Bravo!* And a standing ovation—always and ever. With pleasure—with thanks—and with blessings.

Stratford
1999
Speech

Zeroing In on Arthur Miller

I was nineteen when I first encountered Mister Miller—not in person, but in the form of his play *Death of a Salesman*. I had left school and was working in the foundry of what was then Massey-Harris. I didn't have much spending money, but enough for a seat in the upper balcony of the Royal Alex.

I came out of the theatre in a trance—and since then, I have seen or read almost everything Miller has ever written. And finally, when I was twenty-six. I found myself in the same room with him. We didn't actually meet then, because the room was one in which the McCarthy hearings were taking place—those infamous witch hunts set in motion by the House Committee on Un-American Activities—and Mister Miller was on trial.

It was 1957, and I was working as an actor—in a touring company that had reached Washington, D.C. Except on matinee days, I was seated in those chambers, watching a different kind of theatre unfold—and marvelling at the dignity with which Arthur Miller endured the badgering.

It was over thirty years later that I had lunch with Arthur Miller. Well, to be truthful, we were several tables apart in the same Toronto restaurant. We were both at a Harbourfront International Festival of Authors, and I was confident that at last we would meet. But not at lunch. That would be unforgiveable—to walk over to his table and interrupt his meal. And so, with eyes riveted on the man, I simply ate my shrimp cocktail, and yearned.

And that evening I learned that immediately after lunch Arthur Miller had left Toronto.

I was heartbroken—and several friends at the Festival tried their best to cheer me up.

One of these was publisher Louise Dennys, who fully sympathized with my disappointment, and so a few years later, Louise called me up with the news that Arthur Miller was in town again—and again, reading at Harbourfront. Furthermore, he would be at Louise's apartment afterwards. If I could not make the reading, could I join them later? *Could I!* I had to forgo the reading because I was sitting with a friend who had just returned home from a difficult time in hospital—but it turned out I would therefore be only a few blocks from the rendezvous. Louise gave me her phone number, and told me to start calling around 10:30 in the evening. As soon as there was an answer, I would receive precise directions—and I would finally get to meet Arthur Miller.

I called at 10:30—10:40—10:50 . . . and every few minutes, until after midnight. Obviously something had gone wrong with the plans.

The next day, I discovered what. It was not her unlisted home number Louise Dennys had given me, but—inadvertently—her office number. Well.

A few nights ago, I stood in Arthur Miller's presence once again—but once again, we did not meet. He was accepting a lifetime award on the telecast of the Tony Awards, which Bill and I watched while having supper. Mister Miller was asking the powers of the theatre world to have the courage to take more chances on new playwrights, and I, having risen from my chair, was standing in my kitchen, applauding.

Listening, that night, I was reminded of something Mister Miller had written in his autobiography, *Timebends*—a passage concerning the arrival of television in the 1950s—a time when he perceived that the written word and the arts in general were losing their coinage. *The whole country seemed to be devolving,* he wrote, *into a mania for the distraction it called entertainment, a day and night mimicry of art that menaced nothing, redeemed nothing and meant nothing but forgetfulness.*

Nothing.

Zero.

That's the number of times I've met Arthur Miller, the man. I cannot count the number of times, however, I have met the greatness of his genius and of his spirit. Mister Miller—I salute you.

Stratford
June 11, 1964
Journal

This is only a token entry—in order to remark that I have been here for three days now and was here for three days last week, as well. All in order to secure as many voices for my summer [radio] series as possible. After many title ideas, we settled on "Taping Stratford"—which, having been a suggestion of my own, I was pleased to accept. Thirteen half-hours all told—and I am leaving Stratford with some excellent interviews—a list which I will make below. I have stayed on both occasions with Leo Ciceri—who put me up with great calm and good humour. What a grim time it is, now, for them all. They are deep in the throes of final rehearsals and open on Monday with *Richard II*. Tuesday with *Bourgeois Gentilhomme*. Wednesday with *Lear*. The outcome remains to be seen . . . But my interview with [Michael] Langham was a great moment for me and I fell completely under his spell. He is an unqualified genius . . . he absolutely stunned me with his humility—his sureness—his temerity—his brilliance—his humour—his questioning. His thoughts on *Lear* are lucid—absolute and have just the touch of impracticality.

Stone Orchard
1987
Programme notes

Scandals

The theatre is a powerful resource of social criticism. Playwrights from Aristophanes to Osborne have created a brilliant theatrical looking glass, into which society has stared, amused and appalled by what it has seen.

Not all societies have been forgiving. Aristophanes was run out of town and so, very nearly, was Osborne. But, if the proper study of mankind is man, then no one has delivered a more scathing, savage and comic image of mankind than its playwrights. At its very best, such theatre is merciless. It must be merciless. Tempered, it loses its power to move.

Very often, the social playwright's impetus is rage; but rage can produce the most wonderful comedy. And comedy—in spite of Ibsen—is very often the social playwright's chosen mode. If we can be made to laugh, we can be caught off guard.

Aristophanes, whose politics today would be called right wing, was enraged almost at every turn by his fellow men and he chose to debunk their character in some of the funniest social satires ever written—though *funny* may not be quite the word. In *The Frogs* he attacks his great contemporary, Euripides—a writer whom, today, we could call a humanist. The attack was so vicious, in fact, that Euripides went into exile. In *The Clouds*, Aristophanes' victim is Socrates, whom he turns into a villain and, though it is very much a comedy, this violation of the great philosopher's character is every bit as outrageous as Shakespeare's villainizing of Richard III. And every bit as entertaining. Perhaps Aristophanes' greatest comedy is *The Birds*, from which we get the phrase *cloud cuckoo-land*. In this play, he lampoons religion. Clearly, nothing was sacred to this man; not his friends, not his religion and not, most certainly, his society.

Between the time of the great Greek dramatists and the time of Osborne, Stoppard and Sondheim, there has been a handful of extraordinary playwrights whose genius for social insights has been coupled with a genius for comedy. The names of Molière, Sheridan, Gogol, Wilde and Shaw come instantly to mind.

There is nowhere in the whole of literature a more scathing portrait of hypocrisy than Molière provides in *Tartuffe*; nowhere a more damning portrait of intellectual humbug than in Sheridan's little masterpiece, *The Critic*; nowhere a more accurate and wicked portrait of venal bureaucracy than in Gogol's *The Inspector General*; nowhere a more devastating put-down of social pretensions than in Wilde's *The Importance of Being Earnest* and nowhere a more corrosive portrait of social attitudes to women than in Shaw's *Mrs Warren's Profession*.

Each and every one of these plays has a place in the permanent repertoire of the world's theatres—with very good reason. Every society, since time began, has been rife with hypocrisy, intellectual humbug, a corrupt bueaucracy, social pretension and degrading social attitudes, whether they be directed at women's rights or the rights of a dozen other constituent parts of the social structure, from the racial to the political. These things we have always with us and our attention cannot be drawn too often to their presence.

As for muckraking, the subject of *The School for Scandal*, that, too, is always with us. The very first words in this play, spoken by Lady Sneerwell, the queen of London's scandalmongers, refer to an institution we will recognize too well: the yellow press. *The paragraphs, you say, Mr Snake, were all inserted?*

Indeed, as you shall discover, they have been. Our playwright, Sheridan, has seen to that. And all you have to imagine is a society not the least unlike our own, hanging on every word that is read in *Private Eye*, the *National Enquirer* and *People* magazine.

The Snakes and the Sneerwells of *The School for Scandal* are all still with us. You only have to give them their current names. For my own part, I would not dare to do that here in print. But, if you will meet me in the bar at intermission, I can not only give you their names, I can also point them out. And I will do this, I must add, for more than your edification. I will do it for your protection. That is, if you value whatever you have gained, thus far, in social acceptance.

Stone Orchard
1988
Programme notes

Murder in our Time

Confronted by T.S. Eliot's *Murder in the Cathedral*, I find myself wishing I could say: "this play is out of date. It tells of horrors all but forgotten. . . ." If only this were true. The fact is, *Murder in the Cathedral* might have been written yesterday.

The events depicted here, the politics portrayed, the crisis of confrontation and the violence re-enacted, all have their present-day counterparts. Surely, this is the best of reasons for wishing this play was out of date. But nothing, it seems, has changed since

Murder in the Cathedral was first produced in 1935—let alone since 1170, the year in which Thomas Becket was murdered at Canterbury. In the interim, nothing postive appears to have been done about the use and the abuse of power. Certainly, nothing effective has been done to rid us of those who make their living meddling with our right to live in peace. Fear is still the universal governor.

Think of Ireland, think of Israel, think of Lebanon, think of Nicaragua. The names themselves are drenched in blood. A dozen Beckets perish every week, the victims of church and state; the victims, above all else, of implacable ambitions tricked out in words like *patriot, unity, homeland* and *self-determination.* Meanwhile, men and women of vision and courage—the would-be makers of social reform, the advocates of positive action—continue to be the victims of reactionary governments, of increasing refinements in the torture chamber and of the assassin's sword. In the years since Eliot's play was first produced, the world has borne the loss of Gandhi, King and Steve Biko—each an apostle of radical but peaceful social change and all, the victims of violence.

What were you doing when you heard that Kennedy had been shot? Which Kennedy do you mean? you are forced to ask. Now, as we approach the latter days of the most sophisticated century in human history, this is how we count our awareness of time. By recalling what we were doing when presidents and senators and priests have been murdered. What were you doing when they killed Benigno Aquino? Indira Gandhi? Where were you when they tortured Jacobo Timerman, turned the key on Martha Kumsa, kidnapped Terry Waite?

As things turn out, the play you are about to see is not a comment on the past, at all; it is just a mirror image of the present: what were you doing when you heard that Becket had been murdered in the cathedral at Canterbury?

The seeds of Thomas Becket's murder were sown in the age-old clash of church and state; in the right of each to exist without the interference of the other. But there are other aspects here, perhaps more subtle than the simplistic theme of assassination for political expediency. Think of Martin Luther King, Jr. The analogy is alarming. On the eve of their martyrdom, each of them speaks of his death; each of them gauges precisely why they will die—and, to our sorrow, why they must. T.S. Eliot, writing in the time between their deaths, has provided a profile of all such martyrs that defines precisely why it is always men and women of integrity who pay the ultimate price of our appalling self-interest.

Murder in the Cathedral presents the word *integrity* in its other context: namely, that every act of violent subversion requires the added subversion of someone's integrity. Someone's integrity had to be tampered with in order to accomplish the killing of Martin Luther King, Jr.—just as in the case of Thomas Becket.

But it goes beyond that. Think of Henry II's famous cry of frustration: *will no one rid me of this meddlesome priest!* It would be too coy for words to deny the alarming echo of that cry in a more recent cry from Washington, D.C. Will no one rid me of this meddlesome regime! This way, the names of Hakim, Poindexter and North have entered the common lexicon. Their historical counterparts appear in the second act of *Murder in the Cathedral.*

"No one regrets the necessity for violence more than we do," one of Becket's murderer's says. Unhappily, there are times when violence is the only way in which social justice can be secured. Why do assassins—committing the murder of individuals, states and peoples—always use these words to justify their acts? Perhaps the answer lies in the words of Thornton Wilder, one of Eliot's contemporaries: *Cruelty is nothing more than a failure of the imagination.*

And so, indeed, is violence.

Stone Orchard
1991
Article

Our Town

It always comes as something of a shock to discover that plays and books we now regard as classics were not immediate hits. Such was the case with *Our Town*.

Finished during the autumn months of 1937 while Thornton Wilder was in Switzerland, the play was sent on, scene by scene, to the American director Jed Harris. He had recently achieved a triumph on Broadway with Wilder's adaptation of Ibsen's *A Doll's House*.

Harris was the wunderkind of the American stage throughout the 1930s. Something of a bully, opinionated in the extreme and the object of much star enmity, he was nonetheless an undoubted genius. Daring and endlessly inventive, he had moved from one success to another as if he could not fail.

But things, this time, did not go well. Harris pulled out all the emotional stops and was vituperative during rehearsals. He kept complaining that the play was overwritten and overintellectualized. He and Wilder made war. At one point during their pre-Broadway run, Harris removed several large sections of the play, wrenching them from the text as if he was a butcher performing amputations in an operating theatre. Wilder, in shock, said to Harris: "what have you done to my beautiful prose?" And Harris replied: "prose doesn't play!"

After the opening in Princeton, one reviewer wondered what Harris, *the wonder boy of Broadway, saw in this disjointed, bittersweet affair of small-time New Hampshire life.*

Business and reviews in Boston were no better. The play seemed destined for failure. It was also in Boston that disaster of another kind overtook the company. Jed Harris had been living with Rosamond Pinchot, a wealthy socialite, and without warning, Pinchot committed suicide. Harris considered abandoning *Our Town,* but other voices prevailed and the play at last opened in New York at the Henry Miller Theatre on February 3, 1938. Sensing imminent failure, the producers had withdrawn the original New York booking, and the Henry Miller had been engaged for only one week. Everyone prepared for the worst.

But the worst did not happen.

New York stood up and cheered and four months later *Our Town* and Thornton Wilder were awarded the Pulitzer Prize.

Aside from his adaptation of the Ibsen play, Wilder's only forays into the theatre prior to *Our Town* had been through the medium of one-act plays. The most famous of these is *The Happy Journey from Camden to Trenton.* In this short and beautiful play, Wilder explored the theatrical techniques and devices he was later to augment in writing *Our Town*: the absence of a formal set, actors in plain dress, working without props and a narrator called the Stage Manager.

Happy Journey tells of the Kirby family's trip by automobile through New Jersey on a summer's day. Their car is portrayed by four kitchen chairs. During the course of their travels, they pass not only from early morning to dusk, but also through a lifetime of human situations. The central figure is Ma Kirby, and Wilder liked to demonstrate the difference between an author's intention and his audience's perception of what he is up to by telling the following anecdote.

Backstage on opening night were two of Wilder's oldest friends—both of them women. Suspecting the truth, each one claimed to have recognized elements of Thornton's mother in the character of Ma Kirby. Wilder neither confirmed nor denied their claims, but he was deeply amused by the difference in their perceptions.

The first friend said: "oh, Thornton! How wonderful it is that at last you've been able to pay tribute to your dear and wonderful mother! Such a loving portrait . . ."

The second friend said: "well, Thornton—I see that you've finally put the old battle-axe down on paper!"

Which interpretation was correct?

To Thornton Wilder, it couldn't have mattered less. What the author writes and what the audience takes away from an evening of theatre may be two different things. That is not the point. The point is to carry away something, anything vibrant, and to make it your own.

The theatre, for Thornton Wilder, was the greatest of all art forms because it provides *the most immediate way in which one human being can share with another the experience of being alive.*

Writing specifically about *Our Town*, he quoted Molière, who had said that for the theatre, all he needed was *a platform and a passion or two.* Wilder transcribed this as *five square feet of boarding and the passion to know what life means to us.* He also said that *Our Town* is *an attempt to find a value above all price for the smallest events in our daily life.*

But what have the smallest events in our daily life got to do with that passion he was talking about?

Just about everything. As Wilder demonstrated in *Our Town.*

"I am writing the most beautiful little play you can imagine," he wrote to his friend Gertrude Stein in 1937. "It's a little play with all the big subjects in it; and it's a big play with all the little things of life lovingly impressed into it."

Here in Grover's Corners we have life as it has been lived since humankind first gathered around the earliest fires. Even to this day we continue to gather there in order to endure those elements of nature that most alarm and threaten us: the cold, the dark, the beast at the door and starvation. And more, the subject of our conversation beside those fires is still the vastness of what we do not know. Meaning must be wrenched from the meanest of information—namely, that we live and we are here. And one day we will die. This is what we share as human beings.

"We live in what is," Wilder once said, "but we find a thousand ways not to face it." It was his belief as a writer that theatre strengthens our faculty to face what is. With *Our Town*, using the simplest of recipes, he produced a portrait of human life from birth to death, and he employed the sparest of theatrical tricks and trappings to place that portrait before us. Wilder never pretended for an instant that what we are seeing is anything but theatre. Yet a moment's pause will remind us that we have not come here to be swept back into reality. Quite the opposite. We have come here seeking, with some deliberation, a theatrical reflection of our lives that will clarify their meaning.

In virtually every play he wrote, Thornton Wilder refused us the comfort of realism. Veracity—yes. Reality—no. Part of the magic of *Our Town* lies in Wilder's blatant use of his audience to complete the gestures begun by his players. In this, he was with Shakespeare, the playwright he most admired. In conversation, he used the words *recall, remember* and *conjure up* incessantly. And in all his writing, too, whether for stage or page, he invited us to do the same. It isn't just that he urged us to recall the past. The past in itself is not what's important, but what it meant to be born is important—and what it meant when we first saw grass and knew we were alive.

"It all goes by so fast," someone says in *Our Town*. By the end of this performance we will have seen whole lives go by in a few short hours. That, of course, is one of the tricks of theatre. But also one of the tricks of life.

"All things into all may range," wrote Euripides. "And never that which is shall die." This might have been the motto of *Our Town*—whose veracity is about to be tested again, as it has been tested ten thousand times since it was first produced in 1938. As with *Hamlet*, hardly a day goes by that does not, somewhere, contain a production of this play. And, of course—as with *Hamlet*—there is some good reason for that.

After all, here we all are, yet again about to share with one another the experience of being alive.

"Do any human beings ever realize life while they live it—every, every minute?" Emily asks at the end of this play. Thornton Wilder's most constant urging was: *pay attention.*

Pay attention—every, every minute.

Findley as Playwright

Stone Orchard
1970
Radio Drama

The first of Tiff's plays to be produced was a docudrama written for radio, and broadcast in 1971 on CBC's *Ideas*. It was called *The Journey* and was based on our summer of travel in 1969, when we packed the car with camping equipment and a collapsible kayak and took a round-about route to the Northwest Territories. We drove first to the coast of Maine, to recharge our energies at the Findley family's favourite resort, The Atlantic House. We then headed west through Upper New York State—visiting the bizarre contradictions of wilderness campgrounds endowed with all the urban amenities, followed by a rapid passage through the metropolitan might of Chicago. Finally, turning north in Montana, we traversed Alberta and entered the wilds of the Territories.

I used to tease Tiff over the fact that although he was cast as the passenger in the car, the driver was not played by me, but by an old friend, Gillie Fenwick. I didn't really mind, because Gillie did a splendid job, even though most of his lines were simply announcements of readings from the car's odometer.

It was Frances Hyland who played female roles in the piece. She was a dear friend and drinking buddy of Tiff's, and had preceded me through my Saskatchewan high school and university days. Frannie was magnificent as the epitome of the American campground denizen, as the essence of Chicago and as the spirit of the Native Canadians we met in the North. What follow are three excerpts from *The Journey*. WFW.

The Journey
A Montage for Radio

DRIVER: You write this down, will you? Mileage: 19906. We have to try to make that camp—what'sitsname—at Thompson Lake, New York.

(SOUND: *Car in motion; sparse traffic.*)

DRIVER: Write this down, will you? 20192. We're there.

(MUSIC: *A blast of acid rock, fade and hold under.*)

WOMAN: Hi, honey! Listen—I jus' dropped over t' see if ya could spare me some water. Cookin' water's all I wan'. I mean, c'n anyone find a cookin' water tap roun' this place? Chris! It's gotta be two hours ago I sent my two girls lookin'. But, you know kids, eh? Never senda girl ona fool's erran'. They prob'ly got picked up. I tell ya—that Marilyn! Listen, haven' ya got some cookin' water, fella? Wait a minute! Isn' that Darleen over there now? DARLEEN! Pardon me . . . (*Fading off.*) DARLEEN! Where was you, honey? Where the hell'd you get to? (*Coming back on.*) Sorry again, I forgot my pot, for heaven's sake. (*Going off.*) Listen, you huzzy! Where's your sister? Ya didn' get in nobody's Traila-Home, did ya? I've told you, Darleen: no gettin' inside a strange Traila-Home! Anythin' could happen to ya. Anythin'! Now get back in that tent. An' do up your shirt!

(SOUND: *Fade in moving car.*)

DRIVER: Write this down, will you? 21329.

(MUSIC: "Chicago," *Dixieland version. Establish and fade under.*)

WOMAN: (*As if a rather vapid airline stewardess were welcoming her passengers aboard.*) Chicago: seat of Cook County, is the nation's second largest city—the most important Great Lakes port and the world's railroad terminal. Chicago is now the leading producer of steel, telephone equipment, appliances, electrical equipment, plastic products and diesel engines— and is world leader in nuclear research. CHICAGO: world's largest, biggest, leading, first, best, boldest, brightest, only, longest, shortest, fastest, plastic, electric, nuclear city in the whole god damn world!

(MUSIC: *Up to top.*
SOUND: *Car speeds into distance.*
SOUND: *Red-wing blackbirds.*
MUSIC: *Buffy Sainte-Marie:* "Groundhog.")

TIFF: Somewhere in northern Alberta, between High Level and Meander River, we saw Mary walking by the road. Up there, you call it the Great Dusty, but it's really the Mackenzie Highway. Anyway, Mary was carrying a small suitcase and she had a raincoat draped over her head—I suppose to keep the dust out of her hair.

WOMAN: It's Rae I'm going to. Rae.

TIFF: We didn't know where that was, yet.

WOMAN: Down north there. You go along over the boundary

there, over to Cameron—keep going to Enterprise there, don't turn . . . then you do turn. See? Along over to the ferry there—the River—and keep going down. Don't stop—and then you do stop 'cause you gotta turn down real north there, and that's it. There. That's all. That's it, there. Rae.

TIFF: It sounded like instructions on how to get to the grocery store, five blocks away, but—in fact—what she'd described was closer to 450 miles.

WOMAN: Say! Can I use this ride! Hadda truck ride—guy said he was headed for Enterprise 'n' then broke down. Hadda picture of walkin' all-a-way home, you know. I guess I coulda done it—but I'm sure glad I don' hafta.

DRIVER: What is Rae? Tell me.

WOMAN: Reserve. You know? We got a school there. But they're gonna move our ass, now. You know—some road or somethin'. 'Cause they wants assess to the lake there. Drillin' things—diggin' things—bargin' things. I dunno. Like, I heard about this, you know, when I was up South. 'Cause I thought I might make it away, there—get to Edmonton, you know. But, I got word from my mom to come home now; we needs you. So I got this truck, you see. But he broke down and here I am with you, now. I tell ya! All I want now is to get home. If you can get me to Rae that'll do it. 'Cause all I want is to get there.

DRIVER: Write this down, will you? We got there.

(SOUND: *Cross fade car to loons.*)

Stratford
1999
Notes

The Living Art

I like the world *playwright*. I like it because it so perfectly describes the difference between playwrighting and other forms of writing. A poem, very often, is *composed*. A novel embraces all three dimensions on a flat page. Short fiction is more or less the same, except there are strictures, as well. Journalism, of course, has all those ghastly deadlines, but playwrighting is about STRUCTURE. You MAKE a play, and you make it out of DIALOGUE—ACTION—SETTINGS—LIGHTING—MUSIC—SOUND EFFECTS. And you share it in all these ways with a living present audience. Actors are your allies; directors are like guides who lead you all through the dark until you can find the light.

There is nothing—*nothing*—on the face of the earth that equals the live performance of a play—an opera—a ballet. Playwrighting is a living art.

Stone Orchard
April 8, 1968
Journal

In 1968, a year before the northern trip that led to *The Journey*, Tiff began work on a project that was to last eight years, and that would culminate in the first theatrical production of a Findley play. During that period he published his second novel, *The Butterfly Plague*, but was unable to find a publisher for any of the novels he began in those years. And so, he turned to television, working on adaptations of Mazo de la Roche's *Jalna* series, and Pierre Berton's *The National Dream*, the saga of the building of the Canadian Pacific Railway.

The first version of his play centred on a missionary, Cassandra Wakelin, and on her family. After many false starts, Tiff decided to write it as a radio play, and it was produced by CBC's *Ideas* in 1973 under the title *Missionaries*. He still wanted to see it on stage however, and was thrilled when he was invited to do further work on it while acting as the first playwright-in-residence at the National Arts Centre in Ottawa. The appointment was made by our old friend and former theatre colleague, Jean Roberts, who was then a director of theatre at the NAC, and it was our other old friend and colleague, Marigold Charlesworth, who was director of English theatre and who ultimately directed Tiff's completed play at the NAC in 1976.

By then, Tiff had taken Cassandra and her family into an asylum for the insane, and called the play *Can You See Me Yet?* It was Frances Hyland who played Cassandra. What follow are a series of journal entries chronicling the eight-year journey from page to stage. WFW.

As to the play (made possible by a Canada Council grant) I can hardly believe it is happening. I think I have wanted this play—somewhere inside me—for at least twenty years—at least since I was first moved and taken by a theatre experience—watching Julie Harris and Ethel Waters in *Member of the Wedding* in 1951, when I first realized that it was the *play* that drew me onto the stage—and the actors, performing it, who focused my attention on it—that they were *not* it—that it was itself. Before that, plays were vehicles for actors, in my experience. Of course, only great actors like Harris and Waters could have shown me this—because they, too, were bent on the play and not on themselves. Now I have it in my grasp. It is a great moment.

Stone Orchard
April 25, 1968
Journal

There was another letter from Thornton [Wilder] yesterday. He
seems pleased with the prospect of my writing a play. "Beware,
however, of regarding yourself theatrically . . ." he writes. . . .
Then follows a passage on writing:

> For this play:
> Select your subject carefully. One very real and close to
> you—not autobiographically but inwardly. Take long walks—
> view it from all sides—test its strength—its suitability for the
> stage. Then start blocking out the main crises or stresses. I sug-
> gest (though all writers are different) that you don't begin at the
> beginning, but at some scene within the play that has already
> begun to "express itself in dialogue." Don't hurry. Don't do
> too much a day. In my experience I've found that when I do a
> faithful enforced job of writing every day, the material for the
> next day's writing moves into shape while I'm sleeping.
> Never hesitate to throw away a whole week's good hard-won
> writing if a better idea presents itself.

Stone Orchard
October 9, 1972
Journal

People don't just "say" things. They have to FIND A WAY to
say them. That is the essence of good writing—on the one hand—
and HELL of writing drama, on the other.

Stone Orchard
October 18, 1972
Journal

This morning I woke up with a sense of "new day" that has pervaded not only all my thoughts—but my sense of physical well being and extends to the very *weather* beyond me which is crystal cold and blue and clear. The sun shone—and the wind (which has been constant and battering for days) has died. I watched Bill leaving and for the first time in weeks (I could really say "months") I felt undepressed—but only expectant and hopeful about his going.

This last should be explained. But it's simple: it only means that for a very, *very* long time I have felt incapable of matching his contribution to our welfare—that only *he* was capable of work—or of success—or of bringing in a living—that everything *I* did was either certain to fail or that it was such a minimal contribution that it was almost shaming to offer it.

All right. The very worst things that can happen to a writer have happened to me. But, this morning, getting up—feeling different in so many ways—I realized that the weight had dropped—the weight of failure and defeat had dropped away *in toto*—and I could look at it the way you can look at some terrible sickness you've brought up or at the bandages from a wound that has festered—and see that it is ugly and sick and that it reminds you of how ill you were—of what was in you—the sickness and the festering, and the foreign body syndrome saves you: you look at it and see that "it is gone—it is over—it is out of you." And I found that for the first time in all these weeks and months of being *literally ill* (I guess there's a pun in there!!!) I could be positive—that I could face my contribution and say: "yes—this is either what I am doing or what I will do and certainly these are the things I must do."

I have laughed all morning.

I went out and fed all the birds and came in and watered all the plants and while I was dressing and washing and showering I kept thinking—*this* has been wrong—what a bad idea *that* was—I should never have tried to do *that*—or *this* or the other. *THIS* is what I must do. And God help me (and I won't tell Bill or anyone until it's done) the right play for me to write—the *real* play came in that way the very best things always do—with a rush—almost complete in an instant—as if I had flushed all the bad ideas and the overburdened—over intellectualized—*constipated* ideas out of me and this new fresh water of ideas rushed in and was at home in me—everything sweet and clean and the sourness and the bitterness and meanness all gone.

I don't dare put it on paper—except to say that it comes out of *my* life—and in *my* memories—my own realities—a memory play which is absolutely honest—uncomplicated and filled with the people I really do know—not with people I've only seen in glances and briefly. It has the same setting—the porch and the lawns of my other plays—but it is not so embittered or so hard on its people. *I* am the centre—an autobiographical *me* who assembles the people and the time and the remembered events of a summer. And it's Canadian—and it's filled with all my own images of quiet and despair—and yet—for the first time since *Crazy People*—all of it sighted through *love*. It's a period piece—of both here and now and of the pre-war summers *then* that seem to hold the core of all my writing and of me as a person.

Ottawa
January 1975
Journal

In November of 1974, the role of playwright-in-residence was created by Jean Roberts at the National Arts Centre, Ottawa, and I was asked to fill it for three months—until the end of January 1975.

Roughly speaking, there were four separate facets to the job. One: to complete a final draft of the play I'd submitted to the NAC, called *Missionaries*. Two: to observe all the pre-production activities surrounding Jean Gascon's production of *Riel* by John Coulter. Three: to see and meet as many visiting artists as possible and to see all theatre and musical productions available. Four: to read plays for the Centre—and to submit comments . . .

Riel opened at the NAC on Monday, January 13, 1975. Gascon, his actors (especially Albert [Millaire]) and his cohorts did a masterful job . . . creating a great sense of reality and urgency around the people—and the trial of Riel in particular became a tour de force. It was a fascinating experience—and, so far as I was concerned—invaluable.

In the meantime I was writing—long hours—often late into night and morning—on my own play. It went very badly for a long time. I drank too much—fretted too long—avoided coming to grips with my people—I guess because I didn't want them really to be the people they are—which is to say they are not the best of company. I became quite ill at one point and had to face the very real possibility of cancer in the prostate gland. This created chaos and a great deal of self-indulgent drinking and self-pity. I behaved very badly about it all, and was very sorry to discover how few mature resources I had to draw on of courage and common sense. . . . WFW [Bill] had come, in the meantime, to Ottawa— and the morning of January 22nd he took me to [the urologist's] office where I waited from 11:00 a.m. to 12:30 p.m. before I got in to see him . . . Long silences—lots of poking and prodding— dreadful—and then the happy news that, as WFW later said to Marigold, I was not "dying of cancer"—I was "dying of prostatitis!" Ultimately I discovered this problem will be with me for life, but . . . it is one of those ailments that is a bother but that doesn't normally serialize into a cancerous situation. That was the end of that and I got on with my work. . . .

Then, as if an abscess had broken, I began to write again— rewriting the whole play from scratch. I wrote day and night— with time off to collapse (literally) in between sessions. Many mornings I finished work at 7:00 or 7:30 and went through snow and a couple of blizzards to have breakfast in the Queen's Restaurant, whose eggs, toast and coffee and whose radiators near the windows I will never forget.

All through this blitz I had a compelling sense of wonder that the play was somehow using me to get itself written. This in essence was the fact. It had waited so long—fulminating—gurgling—lying quiet, foetus-like—baby-like—now there was labour and birth . . . I don't give a damn how much people talk (myself included) about the intellectual creation of order—there comes a moment in the creation of every book and poem and play when its own integrity takes precedence—and *your* integrity—your consciousness of being in charge—must be set aside. Later, you can look the whole thing over and make new decisions—qualify—set things in order, etc. but the "moment" must come—and in that moment there has to be—there *must* be total abnegation of rational judgment. Pausing to mutter "this is right" or "this is wrong" can only damage the goods in transit. Not a bad image—for, after all, something is being delivered.

Ottawa
February 3/4, 1975
Journal

I *finished my play.* I got it done by digesting everything Willy had said about making a plan—and then working backward—and by also digesting everything Marigold had said about who we need to meet first, etc. . . . Once I started writing, I didn't stop until it was done . . . The next day, I woke up in a panic: hated the play— knew I had to show it to Jean and Marigold and put both myself and Cassandra [heroine] on the line—and I wasn't willing to do that. *Almost* phoned and said I can't do this, but made myself see that was plain immature and totally unprofessional to boot—and so . . . met Marigold . . . we drove to her place. Jean had made lunch. We were late. Prospect of bad tempers. But, now—we ate—still not mentioning play—and then Jean said: "all right—let's read it through."

We began—in the living-room, with the fire going, and a lovely day on the wane outside. . . .

[We divided up the roles, and] as the reading progressed . . . I realized the characters *worked.* Actors understood them—just because they had got onto the paper *clearly.*

At the end of Act One, both Jean and Marigold were visibly excited. Marigold said it was 100 per cent improved already. *I* got excited.

We read Act Two. . . . At the end, Jean said: "this is a *very* good play. I like it enormously." Pause. Marigold, smiling—looked at Jean and said: "you want to do it, don't you." (It wasn't a question.) Jean said: "yes. Absolutely. Yes." And I cheered.

It was wonderful. Marigold laughed. I danced. I felt *numb* with relief—and pleasure and expectation—as if the world had been lifted away from me. . . . Now, there will be an announcement, coming from Jean—and *I am so proud of this, above all:* "that the instituting of a playwright-in-residence programme has paid off with a producible play—and one which the NAC takes pleasure in mounting for production next season."

So: the thing we all wanted to happen, has happened. They have provided me with experience, expertise, exposure to all elements of production—given freely of their time and their theatre—and I have come back with a play. The crazy idea—that came out of hope and frustration—and a few determined people last autumn—*worked* . . . But I am still the luckiest. It happened for me *first*—and with the best people.

Ottawa
September 1, 1976
Journal

The best news I could possibly have at this juncture came today—Talonbooks is going to publish *Can You See Me Yet?* I'm so excited—gratified for the play's sake—and so *proud* that I am weak-kneed. I rushed into Jean Roberts's office where Marigold was talking to her—apologized for interrupting them—and told them why and we all kissed each other and danced. Naturally—it's good not just for me and for the play—but for the NAC—Jean—Marigold—Bill . . . and *everyone.* It is marvellous. *And the first work accepted for publication since the autumn of 1974.*

Maybe now—things will break on other fronts as well.

When *Can You See Me Yet?* was accepted by Talonbooks, it had been seven years since the publication of a Findley novel. Otherwise, apart from his television work, all Tiff had been able to publish in the early 1970s was a handful of short stories in various literary magazines—each story finally appearing in his 1984 collection, *Dinner along the Amazon.*

What Tiff did not know in 1976 was that the novel he had begun in Ottawa during rehearsals for *Can You See Me Yet?* was not only going to be published in the following year, it was to be considered by many to be his masterpiece. The novel's title was *The Wars.*

And there would be five more plays. WFW.

London, Ontario
1993
Interview

The Stillborn Lover

This play is set in 1972, when Harry Raymond, a Canadian ambassador, is suddenly recalled from his posting in Moscow, following the brutal murder of a young Russian. Raymond is installed in an Ottawa "safe house," along with his wife Marian and daughter Diana. Under RCMP interrogation, he reveals his homosexual relationship with the dead youth. Many questions arise. Who is guilty of the murder? Are Marian's apparently befuddled memories the product of her advancing Alzheimer's, or of her attempts to save her husband? How will the political ambitions of Harry's Ottawa boss affect the ambassador's fate? And why do the atomic bombs dropped on Japan in 1945 play such a major role in the couple's past? WFW.

What informs this play almost more than the first atomic bomb on Hiroshima is the dropping of the second one on Nagasaki—because that is the *compounding* of the will to destroy. How do we know that there wasn't a third and a fourth and a fifth and a sixth bomb—all of them ready to go *boom*? Where would it have ended? Look where it did end. The fact of the second bomb informs the spiritual life of the two leading characters in this play, who spent their honeymoon in Nagasaki in 1946, just one year after the second bomb fell.

Marian had gone through the war as a cipher clerk; Harry, as a career diplomat. They fall deeply and utterly in love and are welded, in fact. They had dedicated their lives to the opposite gesture of that bomb—the gesture of diplomacy. The quest for a nonviolent answer. What runs through the whole play is the phrase: *No, don't.* Sadly, it is the words *no, don't* that destroy Harry and

Marian because, of course, the rest of society is not dedicated to diplomacy at all.

One of the great ironies of 1945 has been revealed in a wonderful book called *The Bodyguard of Lies* by Anthony Cave Hope. It tells the story of World War II as it was fought on the front of coding, ciphers and secrecy—especially at Bletchley Park, an estate in middle England. There, a large group of people was dedicated to the process of encoding all the secrets of the allies and disseminating them and, at the same time, deciphering the codes of the Germans and the Japanese. In the play, I had Marian be the cipher clerk who receives a message called an intercept. The Americans had a transmitter station somewhere on the east coast of Africa where messages on their way from Japan to the rest of the world were intercepted and passed on to Bletchley for decoding. This was one from the Emperor of Japan to the Japanese ambassador in Moscow. That would have been the route that a plea for peace would take, because the USSR was not at war with Japan at that moment. And this message—which is real—read something like, *. . . the Emperor has brought his will to bear in favour of peace . . .* Not a plea for peace, but a *desire* for peace.

Marian waits for the next intercept to come saying: "yes, yes, we'll have peace." Instead, the message that is sent is the Bomb. That message is horrendous news. We could have won the war without the Bomb. The Japanese were ready to quit, but we had to show the world that we were capable of chaos.

The fictional character of Harry Raymond contains elements of two figures in the history of Canadian diplomacy. The first is Herbert Norman, who committed suicide while being investigated by the House Un-American Activities Committee. He had joined the Communist Party in the 1930s when he was at Cambridge with, among others, Burgess and Maclean. He was our ambassador to Egypt when the Suez crisis happened and he was Lester

Pearson's man on the spot. He literally talked to Nasser for something like seventy-two hours straight, listened to him ranting and calmed him down so that he wouldn't go to war against Israel, and would accept having United Nations peacekeeping forces come into the Suez area. It was this action that won Pearson the Nobel Peace Prize. To some, it was Pearson's failure to support Norman through the anti-Communist witch hunt that led to the former ambassador's suicide.

The other historical figure who impinges on Harry Raymond's story was John Watkins—a former Canadian ambassador to the USSR. It so happened that he was our ambassador back in the 1950s when I was in Moscow playing in a British production of *Hamlet*. Watkins was a charming, talented, widely respected man—but he was gay, and this, of course, was highly problematical for a diplomat at that time.

Consequent to Watkins's retirement in the early 1960s and five or six years after I would have known him, the American CIA, working through the RCMP, started pushing Ottawa to get rid of all homosexuals in government—and, most importantly, to get rid of them in the diplomatic corps. So they started going through the files. Somehow, the name of John Watkins came up.

At this time Watkins was living in Paris, where his friends included our ambassador to France, Jules Leger, and his wife, Gabrielle. The RCMP were out to get this man, because they had discovered that yes, Watkins had had an affair with a young Russian poet and yes, there were photographs. The usual. But the fact is, Watkins hadn't caved in. The Russians presented him with the photographs in the hopes that when he got back to Ottawa, he would then work as an advocate for Soviet interests. Watkins refused. When the photographs found their way into the offices of External Affairs, two RCMP officers went off to Paris. They went to the Legers and said: "will you help us trap this man?" The Legers refused. They were honourable people. So, instead of conducting their investigation in Paris, the RCMP took Watkins first to London and then to Canada and held him in a Montreal hotel. By this time, Watkins was suffering from a heart condition. While they were questioning him, he died, and the coroner's report ultimately identified these two men simply as Watkins's friends—and all it said of Watkins was that he died of natural causes.

In 1992, a documentary on my work was being shot at our farm, Stone Orchard, and in Toronto. By then, this play had started to emerge. I'd written a couple of scenes, and in fact a couple of scenes had been published in *Books in Canada*, when they did an issue on playwriting. At any rate, the documentary's director, Terence Macartney-Filgate, had this wonderful idea: to shoot actors playing through the various drafts of a scene to show how a writer arrives at the final version. William Hutt, Martha Henry and Susan Coyne were hired to do this. And suddenly Marian was alive, along with Harry Raymond and Diana, their daughter—and I thought *Oh, God, this is too much. It's wonderful!* But I didn't say anything. I didn't dare hope.

Well, it took about four days to shoot that whole sequence of scenes over and over again—all the different versions. And one night while we were all drinking in a restaurant, Martha suddenly turned to me and said, "Tell me about this play. I'm really very interested in it." She was then artistic director at the Grand Theatre in London, Ontario. "Have you any ideas about where you might want to place it, because I would like to do it at the Grand." That's how it happened.

The problem was, the play wasn't written! There were only those two or three scenes. I was still writing *Headhunter*, and Bill Whitehead had worked out a schedule that was like a train schedule. I had two speeches to do and other assignments and completion of the novel and *then* this play.

It was one of the most extraordinary experiences of writing I have ever had and it will *never* be repeated. I couldn't begin to schedule all these projects, but Bill knew how to pace them against my energies.

I sat at the big blue harvest table. I didn't want to write it at my desk because the novel was all over the desk. I plonked down John Hersey's *Hiroshima*, I plonked down *The Bodyguard of Lies*, I plonked down whatever literature I had about Herbert Norman and John Watkins and the thesaurus and the dictionary and I started writing and in three weeks the play was finished.

But about the play itself, it's probably important to say this: I've talked about the elements of memory and the elements of politics in the play, but there's one word I haven't, oddly enough, mentioned—and that is the word *betrayal*. There's another level of the play which *is* about betrayal and what people *will* do: they'll throw even the most beloved friends over in order to achieve what they want. And there is plenty of betrayal in this world of ours!

Stratford
August 8, 1999
Journal

Martha Henry not only produced *The Stillborn Lover*, she starred in its premiere production in 1993, and repeated her role, Marian, in the Stratford Festival production in 1995.

Meahwhile, for several years another play had been brewing in Tiff's imagination. It was to involve a fictional encounter between two extraordinary people in Shakespeare's time. The first was Queen Elizabeth I—who maintained she had given up her womanhood in order to rule Britain with the strength and vigour of a man. The second was Ned Lowenscroft, the fictional male actor in Shakespeare's company who was the only one capable of playing the Bard's mature and powerful women.

The play was given a workshop by the Stratford Festival in 1997, with Diane D'Aquila magnificent as the queen. A production was planned for 2000, in which Brent Carver would play the actor opposite Diane D'Aquila as the queen. Martha Henry would direct.

In the following journal notes about Tiff's work with Martha before rehearsals began, Martha makes reference to a comment made by Tiff's agent when he first read an early version of *The Wars*, in which it took a long time before World War I made an appearance. The agent, Stan Colbert, said: "It's as if you had promised me a story called *Goldilocks and the Three Bears* and all you gave me was Goldilocks, Goldilocks, Goldilocks. Bring on the bears!!!!"

By the time Tiff and Martha were through, as anyone who saw *Elizabeth Rex* will testify, Tiff had indeed *brought on the play*. WFW.

MARTHA: "Bring on the play!"

Elizabeth and paranoia—"are you telling me something? What?"

These jottings were made during my first meeting with Martha [Henry] re: *Elizabeth Rex.*

She arrived yesterday shortly after 6:00. I was extremely nervous—having no notion what she might think of the play—especially since it has been so greatly altered from the version she read first two years ago.

Well—she likes it *greatly* and said so right off the top . . . especially likes the dialogue, which pleases me. She had no character problems, though she had fascinating things to say about Elizabeth and how she can be expanded in directions I hadn't thought all the way through—i.e., paranoia . . . etc.

She had been reading *Inside Memory* and come across the passage regarding Stan Colbert's visit . . . when he read the first fifty page of *The Wars* and said: "bring on the bears!" Martha pointed out that Elizabeth doesn't come on until twenty-odd minutes have passed—and even once she's there, we stay perhaps too long "introducing" her. Also, perhaps, too long with Will off the top.

We discussed casting . . . Elizabeth—*Diane D'Aquila!!!!!* Enough said. She is perfect casting. Her workshop Elizabeth was stunning. . . .

Stratford
August 9, 1999
Journal

We (Martha and I) sat at the dining-room table, 2:00 till 6:00. I set out bottled water, white wine, lemon slices, glasses, ginger cookies. Also a cup of pencils, a sharpener and ashtrays. It was a perfect place to work.

We got all the way through Act One . . .

The thought occurred between us that this was [Shakespeare's] last play to be performed. Not that he is dead, as I had imagined— but dying—and this is what is on his mind—the unwritten, unful- filled story of a moment that, even as it happened, unfolded as "a play." The fact that everyone there is "playing a role" . . .

Introduce a cart—which the actors begin to load, expecting to return to the city until they learn about the curfew. It could be use- ful on stage . . .

Page 8: Shakespeare can always tell the truth—*and does*. He won't allow obfuscation. "There needs to be a scorecard in the audience's behalf—and he is the scorekeeper." (Martha) . . .

P. 10: Find out more about prop breasts [for male actors play- ing female roles]. What was worn? (Nothing—the costume did it.) . . .

P. 19: Remember that the image of his reading tells us we have lost him as our guide and conduit . . .

P. 29: Elizabeth's entrance comes somewhat late, but I can't imagine getting her on much earlier, given the need to demon- strate the mix of the actors. We'll see . . .

P. 35: Elizabeth's reaction to Jack—"your back, sir, has impudence written on it," etc.—is precisely the same reaction she had to Essex in their final encounters—that he was beyond impudence and had become dangerous.

P. 57: Are we finding "love stories"—and, if we are, does Elizabeth become increasingly agitated that they all turn out so badly . . ."can't there be one that turns out well?"

Act One now ends at the bottom of the page with Elizabeth's "will no one say Amen?"

Stratford
August 13, 1999
Journal

What follows are the page notes transcribed from my script of what Martha and I discussed yesterday re: Act Two:

P. 68: We were left at the end of Act One with Elizabeth's challenge to Ned that if he would teach her how to be a woman, she would teach him how to be a man—so, as Act Two begins, we must bear that promise in mind. . . .

P. 69: Elizabeth catches Will writing something that transpired only minutes before, by *snatching the notebook*. This helps to underscore Elizabeth's paranoia ("what are you writing about me?") and also Will's certainty that *what he is witnessing is a play*—which he then, because of her reaction—and also because of all the forbidden political connotations—fears to write.

P. 71: VERY IMPORTANT. Re: the relationship between Ned and Elizabeth. Martha's analogy is the crossing of three bridges between three islands—but in the present version, *Ned never gets to cross the third bridge* . . . If we accept that the first bridge lies between his respect for her and his anger at having been humiliated in her presence by Jack's drying on "Tarry, sweet

Beatrice . . ." the first island which he reaches is the island of opportunity to demonstrate his reverence of her by falling on his face when he first meets her. Bridge number three leads to the island of "the bargain." But in between there is "the island of attack." How does he get there—from respect to attack? Drink—yes. But more. What? *This is immensely important* . . .

P. 74: Here is the first moment when the actors start playing roles other than their own—Luddy and Jack speaking the lines in Elizabeth's remembrance of her being Towered. Difficult—and must be justified. Another instance of needing a safe anchor for the audience, in order to learn exactly where we are—and where we are going . . .

P. 79: IMPORTANT. Elizabeth's authority overrides the authority of every other character. She would never allow the servants to move her pieces and property, as Ned asks them to. They themselves would refuse. Some other mode is needed here.

P. 82: Their performances of themselves are immensely important, as Ned prods them towards their various revelations (more can be made of these—especially of Elizabeth's and Will's—Ned's is sufficient as it stands)—as Martha said: "this is the crucible in which we understand all."

P. 87: We must be certain that we *know*, when Elizabeth says: "is this a play we are in?" that we are still in 1601—and not merely in Will's mind or reconstruction of it. It *was* a play as he saw it then—and thus the notes he was making and the way he watched it unfold.

April 21, 2000
Letter

Dearest Tiff and Bill,

Thank you so very much for all your hospitality over the months of preparation for *Elizabeth Rex*—the lunches, the wine, the conversations—and most of all for the work itself. Tiff, you cannot imagine what it means to have *such* a writer say, time and again, "Oh! That's wonderful! *And . . .*" and then to hear you come forth with something way beyond anything I had dreamed of in my own often clumsy attempt to tighten or clarify a moment or a bit of text. You are truly sublime and this work has been, and continues to be, thrilling, challenging and stimulating for me (and for all of us), far exceeding even my *great* expectations.

Thank you for being the artist, and the man, that you are. And thank you *both* for a working relationship which continues to be rewarding, all of the above (!) and just a hell of a lot of fun . . . what a gift.

All my love,
Martha

Stratford
November 21/22, 2001
Journal

Home again! After almost three months away—Banff, Calgary, Toronto, followed by a national tour from Halifax to Victoria . . .

Am low—postpartum depression after having to stay "up" for tour. Also, "off," somehow—stomach not right . . . lower back gone . . . legs wobbly. Maybe just age . . . Am religiously faithful to pill regimen, though it drives me mad, both sorting them for day and night and taking the bloody things—about *thirty* a day!

Well—I'm seventy-one, overtired, overworked and with a pow-erful stress load. (So many friends have dire health problems.) I was going to write: *but that's life, Tiff*—and yet there are moments when it feels more appropriate to write: *that's death.*

Must not allow depression to take over. *That* is death.

Stratford
February 25, 2002
Journal

Today, we were supposed to fly to France—but here I sit on the edge of a hospital bed in Stratford . . .

When I was admitted to Intensive Care . . . I realized I was not in an "exercise"—but riding the final wave.

There is—and can be—no describing it. Everyone in the unit is at death's door and you become one of them. Tubes—wires—things in your nose, over your heart, attached to your arms, legs, neck. Blood "by the litre" (so it felt)—masks over your mouth—bottles to pee in (they want to know every ounce you give)—pills by the handful—stethoscopes—blood pressure bindings—thera-pists pounding on your chest and back—and every time you fall asleep, someone wakes you to check this, that and the other.

But wonderful!

It's a good hospital. We're beyond lucky. The caregiving, the dedication, the talent—and, I must add, the *food* (!) are stunning. (They've hired *chefs*, not *cooks*.)

But—I was in crisis. Absolute crisis. My good fortune—beyond where I was—was that I had two terrific doctors—Wayne Parsons (my own GP) and David Tamblyn (Internalist) who monitored my progress every day. I had visits from each every morning. That I survived this episode is due entirely to them—to WFW—to the hospital staff—and—to my own interest in the process of survival.

Stratford
February 27, 2002
Journal

What a curious feeling to be released—pleasure mixed with sadness because everyone has been so kind, thoughtful and supportive.

Outside, it was cold, though the sun shone. I heard birds and distant traffic for the first time in days. Sitting in the car, driving away, I felt the way I used to feel getting on the bus at St. Andrew's College to go home for the holidays—two different worlds, peopled with different souls and running on different tracks, governed by different rules.

When we got to 72 Ontario Street, WFW parked the car in the lane and we went straight into Pazzo for wine and lunch. First wine in five days, which—for me—is something of a record! I hate to confess it, but I also had a cigarette. *Thus runs the world away* . . .

But—I'm home.

Cotignac
March 2002
Play

Before his death in June 2002, Tiff had written *Shadows*, a one-act play for the 2002 Stratford Festival season. He took part in its workshop in 2001, but did not live to attend rehearsals or the performances that were part of the inaugural season in the Festival's new space, The Studio.

The action of the play appears to take place at a dinner party of theatre people, gathered to witness a total eclipse of the moon. Late in the play, it is suddenly revealed that what the audience is watching is actually a public competition among budding playwrights, each of whom has been assigned a role at the "party," while the man playing the host is the judge.

One of the competitors—a young woman—seems to be a sure winner. Everyone is sent home with the promise that a decision will be reported the next day. The host/judge is left alone on the stage—and his cellphone rings.

While clearing up Tiff's papers after his death, I found his copy of the play, with a few scribbled lines to be added to the host's final speech. They were ultimately spoken by the actor Brent Carver, when he had pocketed his cellphone, started to exit and then turned back to the audience. As far as I know, these were the last words Timothy Findley ever wrote. WFW.

BEN: Yes? Oh. Just a minute . . . (*Pretends to offer phone to someone in front row.*) It's for you. (*Smiles.*) Well, no—actually, it *is* for me. Sorry. (*To phone, quietly.*) Where the hell are you? You all just left. Oh . . . So what's . . . No, that's not . . . No! I don't care how good she was . . . Absolutely not. You're still going to win. No—he'll be no problem. Look, I'll take care of everything. Just meet me at the apartment, and . . . Yeah . . . Yeah . . . me too . . . in a big way. OK. 'Bye. (*Pause. Disconnects phone and gestures with it to* AUDIENCE.) Not fair? Deceitful? Dishonest? Isn't that what you came to see? Lies? All those people, pretending to be someone else? Speaking someone else's words as if they were their own? You know? *How do you remember all those words????* That's what theatre is: *lies.* But if we get lucky, the lies may surprise us with some kind of truth.

Who called? One of the women? After all, the men all said they weren't gay. Oh! What if one of them lied??? No. That wasn't part of the play. Tell you what: *always leave room for the audience.* Why don't you decide how this whole thing plays out.

I'm going home. (*He pockets the cellphone, starts to exit, then turns to the* AUDIENCE *and smiles.*) Oh, and . . . keep in touch with the truth. You'll fail, of course. We all do. But at least we have to try. Each in our own way. Be well. Good night.

(BEN *exits.*
The LIGHTS *fade.*)

THE END

Publications

Prologue

THE COUNTRIES OF INVENTION: Canadian Writers in 1984 in 25th anniversary issue of *Canadian Literature.*

Going Places

WINGS: quote from "Bragg and Minna," in *Stones,* Penguin Canada, Toronto, 1988.

THE PINEAPPLE OF PERFECTION: in *Writing Away: The* PEN *Canada Travel Anthology,* (ed. Constance Rooke), McClelland & Stewart, Toronto, 1994.

HOME: Excerpted from *Of Trunks and Burning Barns* in *Writing Home: The* PEN *Canada Anthology,* (ed. Constance Rooke), McClelland & Stewart, Toronto, 1997.

A THANKSGIVING PRAYER: The Globe and Mail, Thanksgiving issue, October 2001.

From Past Imperfect to Future Tense

TIME WAITS: from the play *John A.—Himself,* produced in January 1979 by Theatre London of London, Ontario. An excerpt including the quoted speech was published in *Exile*, Vol. II, #3 in 1986.

LOOKING FOR THE TRUTH: from *A Nation of One*, first delivered as a talk in the Celebrated Writers Series of the Stratford Festival of Canada (1994) and published as a Harbourfront Chapbook, Toronto, 1997.

THE MIND OF ONTARIO: an address to the Ontario Historical Society at McMaster University, Hamilton, Ontario, September 8, 1984.

THE PIANO MAN'S DAUGHTER: a version of this was published in 1995 by HarperCollins Publishers Ltd., Toronto, as a readers' guide to the novel *The Piano Man's Daughter*.

OTHER PEOPLE'S HOUSES; OTHER PEOPLE'S ROOMS: in *Chatelaine*, May 1985.

A LITTLE TOWN IN NORMANDY: a version was translated into French by Nésida Loyer and published in *TransLit*, Vol. 3, 1996.

THE BOB EDWARDS AWARD: a speech given in Calgary in October 2001, in accepting the Bob Edwards Award.

THE ARK IN THE GARDEN: in *The Ark in the Garden: Fables for Our Times* (collected by Alberto Manguel), Macfarlane, Walter & Ross, Toronto, 1998.

Pen Power

MARTHA AND THE MINDER: playlet performed at PEN Gala, Winter Garden Theatre, Toronto, December 1991; published in *Paper Guitar: Twenty-seven Writers Celebrate Twenty-five Years of Descant*, HarperCollins Publishers Ltd., 1995.

INDEFINITE DETENTION, INCOMMUNICADO, IN SOLITARY CONFINEMENT: book supplement, *The Toronto Star*, March 1987.

CANADIAN HEAVEN: excerpt from *A Nation of One*, originally a talk given in the Stratford Festival's Celebrated Writers Series (1992), published as a Harbourfront Chapbook, Toronto, 1997.

THE VALOUR AND THE HORROR: editorial in feature: "Point-Counterpoint: Ethics in the Media," *Journal of Canadian Studies*, Trent University (Vol. 27, No.4, Winter 1992/93).

THE UNICORN AND THE GRAPEVINE: in *The Monkey King and Other Stories*, (ed. Griffin Ondaatje), HarperCollins Publishers Ltd., Toronto, 1995.

NEOLOGISMS: in the *HarperCollins Dictionary of Neologisms*, HarperCollins, New York, 1991.

WILD ANIMALS I HAVE KNOWN: in *Harrowsmith*, July/August 1993.

RIDING OFF IN ALL DIRECTIONS: A Few Wild Words in Search of Stephen Leacock: introduction to a speech delivered at a Leacock Symposium at the University of Ottawa in 1985, later published in *Stephen Leacock: A Reappraisal*, edited and with an introduction by David Staines, University of Ottawa Press, Ottawa, 1986.

W.O.: a tribute to W.O. Mitchell, first given as a speech at a Trent University tribute in 1995; published in *Magic Lies: The Art of W.O. Mitchell*, (ed. Sheila Latham), University of Toronto Press, Toronto, 1997.

MORDECAI RICHLER: read at a Montreal tribute to Morcedai Richler in July 2002.

A WRITER'S CRAFT IN FICTION: notes for a seminar in creative writing given in October 1985 at the University of Winnipeg.

A WRITER'S NIGHTMARES: from a speech given at the Harbourfront International Festival of Authors, November 1999.

Theatre Tours and Final Curtain

CAN YOU SEE ME YET?: a play first presented at the National Arts Centre, Ottawa, in 1976; published by Talonbooks, Vancouver, 1977.

PHANTOMS OF THE CITY: in *Toronto Life*, April 1992.

THE LEAP: in *Standing Naked in the Wings: Anecdotes from Canadian Actors*, Oxford University Press, Toronto, 1997.

KATHARINE HEPBURN AND ROBERT HELPMANN: in *Brushes with Greatness*, Coach House Press, Toronto, 1989.

DIGS: Excerpted from *Of Trunks and Burning Barns* in *Writing Home: The PEN Canada Anthology*, (ed. Constance Rooke), McClelland & Stewart, Toronto, 1997.

AN UNFORGETTABLE JOURNEY TO RUSSIA: in *Bad Trips*, Vintage Books, Random House, New York, 1991.

ANECDOTES: a version of these were published in *Standing Naked in the Wings: Anecdotes from Canadian Actors*, Oxford University Press, Toronto, 1997.

ROBERTSON DAVIES: from an address given at a Davies memorial in Toronto, March 15, 1996.

DONALD DAVIS: sent to be read at a memorial tribute to Donald Davis in Toronto, February 1998.

HERBERT WHITTAKER: speech given at a tribute to Herbert Whittaker in Toronto in September 1993.

WILLIAM HUTT: written for the Canadian Embassy in Berlin, to be used in German newspaper articles about Canadian artists, 1994.

ZEROING IN ON ARTHUR MILLER: speech given at Harbourfront, Toronto, in June 1999—celebrating the 25th anniversary of the Harbourfront International Festival of Authors, an evening of writers talking about their most memorable encounters at the Festival.

SCANDALS: programme notes for *The School for Scandal*, Stratford Festival of Canada, 1987.

MURDER IN OUR TIME: programme notes for *Murder in the Cathedral*, Stratford Festival of Canada, 1988.

OUR TOWN: in *Fanfare*, 1991, to publicize the production that year at the Stratford Festival of Canada.

THE JOURNEY: radio drama: *Ideas.* CBC Radio, 1971.

THE LIVING ART: from notes for a playwrights' panel at the Stratford Festival of Canada, 1999.

THE STILLBORN LOVER: from an interview conducted by Patricia Black, amplified by later comments from the playwright. Parts of the original interview were published in *Scene Magazine*, Vol. 5, No. 1, March 25–April 7, 1993, London, Ontario. The play was co-produced by The Grand Theatre, London, Ontario, and the National Arts Centre, Ottawa. It premiered in London in March 1993 and played in Ottawa in April 1993. It was also part of the 1995 season at the Stratford Festival of Canada.

SHADOWS: one-act play, commissioned by the Stratford Festival of Canada and presented in its Studio Theatre as part of the Festival's 50th season, 2002. Published in *Canadian Theatre Review*, Number 114, Spring 2003, University of Toronto Press, Toronto.

TIMOTHY FINDLEY was one of Canada's most beloved writers, from the publication of his first novel in 1967 until his death in June 2002. His acclaimed novels include *Spadework*, *Pilgrim*, *The Piano Man's Daughter*, *Headhunter*, *Not Wanted on the Voyage*, *Famous Last Words* and *The Wars*. Twice winner of the Governor General's Award, Tiff received many accolades for his work. He was an Officer of the Order of Canada and Chevalier de l'Ordre des Arts et des Lettres in France.

WILLIAM WHITEHEAD studied biology and theatre arts at the University of Saskatchewan, moving to Ontario in 1957 to become an actor and producer. He became Timothy Findley's companion and colleague in 1962, and for the next thirty years worked as an award-winning writer of documentaries, including over one hundred episodes of the CBC TV series *The Nature of Things*.

Timothy Findley
Stone Orchard
Cannington.

Against Despair.